To Chr... [...]

Cond... ... and

on with our

Pros... for ERD —

[signature]

10/29/81

The Ghost
In My Life

Also by Susan B. Anthony, Ph.D.

The Prayer-Supported Apostle
Out of the Kitchen—Into the War
Women During the War and After (co-author)

The Ghost In My Life

Susan B. Anthony

SPECIAL BEFORE AND AFTER CHAPTERS
BY
CATHERINE MARSHALL

chosen for you ✔ chosen books

Washington Depot, Connecticut   06794

Distributed by Fleming H. Revell Company
Old Tappan, New Jersey

To my parents of the flesh and the spirit,
and to my children of the spirit

Acknowledgments

Many people have contributed to *The Ghost in My Life*. I can mention only three. I am deeply indebted to my editor, Van Varner; to The Reverend Louis J. Putz, C.S.C., whose support, spiritual and material, has made this book possible; and to my mother, Charlotte Whetford, whose vivid recall of the early days helped me with *The Ghost*, almost as much as her love and inspiration.

Before

Catherine Marshall Writes . . .

Years ago when Peter Marshall and I were new residents of the Nation's capital, I enjoyed my own kind of solitary sight-seeing: the little house on 10th Street Northwest (across from Ford's Theater where Abraham Lincoln had died); certain places in the old Smithsonian Institution; many a trip to the Lincoln Memorial—my favorite spot in Washington; the nooks and crannies of the Capitol Building.

It was in the Capitol in the dim light of the basement crypt that one day I happened upon the spotlighted Adelaide Johnson bust of Susan B. Anthony. . . . Stark white Cararra marble . . . Miss Anthony's classic head with hair parted in the middle, combed smooth . . . An imposing brow balanced by a sternly modeled jaw, finely drawn lips . . . A strong neck rose from a broad deep chest. Strength and a certain imperious quality had been captured in the marble.

At that time Susan B. Anthony was for me little more than a famous name. If asked, I would probably have tagged her "one of those militant feminists." Oh, I knew vaguely that she had started the movement that led to us women being able to vote. But I had not paused to consider what a tough fight it had been, for it was a full fourteen years after Susan B. Anthony's death that the Nineteenth Amendment to the Constitution finally became law on August 26, 1920.

9

For me, the years passed. Then one afternoon three women sat in the living room of my Florida home. One of them, a tall, striking-looking woman had been introduced as "Susan B. Anthony."

I remember saying hesitantly, half-humorously, "You have a most unusual name. Is it . . . that is, could it be . . . ?"

The look my guest flashed back was a bit rueful. "It could be—and is. Susan was my great-aunt. I was named after her."

Since then I have come to know the second Susan B. Anthony well, indeed to count her among my cherished friends. To comment that the second Susan is an unusual woman is a gross understatement. As a recent convert to Christianity, she came to her faith the hard way after many wanderings in a variety of far countries, so many in fact that it has taken me years to learn a fraction of the alleys, byways, and broad highways of destruction which she has traveled. I've never probed because I've long since dropped out any morbid desire for a detailed map of the Gehenna terrain. Furthermore, Susan as she is today is far more interesting to probe, a woman alive and alight with love for the Lord who rescued her. I *have* marveled sometimes about the number of far-out wayfarers like Susan who are led to my door and end by becoming my close friends. Ex-alcoholics, ex-sexaholics, ex-convicts (such as Starr Daily)—I could go on and on.

Whenever I wonder about this, I remember how often Peter Marshall would look at someone who had broken most of man's codes and God's laws, and comment with rare depth of feeling, "There—but for the grace of God—go I."

Then as likely as not—often with a grin—he would turn to me and protest, "Catherine, when are you going to understand about sin and evil in the world? You've been so shielded, so protected. How can I make you see! It's for *these* folks that Christ came to earth. . . ."

Well, Peter need not have worried. God has even more of a sense of humor than Peter Marshall, and He has arranged my continuous exposure to a procession of friends like Susan who have tasted life's bitterest dregs.

When I read the Gospels, I find that the same kind of far-out folks were Jesus' friends. In fact, over and over He was criticized for this. But He loved them, and, very simply, I do too. Those who have been sunk in the dark night of the soul before the Light found them have something that we "good" church people can never know. Jesus pinpointed what that something is when He commented, "She loved much: but to whom little is forgiven, the same loveth little" (Luke 7:47).

Thus I have learned what Peter knew I had to learn—that no human being can sink too low for the Love and the Light to rescue him; that Christ's forgiveness and restoration are real and contemporary and extremely practical; that heavenly hosannas still ring out so loudly as almost to split the sky, as each lost and straying sheep is hauled back from the abyss of self-destruction.

So this is Susan's story. It is so real and at times so tough that in telling it, Susan has changed the names of many of the participants. I hope that you will not be dismayed or put off by the rough parts, for the Susan of today is very different, a woman of towering spiritual stature. This is part of God's humor too. To put it in the vernacular, He "gets a charge" out of seeing these rescued ones grow so fast in the faith that they overtake and overrun us plodders in the Kingdom.

And whatever your problems and mine may be, if Susan could survive hers and solve them and become a new person in Christ Jesus, then there is hope for each of us too.

The Ghost
In My Life

1 *"...a sacrifice acceptable and pleasing..."*

On the morning of Tuesday, November 2, 1920, when I was four, my mother brushed my dark brown hair, dressed me in my best tan coat and beret and my patent-leather Mary Jane shoes as though I were going to a party. She wore her own best black-and-white-checked coat and her new black turban. Then she and Daddy took me by the hand and walked with me up Northampton Street, Easton, Pennsylvania. The other children stayed home. I was the child chosen for this journey.

We walked past the towering Civil War monument of Center Square, on up to Fourth Street, and turned south past eighteenth-century fieldstone and brick houses. At the corner of Fourth and Ferry stood the Taylor School. This day there were no school-children about; grown-ups stood outside and crowded the class-room that we entered. A woman at a table asked Mother some questions, then handed her a piece of paper and directed her to a booth covered with a green curtain. Another woman smiled and patted my head.

"It's a great day for you, little one," she said.

I knew that this was so, but I was not exactly sure why.

Stately as a queen, Mother took my hand and led me with her behind the green curtain. She marked the paper, folded it, and then we emerged and, as a small crowd watched, Mother walked to a large drum and, still holding tightly to my hand, dropped the paper in it. Then, placing her hands on my shoulders, she looked into my eyes and said in awe-inspiring tones, "I have just voted for the first time, Sue. I want you always to remember this moment. I want you never to forget your Great-Aunt Susan and how hard she worked to make this day possible."

I have never forgotten that moment. I did not forget that moment during the years that I lost the vote Aunt Susan won. And I have never forgotten Aunt Susan.

Forget her? It was never possible. From the beginning she was a presence in my life just as my first memories of her were as a presence in our home. A dozen times each day I saw her photograph, the famous Ellis photograph in which she sat judge-like in a dark robe, stern and forbidding, her white hair parted in the middle and drawn back severely, her arm resting in a statesmanlike pose on the chair. The very mahogany table we ate from each day had been Aunt Susan's. In school another picture, often maligned with mustache, looked out at me from our text books. Her shadowy self was so great that in my childish mind I linked Aunt Susan with another white-haired titan, the red-white-and-blue man in the high hat who pointed his finger and said, "I need you!" I thought that Uncle Sam and Aunt Susan were married.

Even if I myself might have forgotten Susan B. Anthony, other people did not let me. And most of the time I really didn't mind. I enjoyed the spotlight of adult attention. I loved being asked to curtsy and present a bouquet of roses to Lillian Russell when that large and luscious lady brought her aging charms to Easton on a famous visit. In later years, even if it was a bore to me, I was always pleased by the invitations to lay a wreath at Aunt Susan's statue in the New York State Capitol in Albany, to take part in the annual birthday observance at the Capitol in Washington. Sometimes the ceremonies were less to my taste. I cringed at the thought of getting into the dead Susan Anthony's clothing for a commemorative event in Rochester, New York, but I did it just the same. As I grew older I was often of two minds about bearing her name, and there were times when I stopped using it altogether, yet I well knew that there were other times when being Susan B. Anthony worked to my advantage. What it took me years to realize was the extent of Susan B. Anthony's influence on my life, not just because I bore her name, but because of the woman herself. She had been dead ten years when I was born in 1916. She exercised a power within me then. It was a power it took me a long time to understand.

Yet if I feel that Aunt Susan affected my life, shaping it in subtle and mysterious ways, this posthumous pressure was nothing compared to the influence the living woman exerted on the members of her own family. I know well the stories of two members of that family. One is that of my father, Luther Burt Anthony, who had reason all his life to remember his aunt's influence, and the other story belongs to my Aunt Lucy, Dad's older sister, a grim spinster whose existence was so intertwined with Susan B. Anthony's that her own identity was all but lost.

My father and his older sisters, Lucy and Ann, spent their childhoods in Fort Scott, Kansas. My grandfather, Captain Merritt Anthony, had settled there after his exploits as a guerrilla fighter under John Brown at Osawatomie. Later Merritt Anthony fought against slavery in the Civil War and lost an eye in battle. Merritt was Aunt Susan's youngest brother and she was fiercely proud of him, all the while trying, characteristically, to exert her own influence on him. I have often thought of her as "the Unmarried Matriarch." Gertrude Stein and Virgil Thompson called their opera about her *The Mother of Us All,* but nowhere was this matriarchal quality of hers more evident than within her very own family.

Dad grew up seeing far more of his famous aunt than he, in those days of difficult travel, had a right to expect. Susan B. was the most traveled woman of her time. Periodically she would descend upon the household, either while campaigning for woman's right to vote under the Fourteenth Amendment or later for a Kansas state suffrage law. When she would come she would bring with her the excitement of the crowds she had addressed, the great people she had met, the rigors of the fight. She was always the returning warrior, and always the inspector-general taking stock, giving orders, keeping the home militia in line.

My father did not wish to be kept in line. He admired Aunt Susan, but her dreams and his did not match. In that distant prairie town, Dad had been infected with a peculiar disease: he wanted to go on the stage. To Quakers the idea of theater was anathema, and Dad was a mutation from seven generations of Quakers. The Anthonys were unanimous in their horror and opposition. The situation came to a head when he ran away with a touring minstrel show.

No matter, the long arm of Aunt Susan reached out and found Dad, picked him up and dropped him into Drexel Institute in Philadelphia. Dad, temporarily quelled, considered this experience a necessary detour on his way to Broadway, and made the most of it by studying and playing a variety of musical instruments, painting under a famous illustrator, and by acting and directing in every one of the Institute's plays open to him. Finally he sneaked off again, this time to New York where he determined to make his stand. It was brave of him, but ill-starred. He dreamt of being another Drew or Mansfield, but as far as he ever got was a few walk-ons in plays that soon closed. Meanwhile Aunt Susan bided her time.

When Dad would tell the story to me, he never did so jokingly. It was always difficult for him to look back upon the time he nearly starved in New York. The year was 1898 and as he told it, the time came when a fellow actor, also "at liberty," taught him how to stretch both his dwindling funds and his stomach by stuffing himself with pretzels and water. The water bloated the pretzels so that he actually felt full. The trick worked for a while until, with no protein whatsoever in his diet, he grew weak.

One day in his weakened condition he was in his room working on a scene from *Othello* when he answered a knock at the door. There she was, a tall, erect lady of seventy-eight in shiny black silk, a black bonnet perched on her snow-white hair. Aunt Susan. She picked her way through the shabby, littered room, crunching on pretzel crumbs, her aquiline nose sniffing at the stale air. This time the old warhorse was gentle, and she embraced him lovingly.

"You poor boy. You look so thin. I'm going to take you out this very minute for a huge steak dinner."

The word "steak" was more than Dad could withstand. Out the two of them went and when she had won the young man's gratitude in the restaurant, she went still further by producing a handful of crisp, green bills.

"Burtie," she said, "I am not only buying you this dinner, I am giving you this fifty dollars."

Dad could hardly believe his good fortune. He should not have. "The woman who changed the mind of a nation" was then at work on her own nephew. Suddenly Susan B. Anthony laid down the law.

"I am giving you this money on condition that you leave this low life and take a decent job." She hit hard and straight. "Acting is not a man's work. It is not honest work. It is selling your body to the public. You may choose to demean yourself, Burtie, but I will not have you tarnishing the name of Anthony."

Artfully she told Dad about the job she had arranged for him. She described the advantages of three meals a day and money jangling in his pocket. Then she lowered the boom. She produced a one-way ticket to Easton, Pennsylvania, some sixty miles from New York City. To Dad, Pennsylvania sounded like Siberia.

Before the assault was over, Dad had on a brand-new suit, Aunt Susan was at his side, her hand firmly on his arm until she had plopped him down in a seat on a Lehigh Valley train heading west. The last he saw of the old lady that day she was standing on the platform like a sentinel, and he knew for sure that that particular round in the fight was hers. He thought, of course, that there would be other rounds.

Dad started his job at the Easton office of a credit agency called Bradstreet, later to become Dun and Bradstreet, but his mind was on the time when he would again storm Broadway. Meanwhile he sought out what theater the Lehigh Valley offered, organizing the drama societies at Lafayette and other colleges. The time eased by. Before he knew it, and before he realized its meaning for the career he planned for himself, he was in love with a fair-haired girl of eighteen, Grace Dickson, and they were married. Then came the shock of her death while giving birth to twin daughters, one of whom also died.

There were lonely days then, difficult days of finding nursemaids to care for the surviving daughter, Grace, and with that responsibility the utter, inescapable necessity of showing up for work each day. Bradstreet made him supervisor for the Lehigh Valley area, but the promotion meant little to him; he refused to surrender his dream of theater.

Dad maneuvered. If he could not get to New York to act, he would do something meaningful right there in Easton. He would write plays, he would create a publication for theater people to read. He forced himself on to a schedule of writing and editing, a schedule which, even when I was growing up years later, he continued to follow steadfastly. Every night after dinner he would take a short nap and then he would walk to his office downtown where hour in, hour out he would work on his plays and on his quarterly magazine *The Dramatist*. He founded *The Dramatist* in 1909 and for years it maintained a modest circulation and kept his contacts with theater fresh. Gradually he honed his skills, his scripts began to draw serious consideration from Broadway producers, but curiously enough the only real success he ever had was working, not on his own plays, but on other playwrights'. He became known as a play doctor. Because he had a talent for diagnosing a drama's weaknesses, for knowing how to cure an ailing scene or a sick second act, New York producers sought his services to the point that they would bring productions to Easton for their pre-Broadway try-outs. All of these things Dad did while holding down his bread-and-butter job at Bradstreet.

My mother and my father met early in 1910. Her name was Charlotte Agnes Sutherland—they called her "Lottie"—and she was the daughter of a West Indies planter. She and her numerous sisters and brothers had been brought up in considerable ease in a plantation world of servants and British gentility. The year Mother was to go abroad to school was the year my grandfather met financial disaster with an ill-fated citrus crop. Mother left Jamaica anyway, but now to find a job in the United States. She joined the household of the novelist Owen Wister, as a secretary and governess. Wister was then converting his best-selling *The Virginian* into what was to become the enduringly popular play, and it was because of *The Virginian* that the editor and publisher of *The Dramatist* arrived at the Wister home outside Philadelphia. Before the end of the year Mother and Dad were married.

From their first meeting, Dad inspired Mother with his dreams. She believed in them, just as she believed in him, and she went back to Easton to help him make them come true. But it wasn't long before she too had become caught up in the realities of the day-to-day, and Mother who had never cooked an egg or washed a dish, was soon keeping house and watching after her little step-daughter, bearing her own children, reading proof and keeping books for *The Dramatist,* and night after night watching Dad

go off to his office to write his plays. Somehow the years disappeared, the dreams with them.

Still there did come a time when Dad had the chance to live
theater twenty-four hours a day, when theater consumed him,
when it consumed Dad and Mother and all of us gloriously. In
our family we still refer to it as The Year of the Golden Summer.
During that summer Broadway came to stay in our Lehigh Valley.

I was eight then, it was 1924, and we were spending the hot
months, as we regularly did, at Raubsville, five miles south of
Easton. This was the house that we eventually came to think of
as "home." It was a pre-Revolutionary fieldstone cottage, high
over the river road, from which we could glimpse the Delaware
and its canal flowing by. The house backed on a steep, wooded
hill that sloped down to the first floor, giving us a solid backdrop
of summer green. It was furnished—the better word is probably
"jammed"—with the antiques that both Mother and Dad adored,
the walls packed from low, raftered ceiling to polished floor with
books. On the wall was Dad's pastel mural of the ship *Hercules*
on which John Anthony sailed to America in 1634. The place of
honor over the fireplace was given to my grandfather's Civil War
sword.

On his monthly trips to New York for *The Dramatist*, Dad had
become involved in a plan that materialized as one of the nation's
first summer theaters. For three months, New York producers, di-
rectors, actors set up shop in a theater only a few miles away
from us in Bethlehem. The actors who appeared there that summer were important ones, some of the brightest stars of the day:
Nadine Bronson, Florence Reed, Walter Kingsford, Gavin Gordon, Ann Delafield, Vance Powers, Leona Beautelle.

Dad was confident that with these professionals on his own
home ground, with the "angels" that would be lured to the
country, he would be able to get backing for his plays so he
could at last leave Bradstreet for his true vocation in New York.
As it turned out, the producers, the big names, the reviewers
from *Variety* and *Billboard* and some of the New York dailies
did appear. And as they came and as the summer advanced,
my father grew happier than I had ever seen him or, I suppose,
than he had ever been.

Our cottage was packed to the rafters of the attic with the
theater people Dad blithely invited home with him. The house

rang with their voices, the air was spiced with the aromas of Mother's home-made bread and coffee cake, with the mountains of pancakes she made on Sunday mornings following the dip they all took in the Delaware. At the beginning I watched enchantedly from the sidelines and then, unexpectedly, I came into center stage because of a dip in the Delaware that the wondrous Leona Beautelle took.

Miss Beautelle started to drown—at least she *thought* she was drowning—and she screamed for help. I was big for my age and already an expert swimmer and I swam to her rescue, a feat that made me heroine of the day and led to my being honored with large dishes of ice cream at the Bethlehem Hotel. Ice cream was the last thing I needed; I was already showing signs of the weight problem which was soon to become such a big part of my life.

But there was an even more important reward: I was declared the company mascot. This meant that I was permitted the unbelievable privilege of sitting in the dressing rooms while the actresses applied their Miner's cold cream and grease paint. The title carried its duties too; it was my responsibility to stand in the wings during the performance on opening day. This was to bring the company luck.

During these months we all flowered. Mother herself came out of her British reserve as she was fussed over and flattered for her cooking and hospitality. From my bedroom upstairs I would hear the golden-haired, free-wheeling Nadine Bronson calling Mother "Dear Lady Anthony" as she praised her for a lavish midnight supper. The troupers ate like troopers and the expenses soared, but the easy camaraderie of the actors cast a glow over everyone and everything.

If Dad thought of Aunt Susan during these shimmering days, it must have been with a sense of triumph. It was as though the oppressive portrait of Aunt Susan were turned to the wall, the old lady's New England incubus, her Quaker restraint, vanquished by lighter, more carefree spirits. Dad even permitted liquor in the house, something that had never been allowed, but these guests had special license. Dad was among his own at last, surrounded by people who appreciated and admired him, who sought him out for his talent.

When autumn came, the curtain rang down on The Year of the Golden Summer, leaving a bare and silent stage, a darkened

house. For the Anthonys it was like walking out into the gray
dusk of the street after a matinee. The magic faded, real life
took over. For Dad it meant buckling down to his Bradstreet job,
once more stealing the night hours for himself. No "angel" who
came to the country that summer picked up a play of his. No
job in New York was offered. The show simply moved on without
him.

Dad lived for over thirty years after that summer. He eventually succeeded in having a play produced on Broadway; it was
called *Tootlums;* it was a disaster. Another play of his, advanced
for its time, I have heard it said, opened in Canada, but could
struggle no farther. The Year of the Golden Summer, his forty-
eighth year, marked the high-point of Dad's life. Eight years
later, in the Depression, three years before he was to receive a
retirement pension, Bradstreet fired him.

The day this happened I was having my own problems, the
desperate problems of the teen-age wallflower, and Dad came
to pick me up at a party where I'd had a miserable time. I almost
burst into tears when he asked me if I had enjoyed myself, but
something in his manner stopped me. Usually he hummed or
whistled as he drove and I always loved hearing his rich, resonant actor's voice, but now he was silent. I remember looking at
him carefully and seeing that he had grown new lines around
his high-bridged nose and his thin lips. Next day Mother told
me what had happened. He himself would have told me, she
said, but he had not wanted to spoil my evening.

After that, trouble seemed to attract trouble for him. Theater,
as well as everything else in those days, was at an ebb, and
soon Dad could not afford to keep *The Dramatist* going. No
longer did Dad have an office downtown to go to after supper
and no longer was there a reason for going. It seemed to be
Mother's turn for long night hours. Sometimes she sewed far into
the morning, embroidering children's clothes that she sold se-
cretly to an outlet for impoverished gentlewomen, the Women's
Exchange in New York. She even tried door-to-door book selling,
but that produced little, and then Mother and Dad turned their
one-time hobby of collecting antiques into a business. When I
think of those Depression years, I see Mother running breathlessly down and up the lane at Raubsville to the little shop on
the highway beneath us. In the middle of a dinner she had

cooked for us, the bell would ring at the foot of the hill and she would rush down hoping to make a sale.

Added to these problems was the failure of Dad's eyesight. The doctors said he faced blindness. To this day, whenever I see the back of a neck that is too thin for the head it supports, I start to cry. It is the neck of my father as he sat in his chair in a darkened room, day after day, practicing the eye exercises that the doctors offered as his only hope for restored vision. His sight did improve, enough for him to hold down an insignificant administrative job in Harrisburg, the state capital. He went alone to Harrisburg and lived in a small, furnished room, while he earned the pittance that helped the family back home eke through.

There is nothing sadder in my memory of him than the day he left for Harrisburg, when he packed his suitcase with the things he was to take to that furnished room, a few clothes, a few necessities. In one hand he carried the suitcase, in the other hand, a make-up kit, and over his shoulder a banjo. He had kept the make-up and the banjo since the days he had slipped out of Fort Scott with the traveling minstrel show.

2 "...in our image, after our likeness..."

I am sure that Dad knew that he could have failed in the theater just as convincingly in New York as in Pennsylvania, but I also believe that he carried with him a haunting reproach that things might have been better for him if his aunt had taken greater interest in his strengths than in what she considered his weaknesses. Whenever Dad mentioned her, though it was always with pride, I sensed an ambivalence in his feelings.

With Aunt Lucy, my father's sister, there were no such mixed feelings. For her, Aunt Susan represented quite simply, everything worthwhile. Seventeen years older than Dad, Aunt Lucy was the Anthony family's second Unmarried Matriarch. And my bugaboo. To me she was Susan B. Anthony incarnate, as I think she rather liked to picture herself, and as a child I could scarcely separate the two women in my mind.

Susan B. Anthony's will stipulated that Lucy E. Anthony was "the only niece" who had displayed an interest in the cause of woman suffrage and therefore it was Lucy who was the executrix of her estate and Lucy who inherited from her. Dad was not considered as a legatee, not just because of his immoral, theatrical side, but because of his sex. Aunt Susan left everything of historical and monetary value to the female line only, and Lucy became the guardian of the Anthony memorabilia, photographs, furnishings. Most of these things were kept in a house once owned by Dr. Anna Howard Shaw, Aunt Susan's successor in the movement. After Dr. Shaw's death, Aunt Lucy was not only owner but "curator" of this feminist shrine in Moylan, Pennsylvania.

Moylan was a suburb southwest of Philadelphia, just sixty miles from Easton, close enough for us to make periodic motor trips there. We always went there for Thanksgiving, though no matter when we went, I didn't want to go. I am not sure that any of us wanted to go.

I didn't want to go to Moylan because Aunt Lucy was seldom nice to me. She made me suffer because I was fat; I was the only one who seemed to catch the special meaning of her remarks about "How *big* you've grown!" and "What, *another* helping, Susan?" Over the years she wielded dark opinions about apparently everything I did, and in time, Mother caught on and tried to save me from Aunt Lucy's darts.

"Don't talk about how many movies you've seen," Mother would warn me in the car going to Moylan. "Don't talk about boys too much." But, of course, the very things Mother told me not to do, I managed to do, and Aunt Lucy would never fail to let me know that whatever I was doing, I was doing it wrong.

Later Aunt Lucy contributed to my tuition during the first two years of college, but the contributions were always accompanied by a lecture. She seemed to be isolated in Moylan, and yet she must have had spies everywhere, for she always knew of the scrapes I got into at college. Later, when I was married, I was mystified as to how she knew about the wild house-parties we attended or threw. When my first book, *Out of the Kitchen—Into the War*, was published in 1943, she wrote me a letter in which she attacked me for presuming to write on the suffrage movement, as though only those who had lived through part of it, as she had, possessed the right. When I wanted to know more about Aunt Susan, and felt I had proved my professional competence to look at the diaries that she guarded, she forbade me permission. During her lifetime, and she lived to eighty-six, the very same age as Aunt Susan, I gave Aunt Lucy little enough cause for pride in me. And yet I have sometimes wondered if it would have been very different had I led a life of exemplary virtue.

I did not know for a long time why the tacit hostility existed between Aunt Lucy and me, though I should have been able to figure it out. I do recall being surprised by her kind understanding during one phase of my girlhood. That should have been a tip-off. This was the traditional period in which I toyed with the idea of changing my name from Susan to "something beautiful," and I had decided that there was no name in the world more ravishing than "Joyce." Suddenly Aunt Lucy became my ally. "Joyce is a lovely name; it fits you perfectly," she would tell me, and she would remind me of its perfection long after I had ceased to find any loveliness in Joyce at all. The point was, of course, that any name would have been better for me than the one I had been given. Aunt Lucy could not forgive me for bearing the name sacred to her idol.

What Dad himself thought about Aunt Lucy, he never expressed, not to me anyway. With so many years between their ages, Lucy seemed more like a mother or an aunt than a sister. The family loyalty between them was strong, but whether Dad paid his visits to her out of duty or affection, I did not know. I used to think it odd, though, that no matter how often Dad drove us there, along the winding river road, Route 611 following the Delaware and the canal, he always got lost.

The house in Moylan was a large, tan, stuccoed mansion. When we would drive up Aunt Lucy would come out and stand waiting for us in the fan doorway at the end of a long, hedge-lined walk. Tiny, pigeon-breasted, dressed in an ankle-length pongee dress of indeterminate period, her Anthony nose, thin lips and gray eyes marked her as Susan B. Anthony in miniature. But those gray eyes were cold. I found little sympathy in them. Yet one of the disturbing things about Aunt Lucy was something she could not help. She had a withered arm. When I would look at it I would shudder.

As Aunt Lucy would guide us through the broad entrance hall thick with oriental rugs, a hush would fall over us and we would be like tourists in a European cathedral. The house was indeed a shrine, but instead of stained-glass windows we were faced with a gallery of gloomy photographs, all pioneers, all suffrage leaders who had fought alongside Aunt Susan. There was an odor about the house, an odor of papers yellowed with age, of dead embers in the fireplace, of dead days. No matter what room we visited, there were more portraits and pictures; the Thomas Paine of the woman's revolution, Mary Wollstone-

craft; the southern Grimké sisters and the Quaker-bonneted
Lucretia Mott; sausage-curled Elizabeth Cady Stanton, the
theoretician; white-pompadoured Dr. Shaw, surrounded by her
numerous academic degrees. In the place of honor in the long
drawing room, of course, was Aunt Susan.

Everywhere there were sacred objects, tables, chairs, desks
which had once belonged to the founding mothers. Even outdoors one could not escape the memorial atmosphere, for close
to the house was a small forest of trees planted by Dr. Shaw and
Aunt Lucy with an evergreen from every country in Europe they
had visited on their many suffrage tours. The shrine's most valu-
able relics were kept under lock and key in some deeply hidden
recess of the house. As inaccessible as the bones of saints under
an altar stone were the seventy years of diaries which Aunt Susan
began during her teens in Quaker boardingschool. Though Aunt
Lucy hinted mysteriously at their contents, she was so fearful
that the secret thoughts of the public woman might be disclosed
that as long as she lived she permitted no person to look at
them. Priceless as a source for historians and biographers, they
were only shown to a writer a decade after Lucy died, and then
by Dad's other sister, Ann Anthony Bacon, to whom Lucy had
left them.

Eventually the documents and other memorabilia all went to
the Smithsonian Institution, to Aunt Susan's Rochester home
which was turned into a museum, and to the Rare Book Room
of the Library of Congress. There they reside today, and quite
properly, so the public can see them: the red shawl Aunt Susan
often wore for state occasions; the meticulous account books
kept of every penny received and spent for the cause; the famous
scrapbooks with each and every program, clipping, notice, poster,
cartoon, and wisp of evidence of the woman suffrage movement. Susan B. had started this collection at her father's suggestion in the 1850s, the beginning of her long public life.

It was years before I was able to see that house in Moylan for
the extraordinary repository it was, or for the magnificent spirit
it memorialized. The flame that Aunt Lucy kept burning was
no mean one; it burns today. Unfortunately, Aunt Lucy was too
good a guardian; she would part with nothing; she was not even
generous with her recollections. For my own selfish sake I
regret that miserly quality in her. I wish she'd had just a touch

of the showman, like Dad, that would have made a child like
me glory in her and in her cause.

The pictures on the walls were dour, but the women they represented were brilliant and brave. What a difference it would
have made if Aunt Lucy had been able to cuddle me in her lap
and tell me in storybook terms about their deeds. There was
enough material there to last a childhood, and more.

"Up there, dear," Aunt Lucy could have said, "those are the
Grimké sisters, their names were Angelina and Sarah," and then
she could have told the exciting story of how those southern
ladies freed their slaves and then dared to go out and speak
in public, right there in Philadelphia, urging others to do as
they had done. My eyes would have opened wide to have heard
how irate vigilantes burned down the meeting hall the sisters
were in, forcing them to flee from the mob for their lives. I
even might have understood Aunt Lucy's feminist point, that
the mob had been stirred up not so much by the Grimkés abolition message as by the fact that women were rash enough to
speak from a public platform.

With the name I bore, it is embarrassing to think of how long
I went before I understood the fight for woman's rights in this
country. I had no idea that it grew out of the movement to free
the black slave. I had only the dimmest, most superficial idea of
the condition of women before the ladies pictured on Aunt Lucy's
walls went to work, that in addition to lacking the vote, a married woman could own no property, nor have guardianship power
over her own children, and that single women, though preserving
more legal rights, were social pariahs. It was years before I
learned about the woman's bill of rights drafted by Elizabeth
Cady Stanton and presented to the first Woman's Rights convention in 1848. And this, despite the fact that my own Great-
grandfather Daniel Anthony and Great-grandmother Lucy—
Susan B.'s parents—themselves signed that "Declaration of Senti-
ments" that symbolized the start of the longest organized non-
violent campaign in the history of the Western world.

It is ridiculous to hold Aunt Lucy, or anyone, responsible for
my own ignorance, but it would have been wonderful to have
soaked up all that history first-hand rather than to have shied
away from it because the dragon who guarded it was so frightening. I know that it has taken me years to exorcise Aunt Lucy

from my subconscious. But because I myself have done a world
of living in those years, I now see her differently.

When I was growing up, Aunt Lucy was plain, a serious sin
to me at the time, and her withered arm was grotesque. Today
plainness no longer qualifies as sin, and the withered arm I see
not as anything ugly, but as a sad symbol of her whole sacrificial
life. The arm, the austerity, the life—these were the handiwork
of Susan B. Anthony.

In her travels through the wild midwest and the wilder west,
Aunt Susan always carried a gun. And whenever Susan arrived
at my grandfather's house in Fort Scott, she always brought a
toy for Lucy, her favorite niece. On one visit, Aunt Susan delayed in giving Lucy her present, and while the family was talking in the kitchen, the youngster stole into her aunt's room, slid
open the bureau drawer, reached in among the linen, under the
shawl. A shot rang out. Bright red blood soaked through the
sleeve of her dress. When the family rushed into the room, the
little girl was running around like a wounded animal. Aunt Susan
took command immediately. She sent her brother on his horse for
a doctor; she administered a tourniquet; Lucy's life was saved
but she never regained full use of the arm.

Long before the accident, Lucy had adored her aunt. The
wound served to bring the two of them closer together, and it
was only a matter of a few years after that Lucy went back east
to stay with Aunt Susan permanently. Susan B. then lived in
Rochester in a home kept by her younger sister, Mary. This was
battle headquarters for the woman's revolution, and young Lucy
was drilled by its leader as thoroughly as any raw army recruit.
Lucy ate, drank, slept, and read the strategy for winning liberation. At an age when most teen-age girls are practicing how to
attract boys, Lucy was indoctrinated in how to attract women to
the cause. Lucy molded herself to the likeness of her general,
mortifying her own individuality. She lived in the reflected
glory, first of her aunt, and then of the powerful Dr. Shaw.

Lucy was a second-stringer. Not a speaker, not a good cam-
paigner, her services were largely secretarial. She organized
meetings, wrote letters, licked envelopes. But she worked hard
and she was faithful. Today I think of her and am touched by
the paradox of someone who worked so hard for women that she
lost her womanliness. So hidden was the lost Lucy that it threw

up tender shoots only at rare moments, but those were quickly buried in her role as relic-keeper.

These days when I think of all the bric-a-brac in the old house in Moylan, there is only one object that ever brings me pleasure in remembrance. Even with my well-developed sense of the melodramatic, I would turn away from the more impressive items such as the filigreed urn on the mantle in the drawing room that Aunt Lucy kept banked with fresh-cut evergreens from the little forest; the urn contained the ashes of Dr. Shaw. Soon after every arrival I would slip into the drawing room to make sure that my own favorite piece was still there. It always was, nearly hidden among the knick-knacks, a small ceramic of two figures, a handsome man in a brown robe holding a baby in his arms. If I were alone, I would lift the statue from the table and simply hold it, enjoying in silence the tender glance of the man; the enchanting face of the infant. If there were others present my eyes would seek it out and while adult conversation swam above my head, I would commune with it as with a friend. Aunt Lucy had purchased the statue in Italy, certainly not for any religious reason, but simply because it bore the Anthony name. In this whole house of secular reform, how curious that I should have been drawn to this odd little object. It was a statue of St. Anthony and he was holding the Christ Child.

3 "This is my commandment, that you love one another as I have loved you."

A father's banjo, an aunt's frown, a statue of St. Anthony—are these but the trivia of a lifetime? Is it only by accident that some incidents are seared into the memory, and others lost? What memories do we bring with us out of childhood? The significant ones? I think we do, even though they often seem unimportant, unrelated one to another. Sooner or later we all discover that the important moments in life are not the advertised ones, not the birthdays, the graduations, the weddings, not the great goals achieved. The real milestones are less prepossessing. They come to the door of memory unannounced, stray dogs that amble in, sniff around a bit, and simply never leave. Our lives are measured by these.

The phrenologist who read the bumps on my head was just such a stray dog in my memory. This is not to suggest that Miss Jessie A. Fowler was undistinguished in her line. On the contrary, she was distinguished, if for no other reason than that she was the daughter of L. N. Fowler. And L. N. Fowler was the great man of phrenology, that so-called science that swept through the Victorian era like a rage. From his own publishing house, Fowler and Wells, had issued forth the best-selling volumes that studied the relationship between the skull's conformation and mental faculties lodged inside. With his books and his charts, with his talented fingers, L. N. Fowler could adduce the revelatory signs that he called "vitativeness," "approbativeness," "constructiveness," "identity," "sublimity," and some thirty-two other terms that comprised the jargon of his trade. He and his practitioners were everywhere in demand; everyone was having his bumps read.

In Easton, Pennsylvania, during the 1920s there was a residue of interest in phrenology, a sufficient amount at any rate for the Rotary Club to invite Miss Fowler to come and speak to its membership. Miss Fowler's famous father himself had read Aunt Susan's head. He had been able to confirm all the qualities she demonstrated in public every day, her "combativeness," and "firmness" and her ability to make plans and strategy, which in Fowler terminology was "causality." It was arranged that his descendant should read the head of Susan B. Anthony's grand niece.

Miss Fowler sat in our living room at a table upon which she had arranged a number of little green notebooks and a model of a human skull, quite bald, but charted into weird sections. She was a small woman, though powerfully voiced, and I submitted myself to her with a mixture of pleasure and apprehension.

There was silence in the room while she laid both her hands on my head. With all the mystery of a witch stirring a cauldron, she felt through my dark curls, stopping from time to time to reach for a pencil to record something in one of the green note-books. She paused suddenly in her search and turned to Mother and Dad.

"Her mind," she said solemnly, "is already attuned to public work. She is like her great-aunt. She will want to do all the good she can, in the largest possible way, for the largest number of people. She will feel at home when standing before an audience."

I was struck with awe. I was impressed to the core, and some-what confused. Me, like Aunt Susan? Me? No, something was wrong. To be like my great-aunt was to be like Aunt Lucy, grim and spinsterish, and the possibility frightened me.

At the conclusion of the reading, Miss Fowler very nicely left the model of the skull as a gift to my parents and it sat rather proudly on a table in the living room for some months. For all those months I remained affected by Miss Fowler's visit. I saw myself differently. I began to interpret her words to my own understanding, to fit myself into the picture that she so prophet-ically painted. Eventually I came to terms with the matter of being a "public" woman, of being at ease before audiences. These things indicated one thing, that I was to be a movie star.

The fact of the matter was that my soul had been born in the movie houses of Easton. My code, creed, and morals were formed on Friday nights and Saturday afternoons when with Dad's passes, given to him because he was a drama critic, we went to the State, the Seville, or the Embassy theaters. Sitting rapt in the darkened temples, I worshiped Mary Pickford in *Tess of the Storm Country* and Douglas Fairbanks in *Robin Hood* and Betty Bronson in *Peter Pan*. When I learned to write, my first letters were scrawled requests to my idols, asking for their autographed pictures.

The day had come when I was not satisfied with viewing my gods on the screen or in the glossies that papered my walls. The day had come when I would be satisfied with nothing other than their real presence, and so I had written those Hollywood he-men, Ernest and David Torrance, inviting them both to visit me in our home. That our house already was bulging with Mother, Daddy, children, and any number of visiting cousins was not a problem. I decided that I would share my own bedroom with the great ones. I strung a wire across the room, hung up a sheet as a curtain to divide the Torrance brothers, who slept in the beds, from me who slept on the floor. Preparations made, I waited. How my big brothers, Petey and Dan, laughed at me when each day no word came from the west, no star appeared at our door. Finally the postman brought a letter from Ernest Torrance. The star regretted that neither he nor his brother could accept my kind invitation because of prior Hollywood commitments.

It was just at this time, during the period of recovery from the Torrance disappointment, that Miss Fowler had arrived. After that my thinking changed and I felt better because I knew that it was only a question of time before I would be joining Ernest Torrance in Hollywood.

Certainly in the movies I would be giving myself, as Miss Fowler had clearly stated, to "the largest possible number of people." I began to picture myself as I would appear on the silver screen, a sure-fire synthesis of all my favorites. I could see Susan B. Anthony, the siren, form as svelte as Billie Dove's, eyes as large as Mary Astor's, and larger still with dramatic circles

painted around them in the manner of Pola Negri. There I was,
Susan B. Anthony, a voice as golden as Jeritza's; Susan B. An-
thony, draped in silks and satins and an occasional leopard skin.
How wonderful, I would muse to myself while gazing at Miss
Fowler's skull, how wonderful that one could tell all those things
merely from the shape of one's head!

"She is like her great-aunt," Miss Fowler had intoned. As de-
pressing as this pronouncement had been to me at first blush,
I began to work on that too. Surely the old prune could not be
as bad as I imagined her. This marked the very first time in my
life that I showed a genuine curiosity about Aunt Susan. I started
asking Dad and Mother about her. They were pleased that I was
interested, but nothing they told me satisfied my imagination.
Being in the van of the temperance and abolition movements
sounded noble, but not right for me. Woman suffrage sounded
like something dreadful.

At last, however, I was told something about Susan B. Anthony
that was up my alley.

Aunt Susan had worn bloomers. It is a wonderful tale, really,
Aunt Susan and that costume. The more I pushed Dad to tell me
everything he knew about it, the more some of those battle-axes
in Aunt Lucy's feminist gallery began to melt into life, and I
began to get a taste of the meaning of intolerance.

Aunt Susan did not invent bloomers, I am happy to say. Amelia
Bloomer didn't invent the garment either. The honor belongs to
a lady of high fashion, Mrs. Elizabeth Smith Miller, daughter of
the financier who backed John Brown's revolt at Harper's Ferry.
Laced tight into corsets and wrapped in the hoopskirts of the
1850s, Mrs. Miller breathed freely only once a year. That was
each summer when she took the annual water cure at Saratoga
Springs and was permitted the liberation of a loose-fitting tunic
worn over modest pantaloons.

Why not, Mrs. Miller had asked, why not have such freedom
365 days a year? And to ask was to act. Garbed in an adaptation
of this Saratoga costume—no corset, no hoop, a short dress with
pants—she sailed into the fashionable parties of Washington and
New York. When she traveled upstate to visit her cousin Elizabeth Cady Stanton in Seneca Falls, New York, the fiery feminist
too, despite her great girth, cast off her corsets and arrayed herself in pants and tunic. Then, when the editor of a tepid tem-

perance sheet called *The Lily* saw what comfort Mrs. Stanton was experiencing, she too stripped down, and still more significantly she began editorializing about it in her weekly. The editor's name was Amelia Bloomer and soon the costume was known by her name.

Then Aunt Susan entered the picture. When she attended her first woman's right's convention, at Syracuse, in 1852, most of the leading feminists were wearing the bloomer attire. Aunt Susan at first resisted Elizabeth Cady Stanton's coaxing to join in. But finally she capitulated: she took off her corset, cut off her long brown hair, lifted her skirt to the knee and exposed the premature pedal-pushers.

The world was not ready for this innovation. Aunt Susan was 5 feet, 5 inches tall; in those days she weighed 156 pounds; her chest measured 38 inches, and when she projected her voice to a large crowd, she could expand that chest measurement from 38 inches to 43. Going about unbrassiered and uncorseted, she cut quite a figure for herself, though not so full a figure as roly-poly Elizabeth Cady Stanton. But while Mrs. Stanton confined her bloomers to her home and the village of Seneca Falls, Aunt Susan wore her outfit as she did her door-to-door canvassing on behalf of abolition, and battled in the New York State capitol for the first married-women's property act.

Doors slammed hard in her face at the sight of the bloomered apparition on the doorstep. The legislature in Albany nearly erupted in riot when she appeared before it. On the street, gangs of little boys followed her, pelting her with rotten eggs and tomatoes, shouting:

> "Gibbery, gibbery, gab,
> The women had a confab
> And demanded the rights
> To wear the tights
> Gibbery, gibbery, gab."

Aunt Susan submitted to the taunting like a martyr, and when it seemed appropriate, she fought back with logic. "I was obliged to be out every day in all kinds of weather," she wrote later, "and also because I saw women ruined in health by tight lacing and the weight of their clothing, I hoped to establish the princi-

ple of rational dress." The feminist champions dared to believe
that freedom in dress could come before, not after, political and
social freedom.

Gradually Aunt Susan realized the necessity of retreat. She was
hurt when Mrs. Stanton became one of the first to defect. She
was badly wounded when her friends William Lloyd Garrison
and Wendell Phillips hooted as vigorously as the street gangs
had. Those two gentlemen may have been radical abolitionists,
but where female dress was concerned, they proved ultra-con-
servative. Finally, Aunt Susan let down the hem of her dress, let
her hair grow, laced herself once more into a corset with a
resigned farewell to the revolutionary garb.

"I found it a physical comfort but a mental crucifixion," she
said later of the bloomer costume. "The attention of my audience
was fixed upon my clothes instead of my words. I learned the
lesson that to be successful a person must attempt but one reform.
By urging two, both are injured, as the average mind can grasp
and assimilate but one idea at a time."

In Easton, our family was genteelly poor, but we children
never saw this as a hardship. It didn't matter to us that the people we saw the most of were on a higher economic level. We
barely noticed the meat-stretching intent of our frequent stews
and hashes; that I wore hand-me-down shoes from Petey and
Dan never bothered me; I was proud that Mother had learned
to make our coats and dresses. Everyone in the family was very
busy. We all had projects and we had one another.

Dan and Petey were very close. They did everything together.
They went to school together; in the afternoons and on weekends they played together; every night after dinner they would
climb the stairs together, our Belgian Pincer Teddy trotting up
after them. Every night, and this remains one of my indelible
memories, they would have their baths, say their prayers, and
then lie in bed singing songs in harmony. From my room I could
hear them as they went from "My Buddy" to "There's a Long,
Long Trail A-winding" to some of the old Negro songs that Dad
had taught them as he played the banjo. Every night they sang
themselves to sleep.

One year, just as we were on the verge of Easter, Petey, who
was six, became ill. He coughed incessantly, fluid filled his lungs.
Dr. Siebert came, and came again. "Scarlatina," Dr. Siebert said,

and prescribed hot baths to release the liquids, but the baths only seemed to make Petey weaker.

Mother was helpless. She sat with him, sewing new curtains for his room to keep her hands busy. Dad paced back and forth. Dan stayed outside his door. On Saturday afternoon before Easter he didn't even notice the Easter basket packed with the multi-colored hard-boiled eggs that Dan had dyed. He didn't have the strength to pick up the fluffy yellow Easter bunny Mother and Dad had bought. His hand lay on his favorite old toy, the train he always carried to bed. Then, between brutal spasms of cough-ing, he whispered to Mother: "Mother, my arms are so tired."

She leaned over and held his arms gently, stroking them and patting them. He sighed as if content, then he coughed no more. Mother did not leave his side even after the doctor pronounced him dead.

Petey was buried in the Easton cemetery. A Presbyterian min-ister conducted the services at graveside, though the Presbyterian church was not ours; we had no church. Dad was a free-thinker, an Emersonian, not unlike Aunt Susan had been after breaking with the Quakers because she espoused the Civil War. Mother, with her British background, was Church of England, though she had long since given up attending services. We children were everything, sampling Sunday schools more by convenient location than by denomination. Petey's death did not send Mother back to church. But as she and I walked out to Petey's grave each day that spring, I became aware of the number of times that God and heaven came into the conversation.

Up to that time the only real association I had had with God was through the prayers we all said at bedtime. But now I met Him as some unexplained Power responsible, somehow, for life and death. I could not bring myself to ask Mother about this bewildering Power, for Mother in her grief seemed bewildered too.

Mother's grief was heart-rending. Every day we gathered up great armfuls of flowers for the green hillside cemetery, forsythia, dogwood blossoms, purple iris, but it was the pussy willow that Mother treasured. A vase of pussy willow had stood by Petey's bed when he died. On the table between Petey's and Dan's beds, a vase of fresh pussy willow was ever present.

So great was Mother's desolation that eventually, to make life easier for her, I was dispatched to New York for a visit with Mother's brother, Sydney, and his wife Nell. I had been visiting them off and on since the time I was two, and it was always a treat for me. Uncle Sydney was the only member of the Sutherland family—or in all of my family, for that matter—with a talent for making large sums of money. He and Aunt Nell lived in great luxury on Riverside Drive in New York with a chauffeur and a cook, and a lovely room for me. I looked forward to the princesslike splendor of my visits there, but most of all I looked forward to being with Aunt Nell.

To me, Nell Sutherland was beautiful. She was small and blonde and feminine; she was always perfumed and bejeweled; she was soft-voiced, soothing to be near. She had been a nurse— or "Sister" as they were called in her native England—and during the yellow-fever epidemic in Panama she had felt it her mission to travel there to serve. In the Canal Zone she had met Uncle Sydney.

Aunt Nell, too, was deeply stirred by Petey's death. And on this visit of mine she was especially tender toward me. I talked a lot about Petey to her. I told her about our visit to his grave each day. I confessed to her that though I was sad about Petey, I was sadder still about Mother and the awful suffering she seemed to be enduring.

"You mustn't worry about your mother," Aunt Nell told me. "She will be all right. Petey is praying for her now." It was a startling thought that Petey, who I knew was dead, could be praying for Mother. But Aunt Nell spoke with such certitude, with such a weight of adult wisdom, that I accepted and trusted what she said without question.

Aunt Nell was the direct opposite of that other aunt of mine in the gloomy old house in Moylan. Aunt Lucy made me feel as though she were my critic, that nothing I did for her was right. It always seemed to me that Aunt Lucy wanted me to be wrong. Aunt Nell, on the other hand, made me feel that she wanted me to be right. And for her I strove to be right. The most wonderful thing of all about Aunt Nell was that whether I was right or wrong, I knew she loved me. To me Aunt Nell was beautiful and wise, but her most memorable quality was that of love.

She had to have that quality of love in order to put up with Uncle Sydney. He was an arrogant man. Uncle Sydney could purse his lips and squint up his eyes, and destroy those around him with his icy sarcasm. I would sit at the dinner table, fearful of his next cruel, unnecessary remark to a servant. Dining out at a restaurant was worse. He treated all waiters as though they were blacks on his father's plantation in Jamaica—and I had heard the stories of my grandfather's carriage whip. But Nell could soothe his anger and placate the servants.

It was only later I realized Uncle Sydney was an alcoholic. His was periodic alcoholism, long stretches of sobriety interspersed with giant drunks during which Aunt Nell would cover for him at work, telephoning to report his "flu," his "bronchitis," his "attack of ulcers." He got away with his drinking, as some alcoholics do, for the whole of his working life, because when he was good he was very good and guilt drives alcoholics to work harder for time lost.

The love Aunt Nell had for Uncle Sydney, for me, for the world, I eventually was to recognize as an exceptional love. It was unconditional.

It was as though she said, "I love you no matter what you are, no matter what you do. I am on your side. I am your ally."

She didn't just tolerate Uncle Sydney's bad temper. She loved him with no strings attached, no reservations. Her love warmed each word, each little gesture. She could glance in a tender, cherishing kind of way at Sydney, even after he had burst into a temper, as though saying to him: "I understand why you have acted that way. I know something is causing you to do it that is not the real Sydney. I love you anyway."

I felt sorry for Aunt Nell and the life she led with Uncle Sydney. I knew she shielded me from him, yet I was worried about her. I was worried about the onslaughts she received from him. How could I realize that she had her own shield? It was years before I was to know that what she did for me, what she did for Uncle Sydney, were not for us alone, but for Christ. To a child to whom religion was not much more than a meaningless sampling of Sunday schools, Aunt Nell's love of Jesus was a foreign thing. I was fascinated by its mystery and by its symbols, her golden cross, the gilt-edged Bible, the amethyst beads. Because I loved Aunt Nell, I thought that the beautiful aura about these things was Aunt Nell's aura.

When I went home to Easton, I could see how much Dan missed Petey. Now he had to mount the stairs at night alone. Each night Mother would take his hand and lead him up to his room, tuck him in, and read to him as Teddy settled down between the two beds. In an effort to fill the hole in his life, Dan crammed his days with athletics. He went down to the YMCA and signed up for every sport that he could find the time for. In the months and years that followed, his natural coordination, combined with his skill and determination, led him to excel at swimming, diving, track, tumbling, rings and trapeze, boxing, wrestling. All his energies went into strengthening and perfecting his muscles, even to sending for the Earl Leiderman course in body-building and the purchase of a taut elastic push-and-pull chest expander.

Dan sought me out as a convert. His stopwatch was a regular part of my childhood. Timing me in the 50-yard free style in water and the 50-yard dash on land was a regular part of his curriculum and he was a hard tutor. I was a born swimmer and quickly became expert in the eight-beat crawl and backstroke. I did fairly well at track and was not bad at somersaults and nest-hangs, but I couldn't make the grade at boxing. I am not so sure that Dan's spirited coaching, his insistence upon physical prowess, did not eventually save my life—for the time was to come when my body was battered beyond all normal hope of recovery.

What memories do we bring with us out of childhood? The significant ones? If I were to choose my favorite moment from all of my youth, I would select a memory of something that happened when I was eight years old. I didn't understand it then. It was related to nothing else in my experience and I had had little preparation for it.

We were spending that winter in the cottage at Raubsville. We children attended the one-room country school presided over by a frail and ancient spinster, Miss Belle, who valiantly tried to discipline, as well as teach, the pupils who ranged from toddlers to farm boys over 6 feet tall. I shivered constantly as Dan and I trudged through rain, snow or sleet, more than a mile down the trolley tracks each morning and a mile back each afternoon. The school, like our cottage, was heated only by a pot-bellied stove. First I got a sore throat; that developed into tonsilitis, then to fever, and to a swelling in my legs which turned them into lumps of pain.

Dr. Fretz, our family doctor, drove down the narrow icy road from Easton to treat me and to check my heart for damage from the illness that he called rheumatic fever. He prescribed hot compresses constantly changed by Mother and a loving neighbor.

The night before Christmas, feverish and restless and aching, I lay in the second-floor room. I was thirsty and wide awake in the silent night, staring at the blank, black panes of the window beyond which loomed the forest.

And as I lay there, the black window became luminous, revealing a face encircled by a soft yet wondrous light. The face was that of a young boy, about twelve, tender and even wistful. His eyes appealed to me to open the window and let him in out of the winter night. In a mixture of fear and wonder, I lay rigid, awestruck. But his beauty overcame my fear. I determined to rise and fling wide the window so the boy might come in.

A twinge of pain shot through my legs and I sank back. Would he understand that I could not take those steps? I kept my eyes on his in mute apology. And at that moment my pain vanished. Silently, I leaped out of bed and ran to the window, determined to let him in. But even as I reached him, his face vanished. Only the blackness of the night remained outside the cold blank window panes.

I returned to bed, strangely warmed, rejoicing that my legs ached no more, but lonely that he had gone. Quietly I lay pondering him. Who was he? Certainly he was no boy from school. He was nothing like my lost brother Petey. And yet that lovely face, that tender glance I seemed in a strange way to have known all my life.

Whose was that face at the window?

4 "My grace is sufficient for you, my power is made perfect in weakness."

When you want something, and want it desperately, great energy is generated. Some people employ that power creating useful, brilliant lives; others let that power destroy them. When I was young, I wanted something desperately. I wanted to be popular with boys.

As a pre-puberty girl, I seemed an unlikely candidate for male attention. Of all Dad's children, only I had received the thin, convex, high nose with the bump on the bridge which had been inherited from centuries of Anthonys. Dad looked upon it as a badge of distinction, and urged me to take pride in what he termed "the Anthony Nose." My classmates looked at it differently. I was often called "Eagle Beak."

The nose was not my biggest defect, however. It was my weight. Years of homemade bread, pancakes, cocoa, and ice cream had expanded me into a balloon of a girl, all of which I could live with until, at the age of eleven, I fell in love with a neighborhood boy named Joel Bringham. I adored him, that is until one day he broke my heart. He greeted me on the school steps with: "Hi, Fatty."

I burst into tears, ran home and refused to go back to school that day. From that time on my life was a misery. Dan, taut and slim with all his sports, would taunt me about my stomach. I lived in constant fear that Mother would have to let out the seams of my dresses again. And yet I was powerless to stop gorging myself on bread and cookies, candies, pretzels, or the crisp fried potatoes that Emily Wood and I cooked each afternoon in her toy frying pan.

I was not always to be powerless, however. One day I went to Mother and confessed the loathing I felt for myself. I cried, and she tried to comfort me. That very day Mother took me downtown to Dr. Fretz's office.

"Just puppy fat, Mrs. Anthony," Dr. Fretz said. "She'll grow out of it." Then I got on the scale and he all but whistled. That afternoon Dr. Fretz gave me a diet to follow.

The diet was my introduction to will power. Had I been aspiring to sanctity, I could not have been more mortified. Painfully I started to learn the cardinal rules of the ascetic, the sins I had to abjure, the virtues I had to develop to reach my goal. No second helpings, lean meat only, one starch at each meal, and that no more than 100 calories. No Emily Wood potatoes. Exercise, plenty of it. Stand on my feet for at least twenty minutes after each meal.

That first night I got up from the table hungry. The next day after school I walked down College Hill and back, a round-trip distance of three miles. I walked it rain or shine. When I left school in the afternoon, no longer did I run over to Emily's. Now, looking neither right nor left, I walked briskly past the boys, past the mansions dwarfing our tiny house amidst them, past the fraternity houses, where I felt self-conscious about my sprouting breasts, past the early nineteenth-century classic white frame house of the President of Lafayette College, down the hill overlooking the winding Delaware, and the spires of Easton's numerous churches, its tall buildings, three of them; past the shop where Dad printed his magazine.

The daily solitary walks formed a pattern that would never leave me. Gradually I began to observe the changing color of the hillside dropping sheer from the Lafayette campus; the shifting shapes of clouds over the rooftops of the little town. But filling my eyes with beauty did not fill my yawning stomach.

The hardest part of my daily trek came as I approached Mc-Crory's five-and-ten. Wafting out of its doors came the roasting, spattering fragrance of hotdogs. It took every ounce of will power to walk by. I never gave in. It would have been against my religion.

I was even more sorely tempted at bridge parties. On the card table lurked a dish of salted nuts, a dish of candy. At teatime, rich chocolate brownies and cakes, plus ice cream. The choice was mine. I had free will. I could, if I chose, reach out and grab the brownie, but I knew that one would be too many and a thousand not enough.

Each Wednesday I entered the silent, darkened office of Dr. Fretz, to meet a judge more stern than the most severe confessor. This judge would give no absolution, his punishment was implacable. This judge was the tall scale with ugly little numbers on it that would consign me to the hell of a gained pound. I chose not to commit the sin of indulgence at the tea party. Instead, on Wednesday I walked with my empty stomach into the eighteenth-century building which housed the scale. I ascended it while the nurse performed the ritual of adjusting the weights. Breathless, I hardly dared to watch it. Instead I looked at the side of her intent face as she squinted to move the tell-tale gauge forward. The weight went down. She had estimated my weight as more than it was. Carefully, slowly she moved it back, and the weight balanced evenly.

"You've lost half a pound this week!" she congratulated me as I descended. "Keep it up. Doctor will be proud of you."

Cleansed and fortified I entered the next week of fasting. With a steady but slow decline of pounds, I became encouraged. Had a church or even Aunt Nell dared to ask me to fast for Lent, which it happened to be when I went on my diet, I would have balked like a horse at a jump. Yet for the high goal of popularity, no fast was too rigorous.

I could even withstand the ordeal of Straup's Pharmacy. My schoolmates casually ordered their thick, dark chocolate milk shakes, and chewy, toasted cheese sandwiches. Stoically I sipped my orange juice, reciting to myself the litany of the dieter. It's the first milk shake that counts. It's the first candy that counts. Stay away from the first candy.

And I did stay away from the sweets, the starches, the fried foods. A power greater than my food addiction had taken over. Now every time I smelled hotdogs, watched the milk shake froth, heard the sizzle of toasted cheese on the grill, I conjured up the image of Joan Crawford, who had literally starved her way to stardom. Even the greatest goddess of them all, she with the lean and hungry look, Greta Garbo, had been forced to diet when she first came from Sweden to Hollywood. She had mortified herself, even as I was doing, for the reward of hollow cheeks, protruding hip and collar bones. If they could do it, I could do it too.

Nor did I wish for the waistline only of Garbo. I wanted to be completely made over in the image and likeness of the gaunt Swede. And since my goddess usually starred as a lost, as well as a lean, lady I yearned to become dissipated, a *femme fatale*. The outer props were easy. I bought a huge ten-cent-store ring such as hers in *The Green Hat*. I huddled my shoulders, broad like hers, into my polo coat as she did. I clomped in the flat heels she had made popular, let my dark curly hair grow shoulder length, though it would never hang straight and shiny as did hers.

Then came the triumphal day when the scales revealed I had reached my goal: I had taken off eighteen pounds! And to my amazement the first reward I got was an invitation by Joel to walk home with him from a Halloween party. With all the nonchalance of a man of the world he offered me a cigarette. Not wishing to be outdone in sophistication, I accepted. I choked on the alien smoke as it went into my mouth, down my throat, into my lungs. I grew dizzy and had to hold on to his arm.

"Don't inhale at first—just keep it in your mouth," he advised. I knew it was wrong, that my parents didn't approve, but when my peer group called, I answered.

I held the slender tube, I hoped, as gracefully as my idols held theirs on silver screen. I found, what's more, that drawing on the cigarette was comforting. And even more comforting was the fact that it killed my appetite. Looking forward to a cigarette made it easier to withstand the temptations of after-school feasts. Smoking helped me stay on my diet for the next ten years, to maintain the 24-inch wait, 36-inch hips, and 36-inch bust. The bosom measurement, I had to admit, came not from my rather flat chest, but from my broad swimmer's back.

Meanwhile, Mother coached me in the carriage of the body beautiful.

"Do you want a hump on the back of your neck like Aunt Lucy's?" she asked when she caught me in my favorite posture, glued to a book, slumped down on my spine in the corner of the blue sofa. Guiltily I straightened up, lifting my rib cage off my hips. On my College Hill reducing hikes, I tried to hold myself as straight as the Queen of Easton, Dr. Fretz's wife, a stately, gray-haired, beautiful lady. She and I seemed to be the only Eastonians who walked purely for exercise.

But, though I had lost weight, I had gained not one ounce of popularity. While my girl friends quickly started going steady when we entered Easton Senior High School, I was left out in the cold. Each morning I told myself, this would be the day I would find my *own* steady. Each night I tasted defeat. Joel, my long-time buddy, was now off attending a boy's school in the country. The college men next door in the fraternity houses were forbidden as much too old. None of the high school boys really appealed to me, nor I to them. They made no overtures beyond an admiring glance at my figure, and a casual "Hi." Tongue-tied, I could only reply, "Hi," and walk on.

I simply could not think of a follow-up word or expression, other than a big, toothy, over-eager smile. Some girls are born with a patter of small talk in their mouth. I, the Yankee daughter of a shy British mother, was neither born nor bred with this vital weapon. Nor did my Hollywood idols serve as models for small talk. They did not talk at all from the silent screen. Their only words were written in subtitles. All else was mute pantomime, with wide gestures of "Come," or "Go," with appropriate circles of arm and hand, or rolling their big dark eyes as did Pola Negri, or dropping blackened eyelashes on white cheek.

When "talkies" broke the sound barrier, the dialogue was singularly ill-suited to my teen-age needs at the skating rink or the football game. Those first cataclysmic spoken words of Garbo in *Anna Christie* as she drank her whiskey neat, "All my life I have wanted a little baby," were hardly, I felt, good conversational openers. Later dramatic lines by Garbo such as, "Armand, I do not want to die," in *Camille* seemed too rich for conversation with sweaty football heroes or acne-fighting classmates.

Nor did the hundreds of books I read, or plays I saw, teach me "airy nothings" with which to beguile the boys. High school men, I learned, ducked any girl who talked books. Nor could I dare confide in any of them my growing interest in learning from my favorite teacher, Miss Gregory, the rules of putting words down on paper, words that should be, she urged "specific, definite and concrete," of writing in a journal to sharpen my perceptions of what I saw, heard, felt, smelled, and tasted. I kept a close secret even from my girl friends my love of reading and writing, fearing they might rat to the boys that "Sue Anthony is a greasy grind who keeps her nose in a book." I hid the heresy of enjoying Ibsen's *A Doll's House*, or my pleasure in listening to the heroine's climactic curtain speech, which Mother constantly rehearsed for her performance before women's clubs throughout the East.

"When Nora slammed the door, she slammed a door that freed women all over the world," Mother would proclaim.

But despite Ibsen and Aunt Susan, women's goals were not so very different in the 1930s from what they had been in earlier generations. Ten years after suffrage, the average middle-class American girl was still taught as I was that "man's goal is to attain a thing, success; women's goal is to attain a person, a husband." And even Dad quoted the romantic poet Lord Byron, who said, "Man's love is of man's life a thing apart; 'tis woman's whole existence."

"Poor Aunt Susan, she never married" or "Poor Aunt Lucy, without a husband." This was the common scorn expressed not only for maiden aunts, but also for bachelor career girls who occasionally visited us. I resolved that never would I be a victim of the fate worse than death, spinsterhood. That being the case, how was I going to make it with the boys? Nothing seemed to transform me into the "gay lighthearted little coquette with all the village swains dangling at her feet" described by Mother in her review of Helen Hayes playing *Coquette*.

I was flattered but frightened when a handsome college man invited me to the social event of my senior year in high school: Spring Open House at Lafayette College. But I feared he would never ask me out again when he learned that despite my well-groomed, trimmed-down figure and my interesting, though not pretty face, I was tongue-tied.

His name was Harry. And he was tall, blond and older, a junior at Lafayette. After his opening gambits about how beautiful I looked, what a great party his fraternity, Phi Gamma Delta, was giving, he stopped. He expected me to catch the ball and throw it back to him. Weightily I dredged up the fact that my father became an honorary member of Phi Gam when he coached Lafayette's drama club. Next, I pretended to concentrate on some new step Harry was doing, though I could really follow it rather easily. I tried complimenting him on his dancing, his fraternity house. Then I dried up completely. When the set ended we drifted out on the porch. My tongue seemed locked in the cage of my jaw.

Joel, now a freshman Phi Gam, rescued me. He was smiling in an exceedingly devil-may-care manner. He held two glasses in his hands as he walked to where we stood rooted like two trees.

"Here Sue! Harry, you'll have to find your own."

I looked at the amber liquid, sniffed its perfumish odor. Rye and ginger ale, Joel said. What had I to lose? I drank it bottoms up. The elixir warmed my gullet as it went down, flooding the cockles of my heart, sending lively hot blood through my veins. It was as though someone had turned on an electric switch. I lighted up and heard my voice in vivacious chatter. Joel swept me off to dance, where I followed him not on the floor, but above it, floating in perfect rhythm, freed of the floor, freed at last of myself.

Gone was the leaden me of a few minutes before. In her place was the new me, soaring celestially above time and space, bubbling in happy talk and laughter. Something else had taken over. Something that released me, made me feel larger than me, witty, daring, irresistible.

The stag line got the message, cutting in every few steps, surrounding me between sets. The miracle had transformed me from tongue-tied wallflower into the belle of the ball. Cinderella had become the princess sought after by not one, but a dozen adoring princes. What need to search further? I had discovered the secret of transcending the self who felt inferior, unpopular, envious of the other girls. And like all great truths, it was so very simple. One drink turned me on! I became a new and dazzling personality, one radically different from the old, groping, brooding, introvert who hungered not only for food and popularity, but for something that would satisfy an even deeper hunger.

I didn't know it, of course, but I had shown the very first sign of an alcoholic. One drink brought about a personality change, as rapid and transforming as from Dr. Jekyll to Mr. Hyde.

My big problem from that night on became how to conceal my drinking from my parents, Dad especially. Not only was he a teetotaler, he was a strict Prohibitionist, inheriting his hatred of alcohol from his Quaker ancestry. His grandfather, Daniel Anthony, had been a strict abstinence man. His father, Merritt Anthony, had actually gone to battle to bring prohibition to Kansas, his adopted state. And it was quite natural that Aunt Susan should have cut her teeth in temperance crusades. Bred in the bone-dry atmosphere of her Quaker childhood, she once wrote scathingly in her diary after a dance that her partner had drunk too much, made "a fool of himself" and that any future partner must be a "total abstinence man."

She gave her very first public speech on temperance, not only because of her inbred convictions, but because in that day it was the only reform that a lady could espouse publicly. Her carefully prepared address, the first of some ten thousand she would give in the next fifty-seven years was delivered in March 1849 to the Daughters of Temperance in Canajoharie, New York. It was her opening shot as organizer of temperance societies throughout the state.

Only once in our family life had the rules against alcohol been relaxed. That was The Year of the Golden Summer when everything was permitted. Weekend after weekend I saw the actors and actresses sipping what Dad told me was "medicine," the same kind Uncle Sydney drank. I wondered why this "medicine" changed some of my idols into high-pitched demons. One matinee I couldn't imagine what had happened to my favorite idol, the golden-haired Nadine Bronson.

As the company mascot, I was standing in the wings, but not in my usual excitement. Nadine, about ready to go on, looked very sick. She was being supported by two actors. One was holding a cup of black coffee before her drooping face. The stage manager hissed that she had to pull herself together. I caught his words: "Thought you were a good trouper. You're nothing but a drunk!"

And then I watched a miracle. The wavering woman suddenly drew herself straight, shoulders back, chin up. The famous smile lifted her lips. She walked on stage with the spring of youth, her arms outstretched, her voice resonating over the applause. She was my Nadine Bronson, in control of her voice, her body, her every move.

I saw that afternoon what I myself was to put into practice later before the microphone and on the platform. You can give your best when you must give your best to an audience, no matter your physical condition. Some power seems to transform you, bringing together the fragments of your shattered self so that you can go on. Believe in it, I learned, and it will get you on, even perform through you, no matter how shaking your knees, how parched your throat, how throbbing your head.

But back when I was sixteen the audiences from whom I had to hide my drinking were my parents, and Aunt Nell and Uncle Sydney. After that first drink at the Phi Gam dance, my dates and I generally had a pint or flask to carry to college dances or smaller parties at friends' houses. We often wound up the evening six-deep at the bar at the Manichore, a beer-drinking club in South Bethlehem that also served liquor. My drinking began at exactly the time that Prohibition ended, so I did not have to go to the rather dingy speakeasies frequented by Lafayette students in Phillipsburg, New Jersey, across the Delaware. But wherever I drank, my dates and I always finished off the evening at the "Red Pig" or some other barbecue. Already I had learned that I must have a late snack before coming home. First, the snack helped sober me up if I was tight. Second, since chlorophyll breath-killers had not yet been invented, I had to cover my breath with raw onions on hamburgers with milk.

Never after my first drink did I kiss Mother goodnight if I could avoid it. I learned to creep up the stairs with my shoes off, to whisper a goodnight from the safe distance of the hall, then rush to brush my teeth before any confrontation.

Visiting Aunt Nell and Uncle Sydney at Gloucester that summer after graduation from high school called for even more guile. Because of my age they would not allow me to date at night at all. I dated in the afternoons, naturally choosing the hardest-drinking college boy on the beach. Hal, a sophomore at Harvard, picked me up at two most afternoons, racing me in his battered roadster along the North Shore to get ice and a mixer. Parked by the ocean, he tought me how to drink straight alcohol cut only a little with lime rickey. I grew gayer as I downed more of these potent belts, laughing at his funny stories, feeling freed of all restraint, my mind expanded on a trip beyond time, space, and self. But I had to be home at six, for dinner at seven. The moment Hal dropped me off I sneaked in the back door to the kitchen, begged the English butler for a glass of milk to kill my

breath, shot up the back stairs into the bathroom to brush my
teeth before facing Aunt Nell and Uncle Sydney at dinner.

In a few short months I traded in the five years' asceticism
of my diet for incipient alcoholism. In booze, I found the quick
and easy mood-changer that quenched all hunger and thirst. It
won in minutes freedom from self-consciousness, and thus the
popularity I had sought so long. I had found, in fact, a power
greater than myself. For here was a power that seemed to slake
some built-in transcendental thirst.

5 "... journey into a far country."

Aunt Susan was my passport to college.

The Depression was at its nadir, we had no money. Besides, I didn't particularly want to go to college. I wanted my freedom. I wanted freedom from family for my drinking, and for my choice of dates. I wanted to head for where the action is, to the mecca of singers, painters, actors, writers, where without chaperone I could study drawing and painting at the Art Students' League. Mother's reaction to this idea was immediate and final: "I will not let you live alone in New York."

One afternoon, Mother sat, her hands busy as usual, stringing beans, between sprints down the hill for our antique-shop customers.

"Sue," she said suddenly. "Didn't your Aunt Susan have something to do with founding a woman's college in Rochester? I seem to remember Aunt Lucy saying she even left a scholarship there, or her friends did."

On the spot she indulged in the unheard-of extravagance of a long distance call to Aunt Lucy, who said yes, it was true. She invested further in a long night letter to the Dean of the College for Women, University of Rochester, calmly requesting that "Susan B. Anthony, great-niece, honor student, be admitted with the Susan B. Anthony scholarship, detailed transcript following."

When no answer came next day or night, far from idly waiting, she got Dad to drag out her own old trunk from the attic. She

started figuring out what clothes I lacked and how she could cut
groceries to buy material for a new suit. Even when no answer
came the next morning, her hopes were high. Late that night, I
heard my mother walking up and down the stairs, pacing in her
room, the only sound besides the rustle and stir of leaf and insect
in the black backdrop of the forest sloping down to our sleeping
porch. And in the morning she woke me, her voice trembling with
excitement:

"Sue, Western Union called! You are not only admitted, you
have the Susan B. Anthony scholarship!"

We had only six days to get me ready. She sewed round the
clock through the next five nights to finish a tweed suit, two new
skirts, and a monklike, blue wool party dress with high neck and
flowing sleeves. All this dressmaking went on while she ran down
to the antique shop, kept us fed, and tried to figure out how
we could find the balance of tuition and expenses. She made me
sit down and write letters to my rich Cousin Maude in California
and Aunt Lucy, asking for help. Finally, with tears falling from
her eyes, she kissed me goodbye as she and Dad tenderly, appre-
hensively, put me on the Lehigh Valley Black Diamond Coach
for the eight-hour trip to Rochester. Unbelievably, I was off to
college, and on my way into the home territory of the great-aunt
I knew so little about. It would not take me long to discover that
if I were to stay in Rochester with that name of mine, I would
have to know something more about Aunt Susan than mere family
anecdotes.

Actually Aunt Susan had preceded me to Rochester by nearly
a hundred years. I arrived by train; she had arrived by Erie Canal
boat. Her father, Daniel Anthony, had shepherded his depression-
ruined family to a bleak farm three miles west of the city. Only
a few Quaker families were on hand to welcome the Anthonys.
Only a few people had reason to pay attention to the twenty-
five-year-old Susan. When she died sixty-one years later, the fact
was noted by the world. By 1906 she had become the most
talked-about, written-about woman in America. The obituaries
and eulogies to her ran into millions of words; state legislatures
throughout the nation passed resolutions of condolence. Among
women of her time, only Queen Victoria seemed more famous.

So, borne upon the magic carpet of her fame, I came to town.
The Rochester press reported the event as though I were a

crown princess returning to her kingdom. To my amazement, my picture was taken and reporters with notebooks appeared at my side for interviews which, according to *The New York Times*, I did not deign to give.

"Too busy getting off on the right foot in her college work," the story said, "Miss Anthony did not want to take time to talk about her famous grand-aunt, except to tell of unveiling a monument in her memory in Albany last year."

Surprised as I was, it did not take me long to adjust to the new role of celebrity. Soon I was walking confidently up to the receiving line at the President's welcoming tea in the art gallery across from the Susan B. Anthony Gymnasium. The College for Women's Dean Helen Bragdon, whose wand-waving had made my instant admission with scholarship possible, presented me to an ancient, white-haired man. The dean's round face beamed as she introduced me, with considerable fanfare, to President Rush Rhees. I smiled graciously, expecting by now the usual recognition evoked by my name on the Prince Street campus. Instead, an ice-cold hand barely touched mine and quickly withdrew.

"So you're related to that woman!" the president growled. I was caught short by the sharpness in his voice. He looked me over. "You even look a little bit like her. Just be sure you don't act like her." He turned away to someone else, cutting me off completely.

Rush Rhees had been a young man when his and Aunt Susan's paths first crossed. He had been opposed to the idea of woman suffrage. He had been opposed as well to Aunt Susan and her meddling in the status quo of the University. The story was that Aunt Susan long had been galled that young girls in her own home town could not attend the University simply because of tradition. And so in 1891, when at the age of seventy-one she determined to spend more time in the house at 17 Madison Street, she decided the time was ripe to clean up her own back yard, getting women admitted to the University. It would be a short, minor fight for freedom, she thought, nothing major when contrasted with the suffrage amendment struggle.

She didn't know that this "minor" campaign was to cost not only her last penny but almost her last breath. The all-male University Board of Trustees flatly refused her request to let women in, basing their refusal on the added costs it would entail. Susan kept hammering away at them whenever she was home. For seven years she kept at it. Finally in 1898 the Board agreed that if the women could raise $100,000 to meet the additional expense within one year, they would admit the girls to college. Susan, a veteran fund-raiser, knew that was an exorbitant, if not impossible, sum for women to scrape from their slim purses. But she formed a committee anyway. She threw herself into the work of soliciting cash and pledges both in Rochester and on her national campaign trips.

As the year drew to its close, they were still tens of thousands of dollars away from the goal. Susan begged the Board to scale down the required amount. Reluctantly, they cut it in half to $50,000, and under persuasion, extended the deadline another year. Though the Board consisted of millionaires and leading merchants, not one of them offered a penny of his own. They felt they were doing all they could against the hardline opposition to co-education of the alumni and Dr. Rhees, the president.

The new deadline was set for September 8, 1900. Aunt Susan, now eighty, was just recovering from the shock of the death of her younger brother, my grandfather, and from the long, sad funeral journey to Fort Scott, Kansas. She traveled back to Rochester for a week-long suffrage meeting, entertaining at home nine women. Then she made a trip back west to Wyoming. She arrived home near collapse on September 4, a Tuesday. Friday night she was still trying to recover her strength when the phone rang. The secretary of the College Fund committee, Mrs. Fannie Bigelow, told her that the next day, Saturday, was the last day for raising the money. They were short $8,000! There would be no further extension at the next day's Board meeting. She was, she said, the only other committee member in town.

Susan spent a sleepless night mentally marshaling every prospect whom she could visit this final day. She started at dawn tackling her sister Mary, who had planned to bequeath $2,000 to the University if it became coeducational.

"Give it now!" Susan urged. "Don't wait or the girls may never be admitted."

Mary could not say no. Aunt Susan then hired a carriage and she and Mrs. Bigelow set forth to raise the remaining $6,000 in the few hours left. On their first call they struck gold. Mrs. Sarah L. Willis, a friend, gave her $2,000. The two women continued begging at stores, offices, factories for the last $4,000, but by noontime they had raised no more. Mary, seeing the dead-white face of her sister at lunch, begged her to stay home and rest, but at 1:30 she took to the road again. They pled long and hard with one of Rochester's richest women. That lady in her elegant drawing room said that her many expenses barred her from giving anything. Susan sank back into the cushions of the carriage as they drove away. "Thank heaven I am not so poor as she is!" she said to Mrs. Bigelow.

In desperation, Susan called on those who had already given more than they could afford. The Reverend and Mrs. W. C. Gannett loyally scraped the barrel, pledging another $2,000. Now it was three o'clock. The Board was to adjourn at any moment, and they still needed $2,000. As a very last resort, Susan begged from the ailing, ancient Samuel Wilder who had given one cash donation already. She prevailed upon him for a pledge, saying she herself would guarantee this last $2,000. The sick old man told the exhausted old lady, "Yes."

Susan and Mrs. Bigelow sped their carriage to the Board meeting. The men were just about to adjourn, convinced that the women had failed. They were shocked and nettled when Susan took the pledges out of her worn leather satchel and walked over to their board table. Aunt Susan, her voice shaking with excitement and exhaustion, counted out and laid before them the last $8,000 in pledges. The men huddled while Susan's heart pumped in concern. Long-faced and stern, the chairman announced to the anxious women: "We accept six thousand dollars of the pledges, but we cannot accept the two thousand dollars pledged by Mr. Wilder. His age and his health make him an impossible risk. He is apt to die at any moment and his estate cannot be held for the amount."

Aunt Susan's heart began to jump erratically. A veteran of hundreds of major defeats, this relatively minor one seemed too hard to take. So many times she had sprinted to the finish line. So many times she had failed to reach it for want of a few more votes, a few more days, a few more dollars, a few more friends. She lifted her nodding head. In one tremendous effort, the old lady turned warrior once more. She had one shot left. She fired it from a standing position.

"Well, gentlemen, I may as well confess, *I* am the guarantor.

But I asked Mr. Wilder to lend me his name so that the question of coeducation might not be hurt by any connection with woman suffrage. I now pledge my life insurance for the two thousand dollars."

Again the men huddled in consultation. Again they refused to give victory to the women. Now they quibbled, saying they must investigate each and every pledge, that it would take them at least two more days to do so.

Sunday, the old lady waited.

"Went to church today but had a sleepy time," she wrote in her diary that night. "It seemed as if something was the matter with my tongue . . . I had a feeling of strangeness—could not think what I wanted to say."

Ignoring the symptoms, on Monday Susan forced herself to get out of bed and go once more to the Board of Trustees' meeting. Nothing short of death itself would keep her from learning if they confirmed the pledges, yet she sat there in a daze, slipping off from time to time into momentary unconsciousness. Suddenly she started to alertness. The Board chairman announced that the pledges were all valid.

"We must now admit women to the University of Rochester," he said.

Aunt Susan went home and wrote in her diary: "They let the girls in. He said there was no alternative."

The girls crowded the red brick house on Madison Street that night to congratulate the winner, to tell Susan of their plans to enter the University that very semester. Later Mary Anthony looked around for the heroine of the evening. Hurrying up to Aunt Susan's room, she found her unconscious. Evidently she had felt the oncoming attack, and not wishing to spoil the happy evening, had slipped away unnoticed. She no doubt worsened her condition by climbing the steep stairs.

Aunt Susan lay near death for one week unable to utter a word, even when she had moments of consciousness. For a month the eighty-year-old struggled back to life. Two months later, she was a little stronger, but her doctor warned her that a second stroke, sure to be fatal, might come at any time. He ordered her to avoid exhaustion, stay away from crowds. She must, he said, lead the normal life of a woman nearing her eighty-first birthday.

Should she follow his orders? Aunt Susan talked it over with her friend and biographer, Ida Husted Harper. She confessed that never again could she face an audience. Even though she could talk clearly again, the stroke had shaken her confidence. Yes, she should spend the time that was left conserving her health. But how could she spare herself while women still could not vote nationally? Her glance fell on her battle kit, the leather satchel, unopened since the day of her stroke. Aunt Susan knew, Ida Husted Harper knew, that the old lady was not going to act her age.

During my freshman year, such stories as I learned about Aunt Susan impressed me. I began reading more about her. I visited the house at 17 Madison. I went to see her ancient, but still-alive secretary, Mrs. Emma B. Sweet. I began to feel a new sense of pride in the Anthony name. But contrasted with this, and with my rather false, yet satisfying celebrity, was the stark need to supplement my scholarship with a job. So it was that the exalted Miss Susan B. Anthony started working for room and board by washing dishes and scrubbing floors in private homes.

Miss Matthews, the vocational director, figured that I would have to work five hours a day, and an arrangement was made with a Rochester woman, a Mrs. Barton. My first thought when Miss Matthews took me out to my new home was that Mrs. Barton looked like Aunt Lucy. She was white-faced, thin-lipped, and unsmiling. The gloom of her pseudo-Tudor house enveloped me as we walked upstairs. Even as she showed me the dark little room that would be mine, I had a premonition that I would never really succeed as her part-time maid.

As it turned out, I was a faithful drudge of a Cinderella but I, too, could hardly wait for the ball, my weekends. These were my only days off from the chores of washing dishes, cleaning floors, making beds, polishing silver, and my sporadic studying. To blot out my menial status I threw myself into fraternity house dances and parties. Naturally I drew the toughest drinkers at the college for men. Like attracts like in liquor. As I gulped my drinks the message got across that here was a girl who could take it, and wouldn't leave it. Moderate-drinking men bored me. As the year progressed, I dated those whose thirst and capacity matched mine. When Hal, my Harvard date, arrived in Rochester after a drunken journey by taxi from Cambridge, we pub-crawled late and long at my newly discovered bars in Rochester and roadhouses in the suburbs as he proved to me that he could outdrink any local product.

Hal had a capacity even greater than mine. But I think he was not an alcoholic. He deliberately chose to get drunk. I, on the other hand, didn't want to get really drunk, but once I took that first drink, I had to keep going until I was. Hal drank more than I, and more frequently. But quantity does not make an alcoholic, as the classic example of Winston Churchill, who allegedly could put away one-fifth a day, attests. Churchill ran his drinking. It did not run him. There are alcoholics who have no more than two glasses of sherry a day, but the difference between them and the nonalcoholic is that they have a compulsion that drives them to those two sherries.

I did not take Hal into the Barton house. I did not want him to know that I worked for my room and board. I lied, saying airily that the Bartons were friends of the family and that I preferred the freedom of living off campus.

I could not get away with this story to my college classmates. While they played bridge in the student lounge each afternoon, they knew that I usually rushed to board a bus as soon as classes ended. I feared that working at the Bartons' might jeopardize the one thing I wanted that first year, a bid to a sorority. One afternoon, I tried to prevent three classmates from accompanying me to the Bartons' while I changed for the sorority's important rush tea. Unfortunately the tea was being held right across from the Bartons'. My friends insisted on coming with me.

It was a typical Rochester winter day, near-blizzard, freezing cold. We four snow-covered students charged into the house, clomped into the hallway, laughing and chatting. A sharp loud voice stopped us dead:

"Susan Anthony, what do you mean by tracking snow into my house, walking in the front door! Go around to the back door where you should have gone in the first place!"

I stood stock still. Then I wheeled around, and stalked out into the snow, not to the back door—that I would not do—but across the street directly to the sorority tea. There I locked myself in the bathroom and cried in bitter humiliation, convinced that my chances to pledge this sorority I wanted were dead.

Some of the girls beat on the door so insistently that finally I opened up.

"Sue Anthony, stop crying this minute! We heard about that silly old woman. Forget it. Wash your face and come out. Where's the old Anthony fight?"

I cried even more at the contrast between poor little Cinderella Sue, and famous big Susan B. I walked out tear-streaked and messy. But the girls understood and were kind and saw to it that I met the rest of the sorority.

That night, arriving back too late to help with dinner, I sat in silence with Mrs. Barton and her taciturn husband. Mrs. Barton did not refer to the afternoon scene. I did not apologize for tracking snow into her house. As I started to clear the table, she finally broke silence: "Now, Susan, be careful washing that cut-glass fruit bowl. It was a wedding present and our favorite. You must learn to be more careful."

Biting back the words I wanted to lash out at her, I swept the dishes off the table as fast as I could. I wanted at least an hour to look at my history notes. Washing the dishes, I forced myself to slow down when I came to the precious cut-glass bowl. Remembering her warning, I handled it gingerly. Since it was much too large for the drying rack, I set it carefully on the porcelain sink to dry and I went on washing the other glassware and silver. Out of the corner of my eye I suddenly saw the bowl slithering toward the edge of the sink. Before I could grab it, it tobogganed to the floor with a splintering crash. Mrs. Barton came running out to the kitchen.

"Not the bowl!" she cried, her face even whiter than usual.

"Yes," I burst into tears.

"You dreadful girl, how could you be so careless? First you mess up my floor with snow, then you break my favorite dish. Get out of the kitchen, get out, get out!"

I blubbered like the seventeen-year-old I was and ran up to my room, threw myself on the bed sobbing. I had failed completely in my first job. Miss Matthews called me on campus next day, said that Mrs. Barton had phoned and told her I was through. I could pack my bags and get out. The college put me up temporarily in the beautiful, brand-new dormitory I so yearned to afford, while Miss Matthews located another job for me.

At lunch soon after, my junior "Big Sister," Etta Brickell, a brilliant, waspish, music major, glared at me through her thick glasses, and said in her high-pitched voice: "You may not realize it, but in no time at all, you've racked up yourself a least-likely-to-succeed reputation." Etta pointed out that I had got but one bid to a sorority. "Not that I could care less about sororities," she said, "but you seem to."

"I guess I'm not a sorority type either," I tried to hide my disappointment. "I guess they want someone who doesn't work like a servant, who isn't blasted like a servant before her classmates."

"*Au contraire*, my Little Sister," said Etta. "It is just the opposite. Your bid came from the one group that saw you humiliated. Far from thinking of you as socially inferior, most of the girls on campus think you are trying to put one over on them. They think you're stuck-up, trying to get away with murder because of your name. All you ever do is brag about your dates, your Harvard man, your Gloucester summers, your letters from Yale, Lafayette, West Point. I may be blunt but you are an arrogant play girl who drinks too much, and romps through on the family laurels without ever cracking a book."

I fought every word she said, trying to defend myself.

She interrupted: "You have your choice. Go on as you are and be hated. Or make an about-face."

For once I listened to my Big Sister and did what she advised. Next day I began wailing about how many long hours I had put in studying for an English quiz, how tough it was for me to pass biology. Soon I began to notice a change in people's attitudes and soon the blank tablet of my mind actually began to receive some impressions from the courses I attended. I began to learn a bit about the Judeo-Greco Christian civilization which had sired me; the language of Voltaire, the music of Shakespeare. I wound up making the Dean's List with especially high marks in English, history, and the social sciences. Biology continued to elude me.

As my studies improved, so did my off-campus employment. The next couple I was to serve as part-time maid were thrilling people to work for and they had a profound, far-reaching effect on me.

Just as I knew instantly that the Bartons and I were wrong for each other, I fell in love with the Andrews family the very first day Miss Matthews took me there. Even in upstate New York the Andrewses managed to create a Greenwich Village atmosphere in their ramschackle house. It felt in fact like coming home to the world of the theater as I looked at the angular ceilings so like the attic set of *La Bohème;* huge studio windows; a casual cosmopolitan clutter of Spanish shawls and Mexican serapes, a worn-out sofa whose horse-hair had split open to expose the stuffings; prints of French impressionists; a giant photograph over the sofa of the French actress Yvette Guilbert; and huge, colorful posters of Montparnesse, the Comédie Française, and Montmarte. Volumes of plays and novels overflowed from orange-crate shelves; theater programs, yellowed with age, were carefully framed on the walls, some dating back to the nineteenth-century performances of Booth and Modjeska.

Celeste Andrews was a handsome, not pretty woman, in her middle thirties. The first day I saw her, her black hair was parted in the middle, drawn back in a shiny chignon, emphasizing her lovely pierced ears from which hung huge golden hoops. Despite the drafty duplex in the winter cold she was wearing a thin off-the-shoulder embroidered peasant blouse, a bright purple, homespun skirt, and only huaraches on her bare feet. Gerald was about a dozen years older, tall, thin, silvered-dark hair. Triangular eyebrows over his black eyes cast him immediately for a benign Mephistopheles. He was holding their son, Gerry, a small, dark-haired boy of four.

I took the thin little boy in my arms and hugged him. Celeste showed us the tiny whitewash-walled room next to Gerry's that would be mine. She waved her long cigarette holder to indicate that somehow, someday, there would be curtains hung at the bare windows, a spread to cover the bare and narrow cot.

In her deep throaty voice with its non-Rochester broad "a" and soft "r," Celeste indicated vaguely my baby-sitting, dishwashing, cooking, and cleaning chores, in exchange for which I would be given my little cell and board. The Andrewses had come home to Rochester, only because, she explained, she was "at liberty" from Depression-hit Broadway. After Gerald had been laid off from his New York newspaper job, they gave up their Village apartment and drove upstate, where Gerald supported them on a small publicity job. It was only temporary. They were both waiting until they could make it back to New York.

There was no drudgery in the work at Celeste and Gerald's. I would fly through my duties so I could join the two of them in the living room for long stimulating talks on theater, art, books, Paris. After I washed the dinner dishes, instead of studying, I would be drawn like a magnet to the lop-sided, patched leather hassock where I sat at Celeste's feet. She would lie on the serape-covered couch, smoking endlessly, giving monologues compounded of personal history and criticism of plays, books, and the injustice of life.

I gobbled up everything that Celeste said. Seldom did I think of questioning her wisdom. One evening, though, Gerald as usual was holding Gerry in his lap while he sipped his after-dinner highball, his dark eyes looking blank at his wife's familiar recitation.

"Hadn't you better take him up and bathe him?" Celeste asked him. "It's getting late." Then, in an aside to me, she said, "Don't ever have a baby if you want a career. The career has to come first. I would be in Paris performing at this very minute if I hadn't married Gerald and if Gerry had not come along. Yvette had just invited me to come back for a season. But Gerry spoiled everything. You can't act when you have to care for a baby."

I glanced at little Gerry, hoping he had not understood her words, but realizing even at four he could soak up this kind of rejection. I walked over, picked him up, and asked Gerald if I could bathe him. Then I read to Gerry, and told him a story about Tomasina, a pussy cat, hoping to substitute these memories for his mother's words.

With me, on the other hand, Celeste was like a proud parent. She was fascinated by my connection with Aunt Susan and started a scrapbook of clippings about me. She loved it—as much as I hated it—when Mrs. Sweet dressed me up in an old garnet silk gown of Aunt Susan's and paraded me at a women's tea on Aunt Susan's birthday.

When a newspaper picture appeared of me placing a wreath on the snow-covered grave of my ancestor in Mount Hope Cemetery, Celeste clipped it out for the scrapbook as though it were a press clipping of her very own.

Later it was Gerald who became excited when I received an invitation to speak at the annual luncheon of the august Alum-

nae Association. I was honored by the invitation, but scared.
I had never made a speech.

"Nonsense," Gerald said. "Nothing to it. I'll help you." And
he did. With considerable skill Gerald worked out a lead, examples, and a conclusion for a smart little fifteen-minute talk on
world peace. "That's a good subject," he said. "It's like the Bible.
You can say anything you want about it."

Gerald put me through a rigorous rehearsal until finally,
dressed in my best blue suit, I stood before my first lecture
audience.

My solar plexus fluttered with performing butterflies. My
hands were sweating as I rose from the luncheon table after the
chairman's introduction, gulped for air, and began:

"We members of the younger generation are on the threshold
of life, a life that can be happy or tragic, fulfilled or disastrous,
depending upon what we do to keep world peace. In Aunt
Susan's days I would have been pelted with tomatoes and rotten
eggs for trying to speak on this subject in public . . ."

A little ripple of laughter rewarded this remark. It was then
that something else took over. The speech flew on its own wings,
I tasted the elixir of a responsive, alert audience looking at me
with upturned faces. Before I knew it my hands were no longer
lunch hooks hanging at my side; they had freed themselves and
were leading a life of their own, moving like dancers to em-
phasize the content. I finished quoting Aunt Susan's battle cry:

"Failure is impossible!"

The sweet sound of clapping rewarded me. Misted with
perspiration, flushed with excitement, I received the congratula-
tions of the chairman and a steady parade of alumnae who
walked up to the head table.

"A chip off the old block," said one white-mustached man. "I
knew your aunt. You have inherited her eloquence—but you're far
prettier."

My head swelled ten sizes that sunny Saturday afternoon. It
expanded even more the next day when I read the news stories
in the Rochester papers. And Gerald was even more excited
than I was.

"You're a natural on the platform, Susie," he kept telling me,
"a natural! Listen Susie, the world is your oyster." It was Gerald

who first talked about my future in bright, possible terms. He spoke of me as a career woman, a woman with power, a woman in politics. He talked about "feeding some facts" into my brain, really buckling down to the study of political science.

"And for heaven's sake," Celeste added, "don't throw your career away on marriage and babies. You have a head start on your Aunt Susan—she had to make her name, you already have it. What I couldn't have done with a ready-made name like yours!"

My friends the Andrewses held out before me that day a future more intoxicating to my mind than the drink I held in my hand. Now I knew that an audience could warm the blood, shoot the adrenalin, transcend the trivia of daily life as powerfully as liquor. How lucky I was to have Celeste and Gerald to groom me for the fame that lay just around the corner!

Of course, there was one minor problem: I didn't know a thing about politics.

6 *"For your love is better than wine.... We will extol your love more than wine."*

Before the winter was out I distressed Celeste and Gerald enormously. I fell in love. I really think that both of them felt this as some kind of ingratitude, an act of betrayal. No matter, I couldn't help falling in love, and the feelings I had for Richard Winter were genuine and deep. He was my first love, the finest, the best.

I met Richard in the Strong Memorial Hospital where I was taken after a toboggan accident. He was the young doctor who examined my wounded knee. The first sight of him, the first touch of his hand as he probed my "wrenched crucial cartilage"—as he proclaimed it—made pain secondary. Richard was twenty-seven years old, ten years older than I, and he was handsome and brilliant and gentle.

He had been born on his family's estate in North Carolina, a large holding that went back to the eighteenth century. He had graduated from Chapel Hill not only highest in his class, but highest in any class since 1800. He had gone to medical school at Harvard and now he was in his last year of residency at Strong before going back to set up a practice in the south.

By the time I was discharged from the hospital two weeks after our first encounter, I knew I was in love with him. If there were no other way for me to tell, I knew because of the startling change in my drinking. On our first date we went to a softly lighted restaurant where he offered me a highball while he had his. My drink remained untouched in the glass. With Richard there, I didn't need alcohol.

Richard kissed me for the first time that evening. In the darkness of his blue coupé, he was gentle, then firm, and as I responded with the full ardor of awakened love, he held me passionately, as though I were indeed a woman, not a girl. For the first time I truly knew what it was to be kissed. He, not I, broke away, and led me to my door. I could not have found it otherwise.

That evening I knew Richard loved me.

Since he was leaving Rochester in June, we both felt the pressure of time. We both knew that we had only three months in which to be certain of ourselves. They turned out to be months of exquisite tension, months of wonder. My first waking thought to my last at night belonged to Richard. I began wearing lower heels because he was not tall. I ruthlessly cut out every starch because he had commented, inadvertently, that I could lose a few pounds. I said "no" to every invitation that was not his. I studied hard to clear all my work out of the way to be free for him. Present or absent, he was the object of my total attention, time, energy, concern, and I was pleasantly impatient that he had to be away from me so much because of his long shifts at the hospital.

I was aware, of course that Celeste and Gerald looked upon the idea of Richard and me disapprovingly. Celeste, in particular, would twit me about it, as though I were only playing at being in love.

One day Richard and I went horseback riding. He talked of leaving for North Carolina the next month, adding, "It isn't so far, you know. I'll come up whenever I can. And I'll wait for you if you really do want to finish college. You'll love the south. Even as a doctor's wife you can write and paint."

The chestnut mare I was on took advantage of my excitement, shied, and threw me to the bridle path. Richard caught her, helped me mount, and we rode abreast in an enchanted Maytime forest, filled with the fragrance of Rochester's incredible lilacs.

When I rushed in to tell Celeste and Gerald the greatest news of my life, I expected them to break out a bottle of bourbon at least, but there was very little celebration. They were relieved that we didn't plan to be married immediately; that seemed to be the only good news. I almost became angry later when Celeste began to mimic a southern accent, she batting her eyelids, fluttering her cigarette holder like a fan, dropping words like "Mammy" and "Old Black Joe." Then, minus her accent she said, "Your Aunt Susan did not give her life to emancipate women so that you, Sue—her namesake—could bury herself in marriage."

It is an interesting thing for me to look back today and see the numerous ways in which people have interpreted Aunt Susan for me. And yet, in this instance, the actual historical truth about Aunt Susan was that, though unmarried herself, she was not anti-marriage at all, not even antipeople-burying-themselves-in-marriage if they so chose. She waged her fight so that women *would* have a choice, that they should be emancipated for something more than marriage if that was their desire.

At the age of seventeen, the same age I was when I fell in love with Richard, Aunt Susan herself was deeply in love, and yearning for marriage. The man she adored was seven years older than she. He was Aaron McLean, the son of her father's business partner, the same Aaron McLean who had made the journey with the Anthony family by wagon from Adams to Battenville, New York, years before. While at her Quaker boardingschool, Susan wrote letters constantly to Aaron, prim letters on lofty topics, hesitant letters, hesitant because she considered herself unattractive to men, because she lived in fear that Aaron could not care for her. Yet just once with Aaron she was bold.

"If you have anything to say, say it," she wrote, "or if you wish anything, express it in plain English, that I may no longer be left in uncertainty . . ."

In her diary, she was less discreet.

"I dreamed of being married last night," she would begin, and then tell the whole dream.

Aaron's engagement to Susan's older sister Guelma came as an utter shock. Grief-stricken, she hid her feelings, continued her intellectual correspondence with Aaron, pulled herself together to go home for the wedding. She flung herself into the round of picnics and excursions and even turned down an offer of marriage from another man made to her on a ride to Saratoga. With her strict Quaker morality, she could not admit to herself or to anyone that she was in love with her sister's husband. Eventually she found one confidante whom she told of her love for Aaron. That was Elizabeth Cady Stanton.

Psychologists have speculated as to how two such different women as Mrs. Stanton and Aunt Susan could maintain a close friendship for fifty years. The explanation is probably a feminine one. They had the kinship of a secret, lost love; for Elizabeth Cady Stanton had endured a similar experience with her sister's husband, Edward Bayard.

A century ago, a lady who lost in love had only two choices. She could persevere and find another man, if she could. Or she she could resign herself to a dull and dependent spinsterhood in which she was limited to teaching or dressmaking for livelihood, or moving in on the family household as the maiden aunt. Aunt Susan made a hard try for the first alternative. She burst from the chrysalis of Quaker gray and became a butterfly of fashion while headmistress of the Canajoharie Academy. For the first time in her life she spent all of her modest salary on her clothes rather than on her parents' farm in Rochester.

The once plain Quaker maid became the belle of Canajoharie, courted by young men and widowers at parties, picnics, and drives. In her new role, Susan gave up the Quaker "thee" and "thou" in her speech, and took to the dance floor, against all Quaker rules. But she did not take seriously any of her admirers as potential husbands. They could not fill the hollow left in her heart by Aaron.

Susan resigned as headmistress. She fled for the dubious comfort of Aaron and Sister Guelma in their Battenville home. The sight of their happy marriage was a further crucifixion to the twenty-nine-year-old woman. She wanted to escape—to flee—to go west with the men who were in that year of 1849 journeying to make their fortunes in California. But she knew that even that flight was blocked unless she went as a wife. Now she faced the other alternative for the unwed lady. She went back to her parents' farm outside Rochester where she spent her time cooking meals and serving the large crowd of abolitionists and temperance crusaders who gathered about her father's table.

Just as Aunt Susan had dreamed of marriage to Aaron, I longed to be married to Richard. But I feared the long periods of separation we would have to endure before my graduation. And, as Celeste and Gerald pointed out, I hadn't even met his family.

As luck would have it, a valid reason for going to North Carolina materialized at that very time. During the spring I had become mildly interested in the Emergency Peace Campaign sponsored by the American Friends Service Committee. The Congressional hearings exposing the profits made by the munitions-makers had wakened college students to the cause and cure of war. The idealists among them were organizing to do something about another arms build-up. The Quaker position on peace seemed so reasonable to me, so easy to accept. The Anthony family's pacifist stand went back to the very founding of the Society of Friends. Aunt Susan herself had been a strong pacifist. It wasn't until later that I realized she had given up her pacifism, her membership in good standing in the Society, because she put freedom for the slave before pacifism.

The Quaker student peace conference scheduled at Duke University in June, 1934 was very close to Richard's home. It was arranged that Richard and I drive into the south together, a perfect opportunity for me to meet his family.

I loved the south the moment we crossed Washington's Arlington Street Bridge into Virginia. That day we stopped for late tea at the elegant old Jefferson Hotel in Richmond. I was entranced by the soaring three-story lobby, its red-carpeted grand staircase and huge crystal chandelier, the cool, jalousied dining room. The south enveloped me entirely. I loved it first because it belonged to Richard and second because it stirred in me overheard memories of Mother's family, of a softer, more gracious way of life than the one I had known in the sharper north.

The gray neglect of poverty, the unpainted shacks, the lean-to's, contrasted with the fat red barns we had left behind in upstate New York, but I was in love and everything I saw seemed touched by beauty. We slowed down as we drove through the tree-arched main streets of little Virginia towns, glimpsed antebellum houses among the dark green leaves of magnolias and the purple of rhododendron, past their prime, like the south. In the darkness of night, our headlights beamed on the white shirt of a Negro walking at the side of the road with a fishing pole. I clung to Richard's hand, sharing his excitement as we neared his home. Then, almost there, quietly he drew off to the side of the road, turned off the engine, took me in his arms and kissed me.

"That's our goodnight kiss," he said. "We may not see each other alone for a while."

We turned into a long driveway perfumed by sweet olive, drove up toward a huge Georgian mansion with tall, two-story columns gleaming white. I was overwhelmed by its beauty and grandeur.

Mrs. Winter and Richard's sister Mary came out to the verandah when they heard the car approaching.

"Darling boy," Mrs. Winter called, "welcome home."

Richard jumped from the car, kissed his mother, hugged Mary, and rushed around to open the door for me. He introduced me to his mother. I looked into a faded edition of Richard's blue eyes, eyes that examined me carefully.

"You must be exhausted, my dear," she said. "It must be stifling in that heavy tweed suit."

Her accent was more pronounced than Richard's, her voice high, her hand gentle as she led me to the foot of the great curving staircase in the center hall.

Sweetly she said, "My what a tall young lady you are. I do believe you are taller than Richard!" And she laughed before sending me on my way upstairs. "Freshen up and hurry back down. Cook's been waiting impatiently for Richard. He's her favorite, you know, and she has some special treats for him."

Mary went upstairs with me and led the way into the most beautiful room I had ever seen. A giant mahogany four-poster stood regally under the high ceiling. Floor-length windows, their jalousies open to let in the night breeze, were flanked by a low-boy and a highboy. A white Adam mantle over the fireplace, a tilt-top table and Duncan Phyfe chairs with petit-point seats completed the eighteenth-century perfection. Even the dressing room was beautiful with its blue-and-white colonial-pattern wallpaper matching the skirt on the dressing table. My childhood home had been built in the eighteenth century too. But here I saw the peak of the grandeur this period had reached. The high ceilings, the columns holding up broad verandahs were not possible in northern colonial houses built for long cold winters.

The dining room was ivory-paneled. At one end of a vast table were a huge brown-crusted ham and a golden turkey. A shining coffee service with Minton demitasse stood at the far end. In between lay a feast for a city block of hungry people, beaten biscuit, sandwiches, black chocolate cake.

I took only one slice of cold turkey and ham, and black coffee. I was starving myself for Richard.

"My dear Susan," Mrs. Winter said, noticing my plate, "you should eat more—a great, tall girl like you."

I was beginning to feel that five-feet-five qualified me for a freak show. We took our plates into the drawing room with its Aubusson carpet, its Sheraton table, its early nineteenth-century portraits. I chose a straight-backed Windsor.

"We're going to have a party," Mrs. Winter said. "Everyone wants to see you, Richard. And of course they're eager to meet Susan, to see what 'Yankee girl' you've brought home this time." She laughed after "Yankee girl," making certain that I knew it was said in jest.

When Richard drove me to Duke the next morning in the mist of an early heat haze, I could feel a change in our relationship, just slight, just an edge. Suddenly I didn't want to go to the Conference at all. I wanted to say, "Let's play hookey, me from Duke, you from your mother. Let's just go off together."

But I couldn't, and didn't, and I'll never know if that might have made the difference. He dropped me off at one of the Gothic buildings at Duke and as soon as I could I located a Rochester friend, Eldon Garside. Eldon was munching on peanut-butter crackers and drinking a coke. His breakfast, he explained. I thought guiltily of the masses of food I had left untouched the night before, of the luxury in which I was wallowing while Eldon and the four other Rochester students, who would drive me back north, were counting their pennies. Eldon and I went into a classroom where a sweating, shirt-sleeved, older man was demonstrating how to keep cool while canvassing for world peace on hot southern roads. He slapped his belly and his wrists.

"Douse cold water, if you can find any, on your ribs and wrists —that will cool you off fast when you stop at a farmhouse to talk peace with the man or woman of the house. Just go out to the pump, which is all you'll usually find, lift up your shirt—if you're a boy—if you're a girl it's a little more difficult," he laughed at his own joke.

I saw nothing funny about him. In fact I was unimpressed by this room full of college students. The boys were uninteresting

compared with the mature and well-bred Richard—adolescents
in rumpled shirts and unpressed slacks. The girls were worse. It
was obvious they spent more time grooming their minds than
their bodies. Their cotton dresses were pasted to their waistlines
with sweat. Their faces were shiny with heat. And many of them
wore glasses.

And yet there was an intensity, an absorption, a commitment
in the faces of those young people as they sat there sweating in
that classroom. These student pacifists were the forerunners of the
massive numbers of youngsters who would one day form a generation of activists for peace.

Eldon looked uninviting that day. Yet when he drove me back
to the Winters' in the late afternoon, using up his gas in his old
car, his voice rang with conviction about his volunteer mission
for the summer. He would, he said, be carrying the message of
peace to southern farmers, living as poorly as the people he called
upon, no more than five dollars a week. He urged me to join the
peace campaign. I was glad I was safely signed up as camp
counselor at a cool beach on Cape Cod.

That night a number of friends had been invited to dinner at
the Winters', including, I learned to my surprise, an ex-girl friend
of Richard's. I studied her during dinner, a diminutive thing with
soft, brown hair and large, liquid, brown eyes, a girlish accent,
and a frilly cotton dress. She made me feel like a Great Dane
with a tiny white poodle.

When we joined the men on the verandah after dinner, one
genial, portly man in a white linen suit offered me a drink: "Maybe you don't drink, like that prohibitionist aunt of yours. She was
the one who went around hacking up bars with a hatchet, wasn't
she?" He was amused at the thought of it.

I explained that Aunt Susan was not Carrie Nation, but a
suffragist.

He was not impressed.

"Aunt Susan had a varied career," I plunged on. "She was
active in abolishing slavery before she became a feminist. She
helped Lincoln make the Emancipation Proclamation the Thirteenth Amendment."

The after-dinner talk stopped. The portly man turned his back
on me, handed his glass to the butler, "Bring me another drink,
Sam."

Mrs. Winter broke the silence with a little laugh. "And our little Susan B. is following right in her footsteps. Richard took her over to Duke today for a political conference of some sort."

Richard took my arm, "I will show you the garden."

He led me off the verandah, into the fragrant night. The glow from the house showed a serious face, not a romantic one.

"Sue, why on earth did you bring up the subject of abolishing slavery?"

"But Richard, that's what she did. I'm sorry, I guess I was just nervous with your friends."

He seemed to forgive me and took my hand and led me in the half-moonlit night over to an ancient sundial. For a brief moment we were really together again. He put his arms around me and kissed me for the first time since that roadside embrace seemingly a century before. He dropped his arms and moved away. Sam, the butler, loomed in the night.

"Mr. Richard, Mrs. Winter thinks it's too damp out here in the garden. You-all better come in."

I spent a miserable eight hours with the pacifists at Duke the next day, watching the clock for the time when Richard would pick me up for our last night together, our drive to Wrightsville Beach. I rushed to the blue coupé as it drew up to the conference building. It was filled with people.

As it turned out, Mrs. Winter had expanded the expedition, had arranged for others to join us for the elaborate picnic supper.

I wanted to fling out at Richard at that moment, "When are you going to cut the apron strings?" But I knew it would not be wise.

The drive and the picnic, of course, were a fiasco. I was miserable. All I wanted was to be alone with Richard and that had been made impossible.

Under the blazing sun of the southern noon next day, on the baked white concrete campus parking lot, Richard and I said goodbye. We both sensed as we stood helplessly on that sterile lot that this was a final parting. Once in his home, once among his own, Richard had been changed by some alchemy which I was too young and too inexperienced to analyze. I wanted to blame his mother for it, and I did blame her. But there were others to blame, perhaps Richard, perhaps me. I did not know. All I knew was that Richard had been drawn away from me, drawn back into the womb of the south where he would remain.

Richard kissed me. Gently he took my hands from his arms, gave me his handkerchief for my streaming eyes, kissed me once more, and walked to the blue car. I was standing alone on the white hot parking lot as he drove away, watching him with the sightless eyes of those surprised by sudden death.

I could not hide my crying from Eldon and the others who jammed into his old car. I huddled in a corner of the back seat and wept my way throughout the twenty-hour drive north. It was a trip of anguish in which my mind went in circles from Richard to his mother to me to Celeste and Gerald, who seemed to have known all along.

In the morning we pulled into Moylan. Stained by tears and travel I walked into the web, the old familiar family shrine. Aunt Lucy stared at my tear-swollen face, heard my broken explanation of its cause.

"Susan," she said, "pull yourself together. You'll have to help me get breakfast for your friends. Go dry your eyes and wash your face. All this fuss. After all, he's only a man."

7 *"Obedience to God comes before obedience to men..."*

The first real moral decision I was ever called on to make brought me closer to the heart and core of my great-aunt than I had ever been. It was during the autumn of my sophomore year at Rochester, and what I learned about the noblest hour of her life would help me one day in the most excruciating hour of mine.

After the summer at Cape Cod, with Richard gone, I began to fill the empty spaces with super-involvement in campus activities. I started majoring in political science just as Gerald had urged me. I helped organize a political debating club. I went to lots of rallies of both political parties, studying first-hand "the great game of politics" in the 1934 Congressional campaign.

One of the campaigners was Mrs. Franklin D. Roosevelt, who swept into town on behalf of her friend Caroline O'Day, running for congressman-at-large. Mrs. Harper Sibley, a leader of Rochester's social and cultural life, invited me to meet the First Lady at her East Avenue home. The tall lady with the prominent upper teeth, her eyes crinkled by a beautiful smile, asked me to join her while she drank her cup of tea. This was the first of several meetings between us that would continue till the year before her death.

Now with her warm and friendly manner she put an awestruck college sophomore at ease, saying, "My dear Susan, I know what it must be like for you carrying your famous name in your great-aunt's own hometown. My son, Franklin, is having the

same difficulty at Harvard. It's hard for you youngsters. Everything you do is spotlighted. But just be yourself. Don't try to live
up to the name and don't fight it."

But up until that fall I had quite enjoyed the spotlight that
Mrs. Roosevelt had mentioned. The name had been good to me.
It had got me my scholarship and a certain amount of not unap-
preciated attention. Before, in high school, I had always been
simply "Sue Anthony." Now I tended more and more to use the
full "Susan B. Anthony." I had learned the difference that the
"B." could make.

One day shortly after Mrs. Roosevelt's visit, a Republican
Party leader invited me to his Rochester hotel campaign headquarters. He flattered me by asking that I lend my voice and the
luster of "that grand old name" to the campaign during the last
crucial weeks before the election. The idea excited me and impulsively I almost said "yes." After all, this was the prophecy
Gerald had made. This could be the beginning of my real career,
my political career, starting at the age of eighteen in Aunt Susan's
own home town. I was sparked by the thought of getting out
before an audience. Gerald would love it too. He could coach me.

Then a second thought crept in unasked. What did I *really*
know about the issues or candidates involved in either party?

The Republican Party leader, his face glistening in campaign fever, warmed up as he gave me the clincher. He had done
his research. The Anthonys, he said, had all been Republicans,
not only in Rochester, but in Kansas where Cousin Daniel had
gone to Congress eleven times and Great-uncle Daniel had been
a Republican mayor and owner of the Leavenworth *Times*. Susan
B. herself, he said, had been an ardent Republican.

It sounded good, but I didn't obey my first impulse. I thanked
him, and told him that I would like to consider his offer. Then
I went out and tried to learn more about local politics. I also
went to the library to find out what I could about Aunt Susan's
political life. What rich ore I struck! My Republican friend had
done his research all right, but he had not told the whole story.

I discovered that early on Susan B. indeed had backed the
new Republican Party when it declared against slavery. Though
voteless herself, because of her growing influence she was wooed
by the Senate and House party leaders and sought after for the
presidential conventions. Aunt Susan had been among the very

first of the abolitionists to insist that Negroes have a vote, a startling and unpopular idea. Eventually the Republican leaders made a bargain with her. If she would drop temporarily her woman-suffrage fight, if she would throw her weight behind the war for Negro freedom, they would include women, white and black, in the extension of the franchise. Aunt Susan deliberated, then agreed to their proposition. She set up a tiny office in Cooper Union, New York City. Living on twelve dollars a week, she trudged the sidewalks and directed the mammoth task of collecting 400,000 signatures to crystallize public opinion needed by the White House and Congress to legislate the Emancipation Proclamation into the Thirteenth Amendment to the Constitution. Her success was hailed by President Lincoln and Senator Sumner on down through the party ranks, but when she asked the Republican leaders to live up to their bargain, they brushed her aside.

"This is the Negro's hour," they said.

They would not, they said, "jeopardize" the black man's vote for the even more radical enfranchisement of white and black women. The Republicans succeeded in enacting the Fourteenth and later the Fifteenth Amendments, for black men only. Women, white and black, remained voteless. This betrayal broke up the thirty-year alliance between the feminists and the antislavery movement. Hand-in-hand they had fought since the Grimké sisters first had dared to speak from a public platform for abolition. The feminist movement of the nineteenth century had grown out of women's concern for the black man's freedom, even as the "new feminism" of the 1970s has followed upon the civil rights movement of the 1960s.

Aunt Susan was crushed by the party sellout. But she remained Republican when she cast the vote that was heard around the nation. She committed what was probably the first act of civil disobedience by a woman in the cause of women.

Aunt Susan's "crime" was voting. She and fifteen friends went to the polls to vote in order to obtain a Supreme Court decision on what she believed was woman's right to vote under the Fourteenth Amendment. It spelled out: "All persons born or naturalized in the United States are citizens . . . ." Aunt Susan's logic was simple and clear. Women are persons, and the amendment stated that *all* persons are citizens, thus women were enfranchised as persons and citizens.

The "Sweet Sixteen," as the press dubbed them, marched to the 8th Ward polling place in Rochester, a corner grocery store, on November 5, 1872. Aunt Susan overcame the stunned objections of the election officials by reading to them the letter of the Fourteenth Amendment. She also promised the inspectors and officials that she would pay any costs of prosecution if they were arrested for accepting the women's ballots.

That night Susan wrote to her best friend, Mrs. Stanton: "Well, I have gone and done it! Positively voted the Republican ticket, straight, this A.M. at 7 . . . ."

The Republican administration "rewarded" her vote by ordering Rochester to arrest her and the other fifteen women immediately! On Thanksgiving Day, 1872, the doorbell rang at 17 Madison Street. Susan opened the door and saw a man in silk top hat and fine kid gloves. He was, he said, Deputy U.S. Marshal E. J. Keeney. Hemming and hawing in some embarrassment, the marshal handed Susan a warrant for her arrest. But, he said, it certainly wouldn't be necesary for him to escort the prisoner to the courthouse; he was sure he could trust her. Susan, however, insisted upon the full show of force. She followed him on foot to the dingy office of the Commissioner of Elections in the courthouse, the same courthouse where fugitive slaves had been held when captured while fleeing to Canada.

All sixteen pleaded "not guilty" to the charge of illegal voting. They were placed under $500 bail each. Susan, who was selected by the commissioners as the test case, insisted upon a writ of habeas corpus. The other ladies were allowed to go home to their children and grandchildren while Susan was dealt with alone. Susan was remanded to the court in Albany where her writ of habeas corpus was not only denied, but her bail was raised to $1,000. She accepted both defeats with equanimity. Her main goal was to be jailed and to carry her case to the Supreme Court. Instead, her lawyer posted bail for her, saying, "I could not see a lady go to jail."

Now she was disconsolate. She had lost the first attempt to go to jail. She lost again when the Grand Jury in Rochester indicted her. Instead of imprisoning her, the twenty men simply placed her in custody of the same Marshal Keeney. They set her trial for the summer court session.

In January she went to the Rochester station to embark for

her annual suffrage convention in Washington. She saw a man pacing up and down the platform. He approached her swiftly. It was Marshal Keeney. Standing as if to block her way to the train, he officially ordered her to remain in Rochester within the jurisdiction of the court. Susan, smiling sweetly, ignored him and boarded the train, waving goodbye. It was Marshal Keeney's first of many protests. He registered them officially each and every time she shuttled out of Rochester while she stumped the nation with her defense argument, "Is It a Crime for a U.S. Citizen to Vote?"

Her suffrage sisters in Washington and other cities enthusiastically applauded her courageous fight. But they couldn't help her, they said. They had too many domestic duties at home. Susan had to go it alone. There was no committee to support her; no one helped her raise money for her defense. She was already burdened by the $10,000 debt of her now defunct newspaper *The Revolution*. Throughout the winter of 1873 she barnstormed the country, going further in debt in arduous one-night stands.

In a small Indiana town Aunt Susan, now fifty-three, in the midst of her lecture, fell unconscious to the floor. Writhing in pain when she regained consciousness she begged her friends to stop the Associated Press from wiring the story of her collapse, fearing that it might prove fatal to her aged, ailing mother in Rochester. They had to tell her the truth. The news had already gone out on the wire, not that Susan had fainted, but that she was dead! To prove the press wrong, Susan rose from her sick bed, notified the reporters, mounted the platform before a large audience, and gave her full lecture. AP had to wire the nation that Susan B. Anthony was alive and well and speaking in Marion, Indiana.

Far from recovered, she returned to Rochester to gamble further on her life by a crushing marathon of 29 talks in 29 different towns in 30 days. She won so many friends to her defense that the district attorney, fearing she might win any jury selected, sought and won a change of venue, and a further postponement of the trial. The case was moved to the beautiful lakeside town of Canandaigua in the next county, Ontario, almost forty miles from Rochester. This meant that Susan had to begin all over again. In three weeks she had to inform a brand-new territory. Only then did a sister suffragist show up to help her. Mrs.

Matilda Joslyn Gage left her fireside and children and spoke in
16 of the 37 districts. Aunt Susan covered the remaining 21 districts in 21 days. This time the prosecution did not bother to
seek another change of venue. They had been assured that
"Washington would take care of everything."

Washington's intervention first dictated the choice of judge to
sit on the case. In an unprecedented move, a justice of the U.S.
Supreme Court, Ward Hunt, was assigned to a Circuit Court
case. Washington's interference was glaring. This particular justice happened to be the protege of the U.S. senator from New
York, Roscoe Conkling, Republican, an avowed long-time enemy
of woman suffrage. The judge who should have tried the case
had, for some unexplained reason, disqualified himself.

The trial of the *United States* v. *Susan B. Anthony* opened in
the lovely old courthouse on the tree-lined main street of Canandaigua, on June 17, 1873. Crowding the courtroom along with
the other spectators were ex-President Millard Fillmore and
several U.S. congressmen, but not Senator Conkling.

Judge Hunt immediately declared Susan incompetent to testify
on her own behalf, because she was a woman. Her lawyer, former
Circuit Court of Appeals Judge Henry Selden, presented a three-
hour argument supporting woman's right to vote under the Fourteenth Amendment. He documented it with the opinions of other
distinguished jurists. The district attorney made little effort to
persuade the jury of Susan's guilt. He knew that he did not have
to. The jury's work, like his own, had already been done for
them. Justice Hunt took his charge to the jury out of his pocket.
He had actually written it before he had even heard the arguments of the defense or prosecution. He read from this handily
prepared charge, then directed the jury to bring in a verdict of
guilty!

Susan's lawyer immediately objected to this unprecedented
breach of legal procedure.

"Take the verdict, Mr. Clerk," the judge said, ignoring the ob-
jection.

Susan's lawyer requested that the jury be polled. Justice Hunt
ignored him, snapping, "Gentlemen of the jury, you are discharged."

Until this moment Susan had not been allowed a single word in
her own defense. Now the judge surprised her by asking, "Has

the prisoner anything to say why sentence should not be pronounced?"

The prisoner had plenty to say. She had been lecturing the
length and breadth of her land for twenty-five years. She had
testified before Congressional committees, addressed Presidential
conventions, spoken to giant audiences at Chautauquas. Primed
by her years of national oratory she could and did speak with no
notice or notes. In her strong, low-pitched voice, the prisoner
gave the most famous speech of her life.

As I sat in Sibley Library at Rochester, reading that speech
for the first time, I saw an Aunt Susan that I had never fully seen
before. As I, nerves tingling, raced through her words, my respect
for her, my sincere pride in her, flowered. I read the speech twice
and still again that day. In years to come I was to read and
reread it for comfort when I myself was to know what it was
like to have the forces of government arrayed against one. Aunt
Susan spoke out of a deep human revulsion against injustice. She
spoke with the simple eloquence that is given only to a few, and
only in times of deep urgency.

"Yes, Your Honor," she began, "I have many things to say; for
in your ordered verdict of guilty, you have trampled under foot
every vital principle of our government. My natural rights, my
civil rights, my political rights are all alike ignored. Robbed of
that fundamental privilege of citizenship, I am degraded from
the status of citizen to that of a subject; and not only myself
individually but all of my sex are, by Your Honor's verdict,
doomed to political subjection under this so-called republican
government."

Justice Hunt, obviously regretting ever unleashing her ad-
vocacy, interrupted.

"The Court cannot listen to a rehearsal of arguments the
prisoner's counsel has already consumed three hours in present-
ing."

Susan was a veteran at being shut up by men who would not
let her talk.

"May it please Your Honor, I am not arguing the question, but
simply stating the reasons why sentence cannot, in justice, be
pronounced against me. Your denial of my citizen's right to vote
is the denial of my right of consent as one of the governed, the
denial of my right of representation as one of the taxed, the

denial of my right to a trial by a jury of my peers as an offender against the law, the denial of my sacred rights to life, liberty, property, and—"

Judge Hunt again tried to break in. Susan continued:

"But Your Honor will not deny me this one and only poor privilege of protest against this high-handed outrage upon my citizen's rights. May it please the Court to remember that since the day of my arrest last November this is the first time that either myself or any person of my disfranchised class has been allowed a word of defense before judge or jury—"

Hunt barked, "The prisoner must sit down!"

The prisoner did not sit down. She kept standing.

"All my prosecutors from the 8th Ward corner-grocery-store politician, who entered the complaint, to the United States Marshal, Commissioner, District Attorney, District Judge, Your Honor on the bench, not one is my peer, but each and all my political sovereigns; and had Your Honor submitted my case to the jury, *as was clearly your duty,* even then I should have had just cause of protest, for not one of those men was my peer; but native or foreign, white or black, rich or poor, educated or ignorant, awake or asleep, sober or drunk, each and every man of them was my political superior, hence in no sense my peer.

"Even under such circumstances, a commoner of England, tried before a jury of lords, would have had far less cause to complain than should I, a woman, tried before a jury of men. Even my counsel, the Hon. Henry R. Selden, who has argued my cause so ably, so earnestly, so unanswerably before Your Honor, is my political sovereign. Precisely as no disfranchised person is entitled to sit upon a jury, and no woman is entitled to the franchise, so none but a regularly admitted lawyer is allowed to practice in the courts, and no woman can gain admission to the bar—hence, jury, judge, counsel, must all be of the superior class."

Judge Hunt retorted, "The prisoner has been tried according to the established forms of law."

Susan fought back. "Yes, Your Honor, but by forms of law all made by men, interpreted by men, administered by men, in favor of men, and against women; hence Your Honor's ordered verdict of guilty, against a United States citizen for the exercise of 'that citizen's right to vote,' simply because that citizen was a woman and not a man. But yesterday, the same man-made forms of law declared it a crime punishable with a one-thousand-dollar fine and six-months' imprisonment, for you or me, or any of us, to give a cup of cold water, a crust of bread, or a night's shelter to a panting fugitive while he was tracking his way to Canada. And every man or woman in whose veins coursed a drop of human sympathy violated that wicked law, reckless of consequences, and was justified in so doing. As then, the slaves who got their freedom must take it over, or under, or through the unjust forms of law, precisely so now women, to get their right to a voice in this government, take it; and I have taken mine, and mean to take it at every opportunity."

And then she closed saying, "But failing to get this justice—failing, even, to get a trial by a jury *not* of my peers—I ask not leniency at your hands—but to take the full rigors of the law."

Then Susan did sit down. The judge thereupon ordered her to stand up.

He said swiftly, "The sentence of the Court is that you pay a fine of one hundred dollars and the costs of the prosecution."

Susan stood her ground and said firmly: "May it please Your Honor, I shall never pay a dollar of your unjust penalty. All the stock-in-trade that I possess is a ten-thousand-dollar debt, incurred by publishing my paper, *The Revolution,* four years ago, the sole object of which was to educate all women to do precisely as I have done, rebel against your man-made, unjust, unconstitutional forms of law, that tax, fine, imprison, and hang women while they deny them the right of representation in the government: and I shall work on with might and main to pay every dollar of that honest debt, but not a penny will go to this unjust claim. And I shall earnestly and persistently continue to urge all women to the practical recognition of that old revolutionary maxim, that 'Resistance to tyranny is obedience to God.'"

Aunt Susan stuck to both promises. She never did pay one cent of her fine or the costs of prosecution. And she continued until death to urge women to fight against tyranny. But she had lost more than her case, more than her unblemished health record. She had lost the one goal for which she had suffered that lonely, exhausting year, her right to appeal to the U.S. Supreme Court. Justice Hunt had seen to that. He barred her appeal, by simply refusing to abide by the law that she remain in prison until her fine was paid. Had he acted legally, Susan would have gone to jail. She could then have obtained a writ of habeas corpus carrying her case directly to the Supreme Court. The Court would have freed her immediately on the obvious ground that she had been denied trial by jury. But more important to her, she would have obtained a ruling on the Fourteenth Amendment's enfranchisement of women.

During the days that I was reading about Aunt Susan and trying to make up my mind about accepting the Rochester political leader's invitation to speak, it came to me that it would not be just a political decision, it would be a moral decision as well. I did not have a pastor or a spiritual guide, but I did know a young rabbi, Phillip Bernstein, whom I had met while at summer camp and who had impressed me with his unclouded view of the world around him. I knocked at the door of his study in the temple a few blocks from campus. He welcomed me in his friendly, trained rabbi's voice. I told him of my dilemma and asked what I should do.

"Do you agree with the Republicans?" he asked me.

"I'm not sure," I said honestly. "I think I have only begun to study what the Republicans stand for."

"Well, if I were you, I'd think seriously about giving your name and your voice to something you don't know about." He leaned across the desk, his hands lightly clasped before him. "Think of your own heritage of integrity, Susan. You'll be asked a thousand times to give that name of yours to things. Wait until you are informed and really convinced. Integrity is our most important stock-in-trade."

I left his study knowing he was right, went to the phone and told the political leader "no." My decision had nothing to do with his being a Republican. I would have given the same answer to a Democrat.

For the first time, I felt Aunt Susan might have approved.

8 *"We looked for peace, but no good came, for a time of healing, but behold, terror."*

I was never to be involved in local Rochester politics, but by junior year I was very much a political animal. Yet somehow in one way or another, whenever I took to crusading, it always ended in smash-up for me. I never seemed to learn.

While the majority of my classmates were concentrating on romance, the focus of my attention became world peace. At first I was wooed by the oddball minority, the more vocal students who belonged to the American Student Union. They were in favor of collective action against the Nazi and Fascist aggressors. At the extreme right were the pro-Nazi isolationists. At the extreme left were the bitterly anti-Stalinist Trotskyites. All wanted me to join them. They tried to win me over by frequent invitations to lunches and dinners. They wanted my obviously abundant energy, the talent I had shown for organization, but chief of all, I suspected, the name. I tended, however, toward the less vocal, but equally concerned students, the pacifists, very much like those at Duke. Soon I was shuttling about the state as delegate to half a dozen intercollegiate model Leagues of Nations.

There was one student group that did not interest me at all. We politically active students all but snubbed them when we passed them coming from their sessions in the same lounge we used for our meetings. We called them "Christers," "YMCA types," "Holier than thou." When I looked at them I saw only washed-out creatures with little or no make-up, drably dressed.

Political organizations notwithstanding, my chief love throughout the years at Rochester was journalism, the newsroom of the Rochester *Democrat and Chronicle,* in particular. There I blissfully batted out stories as campus correspondent. I was triumphant when the *Democrat* offered me a full-time reporter's job for the summer.

A week before I was to begin, however, the red-haired city editor called me to his desk and told me he had hired an older woman for the job instead.

Panicked at the prospect of my first unemployed summer since I had begun camp counseling at the age of fifteen, I rushed as a last resort to the campus laboratory of Dr. Ethel Luce Clausen.

A gaunt, sallow Englishwoman, prematurely grayed, Dr. Clausen had offered to sponsor me that summer on the Emergency Peace Campaign of the Quakers. Dr. Clausen had evolved from militant feminist to lifelong pacifist after living through "the war to end all wars" in England and France. She had been my biology professor, and though I had absorbed little of the subject from her, we had become friends because of her admiration for Aunt Susan.

I found Dr. Clausen disecting a frog. Nose wrinkling at the smell of formaldehyde, which I detested, I asked if her offer still stood. Her deep-set eyes shone, her cheeks showed a faint pink against the white of her lab coat. "Of course I want you to go!" she said excitedly.

I was stunned at her idealistic faith that our puny student efforts might actually prevent war. We went right into her office where she wrote out a personal check to carry me over the three summer months of the Quaker Crusade.

I took the train to Durham, North Carolina, for the briefing sessions at Duke University. More than a hundred students were on hand to learn how to deploy themselves in the south. One of the leaders of the sessions was Jeanette Rankin, fiery and white-haired, the first woman ever elected to Congress. She had been elected in 1917, even before women themselves could vote nationally. Not only a feminist, she was a militant pacifist with an unbroken record of votes against war and all arms appropriations. She voted against a declaration of war in 1917 and was to cast the single negative vote against World War II. As I walked into her session that day in 1936, she was urging the students to canvass door-to-door in the coming fall elections to defeat candidates in favor of large arms appropriations that could drag us into another tragedy.

I had imagined myself working in remote rural areas, plodding along dusty red roads, stopping in at poverty-stricken sharecropper shacks. But to my relief, my own group of five girls was assigned to a city: Augusta, Georgia.

Our team was to rendezvous in Atlanta before taking the train to Augusta. But when I learned that the overnight stay in Atlanta was to be in that—to me—unloveliest of places, a YWCA, I stayed over at Duke, getting a friend to drive me down. When I arrived at the YWCA in the early morning, I found the four other girls crowded into one room. There was the same odor of disinfectant and stale air that I had associated with "Y's" since my brother Dan's body-building days. Clothes were spilling out of their bags, stockings hung on chair backs; there were empty coke bottles and a dried-up, half-eaten ham sandwich on the floor. The girls were munching on apples.

Pat Knight, a sweet-faced blonde, explained the apples: they had already started our regimen of living on five dollars a week apiece.

A tall brown-haired girl with searching dark eyes, Lyal Maie Reynolds, said warmly, "You're our only Yankee, but we're glad. At least I am. You probably know a lot more than we do about the issues involved in world peace."

I assured her that I did not, but my mind, as I spoke, was on something else. The moment I had walked into that bleak all-woman atmosphere, and gotten a look at what the summer was really going to be like, I had known it was not for me. Even staying home at Raubsville would be better than living with these YWCA types.

Lying, I said that I needed a pack of cigarettes, waved goodbye, and hurriedly picked up my bags at the desk where I had left them. I got a cab to the railroad station, found Western Union, took a blank and composed a wire to Dr. Clausen:

IMPOSSIBLE SITUATION CANNOT GO THROUGH WITH SUMMER HERE STOP RETURNING MONEY AND TO NORTH STOP SUE.

As I walked to the desk with the wire I wondered why I didn't feel more relief at the decision. I had narrowly escaped a long, hot crusade with a group of boring girls. What had been good enough for Aunt Susan was just not good enough for Sue.

But even as I congratulated myself, I felt a tugging. Some unseen hand propelled me away from the Western Union desk and forced me to tear the telegram into little pieces.

On the train ride to Augusta, Lyal Maie began her instruction.

"We are supposed to carry the message of peace to the people of Augusta. The goal, of course, is to take the profits out of war completely, so no arms-makers can build fortunes. We are also supposed to be examples of Christian poverty. We will give talks whenever we are asked, to women's and men's clubs, church socials and young people's groups. We must be prepared to answer questions on the world situation and the hearings on munitions-makers in Congress. We are part of a nationwide movement against war."

I was to surprise myself by falling in love with this crusading for something larger than myself. It was not only a practical experiment in working for peace, it was also an experiment in living in community with others devoted to an ideal. I became converted to working for the common good, not in competitive, prima-donna efforts, but through teamwork, group loyalty, and cohesiveness. All of us that summer felt that we were pioneers, and in a way, as the world has turned, we were.

Augusta was a small southern city redolent still with the gallant tatters of the Confederacy. The Augusta *Herald* and the *Chronicle* covered our entry with pictures and story on page one. We were news because we were a curiosity. Augustans, interested that youth, and particularly young ladies, would be working for world peace, stopped us on the street and asked what we *really* were doing. In those innocent days, long before the invasion of young civil rights crusaders, we were received rather well at first.

We rented one big room in a faded, white, nineteenth-century mansion. With five girls in two beds during the hot Georgia nights, we found it more comfortable to sleep across the beds rather than up and down. Even so, none of us really slept those first nights. Nocturnal itching kept us wide awake. Each morning we awoke with strange welts on our bodies. I walked across the street to the Richmond County Health department and asked the sandy-haired Dr. Thomas Phinizy what on earth these welts could be.

He looked at me long and hard, cleared his throat, then said they might be chiggers, a southern burrowing insect from the woods. Armed with his diagnosis and some soothing ointment, I told our team. They tried to figure out how we could pick up chiggers from the cement sidewalks of Augusta. That night I switched on the overhead light. Scurrying on the white sheet was a brownish creature the size of a lady bug; it oozed red blood when I caught it and mashed it.

"Bedbugs!" shouted Martha, our camellia-skinned beauty from Tennessee.

We kept it as a trophy to show our landlady next day. She tried to explain it away as an alien intruder brought in by the laundress—or possibly, she hinted darkly, *we* had brought it, along with our strange and suspect ideas.

Each morning we sallied forth from Greene Street to the S & W Cafeteria for our fifteen-cent breakfast of greasy eggs, white grits with a hard pat of butter in the center, white tasteless toast, and coffee, thin and boiled. By the time we finished we were already drenched in perspiration. Walking down Broad Street as the sun rose higher, sweat poured down our legs and glued our clothes to our waists.

My own mission was to serve as public relations person and "sociologist" for the crew. My first calls on the two editors had led to news stories, plus radio spots, and invitations to speak at more of the local men's and women's clubs. They were glad to have some new faces in the long, lazy summer. My leg work also led to my first dates with a hard-working, hard-drinking reporter. He began my real southern education with a crash course in 110-proof corn whiskey. I was an apt student.

He also introduced me to the people, classes, industry, and history of Augusta. This led to another new friend, an elderly judge, a gentleman of the Old South complete with white hair, flowing black string tie, immaculate beige pongee suit. The judge had met Aunt Susan on one of her missions. He seemed to enjoy "carrying" me around Augusta in his chauffeur-driven car, lacing his descriptions of Augusta's past and present with corn whiskey.

In no time I learned the answer to how to live on five dollars a week. It was so very simple. Men! Each night I just let a date take me to dinner. One of them was a young stockbroker from Savannah who had come to start a branch office in Augusta. He drove me up to South Carolina to call on Julia Peterkin, author of *Scarlet Sister Mary*, and to the better clubs and restaurants of the area. On the nights that I didn't see him, I was taken swimming and drinking and eating with my newspaper reporter or with a smooth, blond, cotton-mill executive.

Lyal Maie, the leader of our team because of her drive and intellect, lectured me one night as I was about to go out.

"Stay home at least one night to read up on the issues of the day. Please, sit down and read some of these." She gave me a raft of books and magazines and documents on the Nye munitions investigation and La Follette hearings.

Though I didn't stay home that night, I did begin some reading in the hot afternoons. Then I'd discuss what I had read with her. She instructed me on the rise of Fascism and Nazism more thoroughly than any professor had. She showed me how the seeds of war had been sown by the Japanese aggression in Manchuria; the Italian invasion of Abyssinia; and now by the new revolt against the Spanish Republican Government led by Fascist-supported General Francisco Franco. Lyal Maie stressed that so long as munitions-makers could make money out of guns there would be war. The pacifist aim was to force the Congress to nationalize the arms industry, while working for world disarmament and building the dying League of Nations.

Just graduated from the College for Women of the University of North Carolina in her home town, Greensboro, Lyal Maie had plans to enter Union Theological Seminary in New York in September. This stunned me. How could a brilliant, clear-thinking girl concerned for world peace, waste even a year on a myth like religion? Once or twice Lyal Maie started to tell me about that too. "Theology is a science, you know—the science of God." I would smile pityingly at her. All the same, I admired Lyal Maie. I respected her honesty and directness, qualities that emanated from her like beams from headlights.

As the hot weeks went by, I soaked up the phrases, statistics, and facts on peace for an increasing number of talks at Lion's, Rotary, and even Junior League. The lights were going on in my mind even while they were going out in Addis Ababa, Berlin, Rome, Peking, Barcelona, and Madrid.

Paradoxically, we brought not peace but a sword to Augusta. By the end of four weeks our message had torn the town into two warring camps. The more vocal side denounced us as "Reds," saying we should go back to where we came from. The other side, generally Augusta's elite, defended us as lovely college girls of good family. One veterans group attacked us as outside agitators. Another post of the same veterans defended us. Some churches were for us, others against.

When the going got really rough, it was time to call in the big artillery. I wired and called our national sponsors, who promptly wired back their endorsements. Mrs. Roosevelt, William Allen White, and others came to our rescue. I took their wires to the local newspaper editors who printed every word of defense as well as attack. They were glad to have a story to perk up somnolent summer pages. That summer I learned how to keep a good story going with ammunition from both sides and, like Aunt Susan before me, I discovered the importance of keeping the cause in the press.

Meanwhile, neither controversy nor press interfered with my night-time recreation. I continued to sip drinks on cool verandahs and at roadhouses where we brought our own corn whiskey. Wherever I went those summer nights, I carried my favorite record, "Until the Real Thing Comes Along." As I downed my drinks, the now familiar personality change took place. Drunkenly I would call for someone to put my record on the juke box. Then in a husky voice, trying to imitate Ethel Waters, I'd sing along with the music. Later my date and I would hurtle through the dark countryside in the hours when only roosters and wild young folk crowed in sleepy Richmond County.

I savored every drop of life in the dying summer. I couldn't seem to let go of this first crusade of mine. I loved this Deep South city much as I had loved the south Richard had shown me. I loved its broad, shady streets, its mysterious mansions, even the brown and sluggish Savannah River. I stayed after my teammates had gone, visiting friends, going to parties at lovely homes on The Hill and out in the country. Finally, with Labor Day near, I could put off the departure no longer. Lyal Maie was expecting me in Greensboro on my way north.

A friend drove me there in her car while I drank to dull my nostalgia for the summer that had everything: a cause, community, and communication, plus the bonus of southern men.

Lyal Maie was not amused when I almost fell out of the car drunk. The next day, Labor Day, I had a terrible hangover, made worse by the realization that I was actually on my way back to cold, old Rochester. "It's all over. It's all over," I kept saying.

I did not dream how true those words, for me, nearly were . . .

That night, my date helped me drown my nostalgia with bootleg corn poured over ice in paper cups. Long after midnight I found myself treading water in a jet-black pond listening to the story of his life. That is the last thing I remember.

I do not remember getting back into his car, or careening on the slick highway at seventy miles an hour, smashing into the side of a transport truck carrying five cars. Others told me later what happened. He was thrown clear of the wreck on to the shoulder of the road. My body took the brunt of the crash as I was thrown up and over into his seat, carving a seven-inch gash on my skull, slicing, breaking, bruising, tearing bones and muscle on the left side of my body from head to toe. The ambulance drivers carefully laid the young man on the stretcher. Thinking I was dead, they merely put me on the floor of the ambulance. They had found no trace of breathing, no pulse. Blood covered my face from the big head gash. The screaming siren cleared the way from High Point to Greensboro's little Clinic Hospital. Gently they carried him on a stretcher up to surgery, dumping my bloody corpse into a wheelchair to be certified "dead on arrival."

My corpse knew nothing of this. It was slumped over in the wheelchair in the elevator, my blood-stained dress slit, my pumps torn off by the impact of the crash. I was a dead girl, one more victim of drunken driving and a truck's failure to stop at a sign. The attendant opened the elevator door at the surgery floor. Then it was that the dead girl started to rise, her forehead flapping down on her nose. Before his very eyes, she rose up from the wheelchair, then pitched forward into the arms of a nurse.

They rushed me to surgery where a doctor poured glucose into my veins to bring me out of Cheyne-Stokes respiration and total shock. He sewed the flapping scalp together with twenty-seven stitches, taped the broken ribs and ankle, gave the order for full X-rays.

I lay dying in coma for the next week. My forehead, sliced by the rear-view mirror, swelled to such a size that they predicted meningitis. The mirror blow had given me a concussion and two cerebral hemorrhages. Shock distended my abdomen with gas to twice its girth. The gear shift had severed the left long thigh muscle in two, and broken my left ankle. The windshield chipped bone from my chin and cut my upper lip in half. That week of total oblivion I was fed by needle.

Mother and Daddy rushed down by train from Pennsylvania when Lyal Maie called them. Richard Winter kept vigil at my bedside checking each and every medical aid to save my life. It was Richard whose face I first saw when I opened my blurred eyes a week later and began deliriously babbling phrases from my peace talks.

Several days later, I was conscious enough to tell Richard that I saw two, not one of him. He assured me that it was shock. But the next morning when I awoke from my first real sleep I looked out the window. There was a billboard there, with an advertisement showing some girls playing tennis. It seemed odd that there were two identical girls on each side of the net. When Dr. Whittington came in, I told him.

"That will pass away. We have a lot more to think of than just a little double vision. We're waiting to see what happens to those cerebral hemorrhages and concussion."

Even when I was allowed to, I could not lift my head from the pillow. Under its yards of bandages it felt as heavy as a diving helmet. Nor could I eat solid food: instead I sipped the brandy eggnogs the nurses brought me. When my doctor ordered soups instead, a nurse put me in touch with the local bootlegger, a little man who slunk in several times a week with a pint of Cream of Kentucky whiskey. I alibied the fumes to Mother as rubbing alcohol.

Streams of visitors, some of them friends from Augusta, poured in the room. Lyal Maie left for Union Theological Seminary, leaving her fiance, Don Shoemaker, a young reporter, to take over the task of reading to me. Lonely for Lyal Maie, he came often and was the only friend who would read books or articles sufficiently political for me. Now that I had been bitten by the bug of world affairs, I wanted more and more information. Already Don, who later became Editor of the Miami *Herald* was stepping into the tradition of other great North Carolina editors.

One day I looked up to see Rabbi Phillip Bernstein smiling at the foot of my bed. He had read about the accident in Rochester and, lecturing in the south, had detoured many miles to see me. "How are you, now that you've been so very close to death?" he asked, chaplainlike.

I couldn't really answer him. I felt like a mental patient after electric shock treatments. The crash had blotted out the accident itself in what they called "spasmodic amnesia." Also like shock treatments it had erased all trace of the depression I had felt that day before the accident and left me in a high, near-manic mood, totally free of anxiety, except about my continuing double vision. Indeed I acted, not like a young girl recovering from death, but like a gay hostess conducting a levee for my many guests.

Then I came down with a boom. Richard and Mother drove me over to the eye specialist at Duke some fifty miles away. For hours the doctor tested my vision with various instruments. Finally he held a lighted candle one foot away from me. Constantly shifting its position, he asked me dozens of times, "How many images do you see? Where?"

Each time I saw not one image of the candle, but two, nine or more inches apart. Not once did they converge into the single vision of a single light. Though the specialist said nothing, I knew from the care he took that something was seriously wrong. As we left his office I began to collapse. Richard and Mother hurried me to Duke Hospital where I spent the night before returning to my own hospital bed in Greensboro. Dr. Whittington broke the news to me a day later.

"You cannot go back to finish college. That's the first thing. You must rest. The blood clots in your system might break loose at any time. That would be fatal. Second, you cannot read and write normally at all, now and perhaps never. Right now, Susan, healing your eyes would have to be some kind of miracle."

I couldn't say a word.

"The specialist at Durham says that your double vision is caused by one of the blood clots resting on the optical nerve. Until the clots clear, and they may never clear, you can only read with a black patch over one eye. He doesn't want you doing that for more than a few minutes each day. Try to be thankful. You survived what would have killed most people."

He patted me on the shoulder. "Remember. You were really dead when they brought you here. If you hadn't stood up in that elevator, if we hadn't started the glucose right away, you would be dead. Somebody must be praying for you."

Who that "somebody" was I learned more than thirty years later at a banquet at my adored Jefferson Hotel in Richmond, Virginia, the same hotel in which Richard and I had stopped on the journey south. In 1967 an attractive woman in her early forties came up after I had finished the talk I was there to give.

"Are you the Susan Anthony who nearly died in an auto crash years ago in Greensboro?"

"I certainly am."

"You don't know me, never met me. I was a little girl at the time, eleven years old. But when I read in the paper about your dying, and saw the horrible picture of the car crumpled like an accordion, I prayed that you might live. I told God that this was my first prayer to save someone's life. I begged Him to save your body and your soul. I told Him that if you lived I would devote myself to prayer forever after. When I read that you were well enough to leave the hospital, I knew my prayer had been answered."

I held her hand with both of mine. I could say only, "Thank you."

Dr. Whittington left me alone with his verdict. And then the delayed shock reaction hit. Hysterics began that day, hysterics, because I could face the loss of life, but not the loss of sight. I did not hear the nurse come into the room. She touched me on the shoulder: "Sue, take this pill the doctor has ordered for you. And I have a surprise. Someone left this package for you."

Curiosity conquered tears. I opened the package, a plain

manila envelope. The broken black fragments of the record I had carried all summer spilled out on the bed. Part of the blue label had survived the crash. I didn't need single vision to know its title, "Until the Real Thing Comes Along." And then I cried again, mourning my favorite record, shattered like my body in the wreck.

9 *"The light of the body is the eye: if therefore thine eye be single, thy whole body shall be full of light."*

"Some sort of miracle," Dr. Whittington had said. But I couldn't sit around North Carolina waiting for one. And seeing double, I couldn't go back to school either. Just where I was to go and what I was to do was resolved suddenly when a friend of Mother's offered us her beach cottage in Fort Lauderdale, Florida.

The first thing I did after we had set our bags down was to go out and find a bar. From the time I took my first drink in Easton when I was 16 I was destined some day to cross the line to alcoholism. Nobody, not I certainly, could have foreseen that that day would come so soon. But it did. At the age of twenty the enforced inactivity of that winter in Fort Lauderdale prodded me over the line. My days, now devoid of hyper-activity on campus, were filled with frozen daiquiris, cuba libras, and cold beer. Liquor which had been my quick and easy way to popularity, now became the anesthesia to blot out each unwelcome day. No longer did I drink because I wanted to. I now drank because I had to.

Mother implored me to stop my day-and-night pub-crawling with hard-drinking older men. She nagged at me to come home to dinner. She lay awake each night fearful of another drunken crash. She wept when she couldn't wake me from my drunken noontime sleep.

My only response was to rush from her as soon as I awoke and start the day's search for the first drink. The fact that I had no money at all did not stop me. It never stops an alcoholic. My new drinking partner was an alcoholic himself, a divorced man with an unsavory reputation. Mother warned me that the blood clots would kill me if I did not stop pouring alcohol into my bloodstream. She warned that my wild late-night carousing would be used as evidence by insurance investigators to prove that I was well enough to frequent bars, and hence suffered no lasting damage from the accident. I was, she said, jeopardizing our only chance of paying the medical bills: our lawyer had claimed permanent damage to my body as grounds for collecting.

Periodically I made an effort to take Mother's advice and "do something worthwhile" with my time. I sat through some of the meetings of the Fort Lauderdale writers' group. In no time their coffee-oriented evenings palled. Price Day, a Pulitzer Prize-winning reporter, and his wife, Allie, very kindly offered to read to me, but the book I chose was one someone had given me in the hospital, Trotsky's *History of the Russian Revolution,* and all of us soon got bogged down in its unpronounceable Russian names and prolix style. I even tried to launch a peace crusade. My only convert was a pimply-faced adolescent boy. Finally, a noted labor economist, just retired from the University of Wisconsin, Dr. John R. Commons, suggested that we simply talk together about the subject of economics. He was a sweet man and brilliant, but I could not bear conversation with him for the simple reason that I could never look him in the eye. When I tried to, I saw Dr. Commons' two faces nine inches apart, one image up at the right, the identical, old leathery face down at the left.

Strangely enough, years later I was to discover that Aunt Susan had a serious eye problem of her own. That problem was kept a secret from everyone but her closest friends; even her early biographers did not know of it, because Aunt Susan's shame was so great.

The story of Aunt Susan's eyes began when she was three years old and living in Adams, Massachusetts. When her mother, Lucy Anthony, was expecting her fourth child, Susan and her older sister Guelma were packed off to stay with their Grandmother Anthony. While there, the two children came down with whooping cough. As they got better, the grandmother found a way to fill the long, boring days of recuperation indoors; a teacher in the family school, Miss Rhoda Brownell, taught the two little girls to read.

Three-year-old Susan quickly grasped the fact that letters came together in words; words soon became sentences for her, then paragraphs and pages. She spent the remainder of the six weeks at her grandmother's reading children's books and the Bible. She could hardly wait to get home to show off her brand-new skill; certainly she was unprepared for the reception she got. Her mother took one anguished look at her, and burst into tears.

Susan couldn't comprehend what had gone wrong. She too began to cry. Her mother took her by the shoulders, shuddering and sobbing. "Your eyes, your beautiful eyes," she wailed, "what has happened to the prettiest eyes of any child I ever saw?" She led Susan to a mirror and showed her. The "prettiest eyes" had turned completely crossed toward her nose.

Lucy Anthony did nothing to conceal the fact she thought her daughter disfigured forever. She blamed it all on Susan herself, on her precocious, overambitious reading. Daniel, Susan's father, suggested that perhaps reading while coughing had simply strained the muscles of the young eyes. He was sure that rest would restore them to their original perfection. They forbade her to look at a book and kept her for a time in a darkened room. Later she wandered about the house and yard begging Guelma or anyone around to read to her. Slowly the rest restored the left eye, but it did not help the right. It remained recalcitrant, moving inward in a direction of its own.

People tried to assure Susan that only she noticed the cast in her right eye, but Susan did not believe them. As a teen-ager she lived in an agony of self-consciousness, convinced that she was ugly. She felt that no man could truly love her, looking as she did. Despite invitations from boys to village picnics and rides, despite Aaron's constant correspondence, Susan retained the trauma of her mother's horrified expression. This sense of homeliness put her at a distance from young men, and fostered her extreme reserve with Aaron at the time when she still had the chance to win him. Only after she had lost him did she make one final effort to become a desirable woman.

She was twenty years old then—the same age as I that winter in Fort Lauderdale—and teaching school in Center Falls, New

York, when she heard of a "miracle" doctor who could straighten crossed eyes. Feeling that she had nothing now to lose, she begged her father to take her to the surgeon for this great chance. Daniel drove her in the buggy to Union Village a few miles away and stayed with her during the painful operation. He prayed with her that the miracle she had awaited for seventeen years would now occur. He encouraged her during the long weeks she kept the bandages' on, and drove her back to the doctor's for their removal. He believed firmly that the "prettiest eyes" would once more be revealed.

The doctor unwound the bandages from around her head, then lifted them off her eyes. Susan blinked in the light. Everything was at first completely blurred. Then her father's anxious face came into focus. His face, though, was not smiling. Susan asked for a mirror. The doctor handed it to her in silence. She peered into it, holding it close to examine the results of the "miracle" surgery. The eye had indeed been changed by surgery! Now the iris turned no longer inward as it had for seventeen years. It turned outward instead. The doctor's knife had cut the muscle too much, and thrown the injured eye in the opposite direction.

Daniel begged the doctor for advice.

"If she can find anything at all to see through—let her put them on," he said, admitting total failure in his effort.

Susan and her father returned in gloom to Battenville. In desperation she tried her mother's glasses, hiding herself even from her brothers and sister. In those days a twenty-year-old girl wearing glasses was unheard-of. That her eyes survived the abuse of wearing glasses prescribed for her forty-seven-year-old mother, proved their strength. Later she was fitted with her own prescription. And even later a "miracle" did happen. In some unexplained way as she grew older, her eyes grew better. Susan used those eyes far more than most women of her time. She used them to study the legal fine print of the laws she sought to abolish. She used them to read by dim kerosene lamps, in stagecoaches, trains and meeting halls, right up to the age of eighty-six.

But despite her clear vision, she carried to her grave the conviction that she was disfigured by the cast. Even though the full-faced photographs taken when she was twenty-eight, thirty-two and thirty-eight years old show no sign of a cast, she would permit only profile photographs to be taken of her for the remainder of her life. She kept her glasses on to hide the offending eye even for the formal portrait by Ellis that I grew up with in our home.

At the age of twenty my eye problem too had resisted the efforts of the medical profession. But help in other areas of my life was on its way. Principally, it came from two people: one was an ex-Follies girl; the other a former gangster from Chicago.

One day at Fort Lauderdale I wandered idly into a large Spanish-style building with red-tiled roof across from the broad, white stretch of beach. I mounted the curving, graceful stairway, went through the cloisterlike arches. There, stretched out before me, lay a gorgeous Olympic-sized swimming pool. I had not been swimming since the night of the accident. Turquoise blue and flat calm, I wanted to try this water right away. I paid my last quarter for admission and walked in.

A woman in her forties with dyed black curly hair was trying to oil out the lines on her world-used face. She smiled both with bright blue eyes and with crimson lips.

"Go on in, the water's fine," she said in a gravelly voice.

I gazed at the tempting pool, comfortingly shallow at one end with steps leading down to it.

"I'm just over an accident. I'm afraid for my head."

"Don't dive then. Just slip in over the side or down the steps," said a male voice from the diving board.

Like a fearful child I let myself into two feet of water. I tried a cautious sidestroke to keep my head out of water. Then I bent down and submerged first my forehead, then my nose, and finally my mouth. I stretched my rib cage, and my leg and mending ankle for the crawl. The salt water held me up and I let go, pulling through its silken texture with my arms, and breathing now in time-trained synchronization. But as I reached the poolside to make my racing turn, my arms went leaden. Panicked, I found the bottom of the pool with my feet.

The white-haired man on the diving board hurried over and helped me. This was Al Gordon, the pool coach and manager. Right then and there he taught me how to slow down my eight-beat kick to six beats and conserve my strength, while congratulating me on the free-style form that brother Dan had taught me. He said I should train daily till I built up my distance

once more. I smiled for the first time in months. But I knew
Mother would not let me "waste" money on a pool when the
ocean was free.

"Be my guest," said the woman, whose name turned out to be
Rippy Carson. "Let me give you a season ticket to the pool."

It was suddenly an enchanted day. Almost instantly, I had
gained friends and hope and something to do besides drink.

Lured by the life-giving water I returned next day and accepted Rippy's gift. Every day Rippy would be there, sunning,
watching while I gradually extended my distance from 25 yards
to 50 to 100 to 220 and one triumphant day to a 440. The work-
out at the pool was the sole constructive period of each day.
I showed up for it each noon even when my shaking hands and
bloodshot eyes betrayed the night-time destruction. I didn't have
to hide anything from Rippy. She was a veteran of a thousand
all-night parties. She could match my tales of pranks and parties
with her own past in speakeasies and two-week blasts. She
encouraged me to talk about my night life; and then one day
she talked to me seriously.

Rippy began to tell me about her life and the fight she'd had
to come up in the world. It was a rough story told with flair, of
love affairs and then marriage, of a wild girl who got smart.
She was a woman who as she began to lose her looks, taught
herself to read and write better, even to gain a little culture.
When I met her at forty-nine, she had a bank account, her own
home, "and best of all, a mind that can still learn."

I listened to Rippy Carson as I had listened to no one else.
Her story was real. She told it with love and with concern for
me. She made me want to do something with my mind.

Just at that time I met Johnny Danton. He wandered over to
me at a huge cocktail party. I was not complimented by his attention: he was a squat, ugly, powerfully built man with eyes
like black marbles popping out under thick lids. He had a broad,
monkeylike upper lip, a wide spatulate nose, a deep, black tan,
and a huge, overhanging paunch. But after Johnny Danton
opened that monkey face of his into a broad grin and said, "Hello,
kid," in his deep resonant voice, I forgot all about his looks.

I had never before had contact with anybody even remotely
like Johnny. Once he had been a member of the Toughy gang—
the "Terrible Toughys" they called them in Chicago. He had

served time in jails and penitentiaries, and then, though he never told me the story behind it, he went straight. He had wound up in Fort Lauderdale raising chickens.

Johnny wasn't on the make for me, and I, virgin that I was in spite of my wild drinking habits, was grateful for this. No, Johnny was drawn to me because he liked me. He saw some-one else beneath the wild young girl. While the nice ladies who sat with Mother on the beach each day clucked their tongues and eyed my activities disapprovingly, Johnny reached out to help me.

He began by picking me up at the pool in his old black jalopy before I had time to get plastered after my noontime swim. He took me to Joe's on New River for a hamburger and milk shake that began the afternoon "class." This was a driving lesson. I protested that I couldn't see well enough to drive be-cause of my double vision.

"That's what you think," he said. "You've got a built-in ad-vantage, kid. You can keep one set of eyes looking in front and another in the rear view mirror." True to his predictions, under Johnny's tutelage, I learned to drive.

One day after our driving lesson, he invited me to dinner. I hesitated, and he caught the hesitation.

"What's the matter?" he asked, "Not in your class?"

I double-talked a bit.

"What about some of them bums you get drunk with?" he broke in. "Any bum is OK if he's in the right class?"

I blushed clear to the scar-line under my hair. "O.K. Johnny, dinner it is. Great!" He took me to my favorite hangout, The Deck, on the north side of New River. Hank, the bartender, was polishing glasses when we came in. He looked up, surprised— not because I was with Johnny, but because I was sober, and because I wore a dress. Generally at six in the evening I was al-ready loaded, a long shirt pulled hastily over my bathing suit.

Johnny cut off my drinks after two, then led me across the street to Elmer's for dinner. He himself had put on a clean sport shirt and combed his fine, thin black hair. He rationed out one more drink before I ate the Florida crawfish.

He was still simmering at my near-refusal to dine with him.

"Maybe if I'd growed up like you in a clean little town like Easton, Pennsylvania, not that I want an alibi, but maybe it would have been different. The streets I lived in on the South Side weren't so clean." I could tell he had done a lot of thinking about how he had got into the gang that led to the reformatory, that led to the big-time gang, that led to prison. "Why do you have to knock yourself out? What ails you kid?"

"What have I to live for?" I said bitterly. "I might die at any moment. I can't read or write. I'm not good for anything really."

"You think about yourself too much. Did you ever try to help someone else?"

"I spent all last summer helping people. I helped humanity, I crusaded for world peace. And all I got for it was a smash-up."

"Come off it. I don't mean great big humanity, that's easy. I mean did you ever help people, a person?"

He pointed toward our waitress. "She works hard. Do you wonder where her kids are while she's waiting on us tonight? I bet I know. They're out running wild in the street, no one to care for them, just like I did. My mother went out as a maid. Ever think that perhaps you and some of your fancy friends could help those kids? It's just a 'for instance' but those kids need a place to go and someone to care for them."

"You mean me? You mean *I* could do it?"

"Because you need to stop feeling sorry for yourself. You're not doing a thing now but lousing up your life. And that bunch of rich bums, what do they do but sit around and get slopped up at cocktail parties?"

When our waitress gave us our check, I looked at her for the first time that evening. Johnny drove me home at the early hour of 11 o'clock. I was sober and as I went to bed our conversation stirred in my mind. When I awoke the next morning, my first thought was not, how could I fill my day, but was there something I could do for someone else, something as specific as helping the children of waitresses?

I rode my bike over to Ginny Gamble's apartment. An intelligent leader of Lauderdale's young matrons, Ginny listened with interest. She got on the phone, called up some of her friends and invited them to drinks three days from then.

At the cocktail party, Ginny and I presented an idea to them: the need for a center to care for the children of working mothers, a place where they could receive supervised care day and night. Before the third cocktail had been drunk, we had launched the organization with a fund-raising plan. Today when Ginny and I are listed as founders of what later became the Junior League of Fort Lauderdale, I often wonder if the League knows that their real founding father was a retired Chicago gangster!

The children, ranging from three to eleven years of age, began coming to rooms given us by local businessmen. Ginny's friends scheduled their volunteer time and hired paid help for the continuing care. I can still see the little children opening up like a night-blooming cereus under the warmth of the attention the ladies gave them. We played games with them, helped them draw and paint, took them to the beach. The miracle of love-in-action not only broke through to the children, but thawed the freeze in me, drawing my eyes away from the mirror of myself. I cannot today ever look at children in a play group without wanting to hug all of them; and even more to include all neglected little children, like my lonely little Gerry Andrews in Rochester, in good child-care centers.

As the warm Florida summer began, Johnny had other ideas for my eight hours a day. I must, he said, get back to work at my trade, newspaper reporting. Leave the volunteer work to the young married women. Again I protested, saying that my eyes would bar me.

"You can type, can't you? You don't need no eyes to type. You only need your eyes to look at the people you're writing about, and you see them better than most, you see two of them."

We walked up the steep stairs of the tiny little building then housing *The Fort Lauderdale Daily News,* to the city room on the second floor. It looked like a trailer after the big news room of the *Rochester Democrat* and *Chronicle.* But I savored the clatter of typewriters, the clutter and confusion and shouts, and sniffed the glorious smell of printer's ink. Johnny took me over to a desk, where a man with a green eyeshade hunched over some copy. He introduced me and wasted no time.

"Got a job for Sue?"

The man looked at me and shrugged. "Johnny, you know I always want to do any favor I can for you, but the season's long over and there just isn't a thing. She can fill out an application though."

"I don't think you understood me," Johnny said deliberately. "Sue needs a job."

I gaped at him. My kind, gentle Johnny had suddenly become
a man with a gun in his voice. Then he cocked the trigger.

"Come on, you know you need help for the summer, with all
them snowbirds flown north. This gal knows her stuff, and she's
got class—more than you got in this room right now. What time
do you want her tomorrow morning?"

The newspaperman looked down at his desk, shuffled some
papers around, jabbed one on the spindle.

"Come in at eight tomorrow," he said.

Back in the jalopy I asked Johnny for his secret.

"Don't ask. You got your job. Now make good and don't be
late tomorrow morning. Cut down on your booze tonight and
get to bed early."

I did as I was told. Aften seven months of daily drinking, of
staying up till four, of sleeping till noon, I went to bed with only
one drink offered by Johnny to celebrate my new job. Effort-
lessly I moved back into the swing of reporting and writing, my
task a 24-page mail-away edition called "Beautiful Florida
Homes."

Johnny liked to come along on my assignments. He and our
friend, reporter Phil Weidling, filled me in. Phil knew every
grain of sand in Broward County. He had grown up there and
had covered every facet of its life for newspapers and his books.
In the black jalopy the three of us drove out to meet the earliest
residents of the country, the Seminole Indians, now segregated
on their reservation. Phil introduced me to a pioneer white
settler of Fort Lauderdale, Mrs. Frank Stranahan, in her old
frame house hanging over New River that had been her husband's trading post at the turn of the century. Phil told me all
the inside stories of the families who had built the boom-time
Spanish-style mansions, some now empty since the 1926 crash.
The reporter's omniscience lighted up this town, once hated, now
alive and loved, as I began to penetrate its past, its present, and
its people.

The way I expressed my gratitude to Johnny for all the things
he had done for me remains one of the great guilts of my life.
Seeing me happy and productive, Mother went back to Pennsylvania, while I divided my time between Rippy and Ginny
and a steady stream of dates. There was one college boy in
particular, Bronson, whom I liked, but Bronson could not bear

Johnny. Gradually Bronson put the pressure on me to stop seeing him. Johnny, of course, sensitive as always, picked up the emanations and threw them back at me in what turned out to be a hurtful exchange. It was I who did the hurting.

"You're ruining my reputation," I told him, which, even then I probably knew was a ludicrous thought. "With Mother back north," I said, "I simply cannot afford to have you be seen entering and leaving my house at all hours."

Johnny's black eyes dilated. He growled, "O.K. Kid, I get the picture. You don't need Johnny now that you got a job and a college kid hanging around. If you think you're too good for me, Sue, I won't bother you no more."

He wheeled around in his white shirt and white duck pants, climbed into the old black battered car and drove off in a burst of exhaust. As it turned out, only a few weeks later I went back home. All through the following months I worried about what I had done to Johnny. I didn't write to tell him. I wanted to apologize in person. At Christmas, back in Lauderdale on a visit, I ran all over town trying to find him. Finally I looked up Phil Weidling at The Deck. Phil raised his golden-brown eyes from his beer. "The train smashed him and his jalopy to smithereens," Phil said.

It had happened one week before.

Back in Pennsylvania the previous fall, Mother had suggested various ways that a handicapped twenty-one-year-old girl might earn a living. In a few weeks October rain and cold would send her back to Harrisburg to her and Dad's apartment, too small for two, let alone for three. My solution was to slink off on solitary walks in the woods, then head down to the towpath beside the canal, crossing the ancient wooden bridge to the old Raubsville tavern. There I furtively drank my beers, hoping Raubsville natives would not report me. I dreaded trips to Easton. The store windows mocked me with their back-to-college browns and rusty reds. My friends seemed of another world, their going-away parties an affront. Everyone was going somewhere, doing something, in the new year that September always signals.

One September morning I awoke on the sleeping porch dreading another day. Sunlight dappled through the curtain of green forest beyond the screen. I tested my vision as always, first on the bedside table, peering at the glass, the ashtray, to see if there were one or two images. I glanced back at the sun illumining the forest, postponing getting up. What was there to get up for? Then something drew my eyes back to the table. I sat upright and stared at the ashtray and the water glass. I must be still asleep. For now I saw, not two, but one ashtray, one glass! Quickly I tested my new single vision on the swing, the chairs beyond, the apple tree outdoors. I walked into the kitchen, saw one stove, one kitchen cabinet, one sink. I shouted: "Mother!"

She came running down the stairs, saw my face and exclaimed: "You can see!"

"I see—I see!" I threw my arms around her and we wept together.

A week later the great eye specialist in New York, Dr. Webb Weeks, could not explain the healing, but his careful tests revealed a consistent single image, 20-20 vision, no impairment in the eyes. It was a miracle, he said, and he congratulated me on it. Dr. Whittington in North Carolina had said it would take "some kind of miracle," and now just that had happened.

Many times after the accident I had flung out "Why?" at an unfeeling universe. About the healing it never occurred to me to ask.

10 *"And if one look to the land, behold, darkness and distress; and the light is darkened by its clouds."*

With eyes to see again I raced back to college for senior year. The enforced idleness of Fort Lauderdale had made me determined to live fully, totally, to learn, to do. I studied hard that year and drank hard, and my extracurricular schedule was fuller than ever. When the insurance money for my accident came through, I plotted a postgraduation trip to Europe for more learning and working and living. A major item on the summer's agenda had to do with what I deemed my complete emancipation as a woman. I made a carefully pondered, objective decision to do something drastic about my virgin status. I had no particular man in mind. Europe, I figured, would produce him. It did, immediately.

When I graduated in June, I went forth with a B.A. degree, *magna cum laude*, even though in May there had been a moment when I wasn't sure I would be getting a diploma at all. The new college president, young Alan Valentine, had summoned me to his office for a reprimand. It wasn't for my drinking. It was for political activity on campus. I had organized a peace strike.

An organized peace strike sounds like a major achievement. I often think of it today and smile sadly, for our strike wasn't very potent and it wasn't even very dramatic. I simply had sent out a call to all those on campus who took their pacifism seriously, asking them to show their support for the student peace movement then spreading across the nation.

111

Most students in 1938 didn't even look up from their bridge hands. Still, on a fresh green day a little band of some twenty-five forlorn coeds straggled together and stood in front of the campus administration building. For one minute between classes, we stood there in silence. We felt staggered by our boldness.

When President Valentine called me in, he was angry. He had considered sending me home, he said. Instead, he warned that I would be expelled immediately should I ever again dare to issue a call for any political activity without his expressed permission. How quaint it all seems today.

The crisis passed and in the waning weeks at Rochester, most of my thoughts were of the approaching summer. The trip ahead was built around my joining a group of pacifists in England and going with them across the channel to a peace conference in The Netherlands. I had charted a lot of sightseeing in a number of countries as well, and despite the rumblings of war getting louder every week, I had it in mind to try to find work somewhere in Europe and remain for a year or so. I had booked third-class passage on the glorious *Ile de France* and already my mind had fashioned a fantasy of what the future would be like. These were the days when women reporters were coming into their own. Exciting ladies of the press such as Dorothy Thompson and Martha Gellhorn were in the thick of peril and intrigue, sending back copy from the trouble spots. That was the life for me. I pictured myself as a combination reporter and *femme fatale* working and sleeping and drinking my way through the capitals of power.

When the *Ile de France* pulled away from the dock I was eager to be going. Among other things, I was glad to be leaving Aunt Susan behind. She had been a dominating presence all those years in Rochester, and long since I had tired of being introduced as her great-niece. It would be good to get away to Europe where the name was unknown. Yet I had no sooner set down my precious new portable typewriter in the cabin which I was to share with three other girls, when a gray-haired woman with large, yellowish buck teeth appeared in the doorway.

"Miss Anthony?" she said. I nodded. "Ah, good. I saw your name on the passenger list and I hurried down to see if you wouldn't join us at our table on the voyage." She told me her name—Sarah Watson. "I heard your aunt speak once, when I was

very young, of course. I myself marched in the Victory Parade
in 1920. I can't tell you how pleased I'd be to have you at my
table. We could have such nice long talks."

Trapped, I thought. But she was pleasant enough, and it was
nice to have a friend.

Friends, however, were no problem aboard the *Ile*. Third class
was a fascinating melange of people from everywhere, people
with different tongues and backgrounds, people of cultivation,
all traveling with purpose. In Depression years fewer people
traveled for the lark of it, not in third class, anyway. Young or
old, everyone I met seemed to have a story, seemed to have sub-
stance to him. Of course, according to my plan, it wasn't sub-
stance or story or cultivation I was seeking. I was looking for a
man. And on the very first day out, I met not one, but two. A
young German exchange student and an English artist.

I preferred the German. Quite simply he was the most mascu-
line man I had ever known. He was bronzed and blond; he was
tall and broad-shouldered. And he actually had a dueling scar
on his strong Teutonic face. His name was Otto Speidel. Otto
had been studying as an American exchange scholar at a college
in the middle west; his English was unbelievably good. I was
entranced by him.

Val Wylie was the Englishman, and though he was handsome
too, the quality was altogether different. There was a gypsylike
feeling to him. He had dark eyes; dark curly hair, longish for
that time; deep tanned skin; teeth much too white and healthy
for what I had heard of British dentistry. The crinkles at the
corner of his eyes showed that he was older than his slim young
body suggested. Val was forty-two. He was on his way home to
Hampstead from Mexico, where he had been painting for eighteen months. He was a graduate of Oxford; he spoke with a
clipped Oxford accent; he was a man of the world, a free-moving
Bohemian who was not only single but unattached.

Otto was devastating, but Val was fascinating. Either one
would do for my summer's plan.

I settled easily and quickly into the routine of shipboard.
There was only one awkward moment and that came the very
first day at sea. When I arrived at Mrs. Watson's table, I found
that I had been seated next to a Negro. I didn't notice that first
instant that he was tall and young and handsome; I saw only

that he was black. In all the college years that I had spouted
phrases about equality with our black brothers, I had never .
actually known a Negro on an equal footing—and for a self-
conscious moment I wondered what we would find to talk about
three times a day. Fortunately, Alan Boulet proved to have social and conversational savoir for two, and after that meal I never
saw his color again.

There were five of us at the table. Mrs. Watson consistently
sounded us out on our views on everything. She was in the
process of founding the Descendants of the American Revolution, which she described as a civil liberties organization, a
group of sons and daughters of the American Revolution who
believed that democracy was being threatened by the current
treatment of minority groups, racial and political. I became in-
trigued by Mrs. Watson and pleased that she wanted me to look
her up in Washington when the summer was over. For the present, though, I was much more interested in Otto and Val and in
the lovely French custom of wine at every meal. My tablemates
were all moderate drinkers and so I was able to consume their
wine as well as my own and thereby managed to be in a gentle
fruit-of-the-vine glow for the entire voyage. I also went completely off my diet for the first time since Joel had called me
"Fatty."

Three days at sea, Otto and I, who had been finding one another increasingly desirable, ran into trouble. The cause was
Alan Boulet. Our argument began when Otto suggested that I
should change my table.

"It is not right," he told me, "that a fine girl like you should
consort with such people."

"What people?" I knew exactly whom he meant because he
had made a few remarks about Alan before, but now I wanted
him to say it.

"That black man from Martinique. I cannot understand how
you can permit this to continue, this eating together. It is re-
pulsive. It does not befit you."

Perhaps out of shame for my own original uneasiness with
Alan, I took offense at these words. I lied and told him that it
had been my own idea to sit next to Alan. Otto went into a
frightening rage.

"I cannot permit this!" he shouted. "I *order* you to change your table!"

That was enough. I left him standing on the deck, clenched and white.

As if to shelter, I flew right to Val. I found him sunning himself on the deck. Until that moment I thought I had been fairly successful at dangling two men on my string, but Val was too knowing, too confident of himself to be dangled. He liked me for my zest and earnestness and even for my flirtatiousness, but he knew my game far better than I did.

"You've had a fight," he said to me with an impressive display of omniscience.

I didn't know how he knew but I was glad he did. He was a man of insight.

"Yes."

"And I thought you were a pacifist." He was also a man who liked to take gentle jabs at my political convictions. In all of our discussions, he never disagreed with me outright, but somehow I always seemed to come away from him with something to think about.

"But this was for a good cause, Val. That boy is a bigot. He is so arrogant, so imperious—"

"Pacifists fight then, if the cause is good?"

Once more I felt very young with Val, very green, very stupid. I knew he was only sparring lightly with me, in half-jest, keeping life and politics buoyant. I also knew that he stood firm in his view of the world in 1938. The first time we had talked of pacifism, he had shaken his head slowly, "It's just too late," he said wistfully, "it's just too late."

For the rest of the voyage I was under Val's sway, and I loved it. He was charming and experienced, the perpetual traveler, the worldly guide. He knew how to amuse me and how to impress me. Dramatically, without telling me, he had the steward change his table, and one day when I came into the dining room he was sitting there next to Mrs. Watson as though he'd been there all along. Mrs. Watson and the others—and I—couldn't have been more pleased. From a distance, "the Nazi," as we came to call Otto, glowered.

Soon I knew for certain that Val was the man who should accomplish my summer's objective for me. It was quite clear that he was not opposed to the idea, but on shipboard, especially in cramped third class, this feat was not easily accomplished. In fact, with four men in his cabin and four women in mine, it was impossible: we had difficulty finding privacy even for a kiss.

But only when we slept were Val and I apart. We sunned and read during the day, and in the evenings we joined friends in the bar to drink and talk the night away. One of our group was an American girl named Sylvia Rank who was on her way to Spain to be a medical aide in the North American Ambulance Brigade. She had many friends in the International Brigade, she said, especially the young Americans who had enlisted to help the Spanish government fight against the insurgent General Franco.

With my pacifist leanings, I did not take easily to this girl and what she had to say. Behind thick glasses, her eyes glowed fanatically. I'd always heard of religious fervor; when she talked about Spain, she seemed to have such a fervor. She was given to picturesque speech and elaborate metaphors, most of which I found cumbersome, but I couldn't help but be touched by her earnestness, her desperate seriousness, when one evening she described Spain as "the world's hourglass."

"It's silly, I know, but I'm going to Spain to do what I can to keep the sands from running out of that glass."

On our last night at sea, Val asked me if I would stay over with him a day or so in Plymouth. I had made plans to travel with a bevy of Bennington College girls as far as London where I would meet with the English members of the Fellowship of Reconciliation. It took me less than a second to change my itinerary.

The next day, as we went through customs and immigration, I suddenly wondered if I hadn't been a trifle hasty. A strange land, a strange man. At least, I hadn't known Val long and perhaps I really didn't know him well enough, this man whom Mother would have said wanted "just one thing." The old Puritan conscience came up to the surface. I thought of all the disasters that could happen. The hotel might catch on fire. Val might drop dead of a heart attack in my arms.

I fought my fears all the time Val was pointing out the first pre-seventeenth-century buildings I had ever seen. I nearly panicked again when we arrived at the decayed elegance of the Grand Hotel. While Val, carrying his paintings rolled up in a leather portfolio, walked up to the desk, I hung back. I was glad my gloves hid my ringless finger as the bellboy picked up our overnight bags. Could he tell we were not married? We followed him through the dark, ornate lobby and into the creaky, filigreed iron elevator. We were shown into a baroque, high-ceilinged room, with dark red brocade drapes and dark red rug. Dominating the room was a huge double bed.

When the boy left, Val took me gently in his arms.

"Susan, lesson number one in hotels. March right up to the desk with me and insist upon a bath or a shower, or a twin or double bed. A married woman will always do that."

I walked over to the window and looked out at the long gray twilight. There was a knock on the door. Val opened it to a chambermaid.

"Shall I turn down the bed, Madame?" She looked at me.

"Why, yes," I faltered. I had never been called "Madame" before. I didn't know what to do while she was in the room. I stayed rooted at the window.

"What time would you like tea, Madame?"

"We've had tea," I said.

"Early tea, Madame, in the morning," she said sternly.

"Just a moment. Val, what time do you want tea?"

"We'd better have it about seven since our train leaves at nine," he said smoothly.

The maid left. Val hugged me, smiling, "Well, Madame, how does it feel to order early tea in a man's room?" Then he gave me another lesson in the wifely thing to do. "Be unpacking my things. You could have been taking out my shirts, or even examining a sock for holes. That's what wives do. Mistresses couldn't care less. Now, let's have dinner up here and make it an early-to-bed night." By this time all I wanted was a drink.

We had dinner, the coffee was cleared away, and then we went to bed.

It is difficult to say which one of us was more to be pitied. Val, I think. Val, the man who knew me so completely, who knew so much about everything in the world, did not know that this seemingly daring girl he had taken to bed with him was a total innocent. For the first and only time of our relationship, Val was shocked.

He refused to have anything to do with me.

But the next morning he invited me to go home with him and visit his mother. Again I put off joining the pacifists. On the train to London I wondered why it was that I seemed to be fated to meet men's mothers. At any rate we traveled on platonically while I held on to the hope that with a little time, Val might recover from his shock.

If I had thought for an instant that Val's mother would be like Richard's in North Carolina, I was wrong. Mrs. Wylie greeted us at the doorway of their huge eighteenth-century townhouse just off Hampstead Heath. She was a Bloomsbury version of Queen Victoria with a long black dress and lace fichu, but there the comparison ended. She was quite accustomed to Val's bringing girls home with him. The last girl had been an American, too. I got the feeling that there had been a procession of nationalities before me. Many had been called, none chosen.

One of the surprises of the whole trip to Europe came when Mrs. Wylie instantly recognized my name. Leave Aunt Susan behind? Oh, no. And to top that, I discovered I had come back to the very place, Hampstead, where John Anthony, who had sired our clan, had been born 331 years before.

Aunt Susan, it turned out, had made her mark in England. The lady was eighty-four years old when she spoke in Manchester in 1904. Christabel Pankhurst heard her speak and was "filled with sorrow and indignation that such a splendid worker for humanity was destined to die without seeing the hopes of her life realized. It is unendurable," Miss Pankhurst said, "to think of another generation of women wasting their lives begging for the vote. We must not lose any more time. We must act."

And act they did. They went militant. They refused to accept the shilly-shallying of Parliament and demonstrated outside its doors; the women were led by Christabel and her mother, Emmeline.

When their picket lines and parades grew larger the women were roughed up by the police and jailed, and when they went on hunger strikes, they were subjected to the torture of forced feeding. Parliament passed one act after another to harass them, including the notorious "cat-and-mouse" act by which a protester could be rearrested as soon as she had recovered physically from the abuse of her previous incarceration. Only when World War I came did Mrs. Pankhurst and her followers relent. Like the

American suffragists in the Civil War, they waited for peace to renew their own fight. Finally, in 1928, eight years after their American sisters, they won the vote.

In the next days, which stretched into four weeks, I stayed with the Wylies. While the pacifists were holding meetings and speaking throughout England, I was seeing London. Val took me everywhere with him. I was to discover that he had a genius for long-time relationships, with men as well as with women. These friends all had several qualities in common. They were cosmopolitan, internationally minded, artistic, and distinguished in their fields. They were all fervently anti-Nazi and anti-Fascist. We spent afternoons and evenings with the scientist J. B. S. Haldane and the sculptor Henry Moore, with Marc Gertler and dozens of painters who owed their fame to Peggy Guggenheim. Val showed me his beautiful London, whole and intact, as it would never be again. He taught me how to look at the masterpieces of Van Eyck and Vermeer and Velasquez at the National Gallery. He took me to the Tate and to the great British Museum which housed his own collection of East African art, and to the Tower and Westminster Abbey, and to Hampton Court.

One day I went alone with a letter of introduction I had brought from America to a veteran foreign correspondent. I still wanted to find a job as a reporter. Webb Miller was the head of the United Press for all of Europe and I found him in his office in Bouverie Street, just off Fleet. He was an older man, tailored and distinguished, not at all like the sloppy, trench-coated Hollywood version of a newsman. Once a farm boy in Dowagiac, Michigan, he had become a star reporter, covering all continents, and all major European stories since World War I. Webb became the second hero of my trip.

He took me to the Savoy for a drink, and then to Quaglino's for a lunch that went on for four hours. Very soon I knew that Webb was to become, not just a possible employer, but a friend to cherish. For a young American just out of college who wanted to work on newspapers, this was Mount Olympus. I was confident that he was going to give me a job with UP at summer's end, even though he warned that "war might come soon, even before the fall."

That was the refrain of the summer. "Treasure these weeks," people would say. It made me feel guilty that I was doing nothing about the pacifism I was supposed to be espousing. But England and Val were too powerful a call. Besides, increasingly I was having doubts about the very conference I was to attend in The Netherlands.

One day Val and I had lunch in Soho with a faded, beautiful, red-haired girl on leave from the Spanish government press bureau. She and Val were old buddies. She had been trying futilely to win support for the besieged republic from England and America and I could tell she was at the point of exhaustion. It was like talking again to the girl on the *Ile de France,* except that Sybil had been there. She had seen Hitler's and Mussolini's planes, seen their bombs explode and had watched people die. I couldn't talk to her about peace; I found I didn't want to. I began to believe that Spain was, as she said, a curtain-raiser, that Hitler should be stopped now—or else.

A week before I sailed by channel boat to Holland, Val made love to me. We had spent almost every minute of the precious weeks together as he had guided me in my choice of food and drink, and opened my eyes to the beauty of painting and sculpture. With Val, even my sense of smell had been quickened; I had new pleasures in the fragrance of soap, and the sharp clean essence of turpentine in Val's studio at the bottom of the Wylies' garden. One night, after the old townhouse had gone to sleep, we went up to Val's suite on the third floor and there consummated our relationship.

When it was over, I was not sorry, but I was disappointed. Not in Val, in the act. The expectation had been greater than the deed.

Would it have been better if I had been wholly in love with Val? A question worth pondering, but without answer.

First thing I did when I arrived in The Hague was to see the Rembrandts at the Mauritshuis. Val had taught me well. It was my own idea, however, to cycle out to the sea at Scheveningen and buy some golden wooden shoes. In a way I was still putting off the Fellowship of Reconciliation. Finally, at long last, in the tiny town of Luntern I joined the hundreds of pacifists who had come from all over Europe and England to confer. But the weeks aboard ship and in London had changed me. Just as I had come to the conference reluctantly, I was reluctant to take up their way of thinking. I listened to the "peace at any price" message of white-haired George Lansbury, the pacifist M.P., but during his speech I kept hearing the voices of Val's friends.

It upset me too to see dozens of tow-headed German youths cycling to the conference from the Third Reich; to me they all looked like Otto Speidel. Little by little the pacifists who sat and listened and cheered around me began to look less like people. Gradually I saw them as ostriches ignoring what was actually happening in Europe. I left the conference before it was over; I knew that I would not go on to the peace meetings in Geneva either.

On my own I traveled, picking up from time to time with other vacationers, visiting new friends, stopping when I wanted, sightseeing at my own speed, making arrangements for a meeting with Val in the South of France. At Cassis-sur-Mer on the Côte d'Azur, Val rented a room in an ancient stuccoed house with red-tiled roof. The room, where Val painted, had a big double bed but no bath. We shared the toilet and sink with the owners. For a real hot bath in a tub I had to be invited to the glamorous villa on the hillside owned by a friendly English bachelor. He made an almost liturgical rite of it: water was heated and poured by servants in the Roman-sized tub, while Val and his friends were served tea and drinks to celebrate the rare event.

Every morning I arose long before Val. Ravenous from my diet of sea air, I would walk alone past the fishing boats in the harbor, watching the Mediterranean stirred up by the mistral. I would go into the patisserie and buy my daily croissant, then to the sidewalk café, to order the good chicory-flavored French coffee.

I was at peace with Val at Cassis, but even as we swam and made love we could never forget how close we were to Spain. Cassis was not very far from Perpignan, where Spanish Loyalist refugees had fled Franco firing squads to the crowded French concentration camps. The stories came to us fresh. At night we partied, exerting ourselves to extremes to have fun. One night we drank at a notorious bordello in Marseille and grew sober listening to some German homosexuals tell how the Nazis were throwing their kind into concentration camps along with Jews, liberals, and Communists. Europe was filled with birds fleeing before the storm.

Then a letter came from Webb. He was off, he said, to cover the last-ditch peace talks of Chamberlain and Hitler at Berchtesgaden. War was sure to come at any moment.

It was obvious that I had to make a decision. With the UP reporter's job far from certain in London, I could still return there to stay at Val's home while I studied at the London School of Economics on my fellowships. Or I could return to America, to the government job that waited for me in Washington.

A second letter from Webb made the choice for me. It came from Berchtesgaden.

"God only knows what is going to happen. War is inevitable. I'd strongly advise you to go home and not get caught in the mess that's coming up here. Go on back to America and try to get on a paper there. If war doesn't come, I'll see what we can work out in London."

When Val saw my disappointment, he made, for him, the ultimate offer. He asked me to marry him. I could not accept. It had been good and fine of him to ask me; but I told him I honestly was not ready to settle down.

Sadly we went to Marseille and booked my passage home on the *Paris,* and did some sober sightseeing at the Basilica of Notre Dame de la Garde and ate bouillabaisse at the Vieux Port. We spent our last days together in Paris at the Louvre and Fontainebleau, our nights at the cafés Dome and Rotonde with his artist friends.

On a chill day we went to Le Havre, sat over a farewell drink while a brisk breeze from the channel almost blew Val's words away.

"Unless there's a war, I'll be over to see you next summer. We'll go to Mexico together," he said. I smiled.

Then as if in benediction, Val took my hand in his.

"Susan, all the wildness I have seen is not really you. Underneath this drinking, pleasure-seeking self there is something in you that wants a larger life. It's a mystical self that tries to emerge when you are not blotting it out with drink."

It was a curious thing for Val to say. Not understanding, I was moved by it nonetheless.

I stood on the deck while Val receded into a tiny, waving figure. I watched until the shore of France had vanished, and then, too depressed to go to my dark, third-class cabin, I walked

into the brightly lighted bar. Among the tourists drinking there
was a group of young men, about a dozen of them. They stood
out because they wore a kind of uniform of mismatched jackets
and pants. Some wore berets. One of the young men had an
empty sleeve that hung limply from his shoulder. Another supported himself on a crude cane.

They saw me come in. A tall, thin man whose boyish face was
lined and weathered came to greet me. "You're an American!"
he said. "Join us for a drink. Help us celebrate exactly nothing."

Jim, Sol, Frank, George, and the other boys from farms, towns,
and cities across the country I met that day had fought in the
Abraham Lincoln Battalion, part of the International Brigade of
volunteers in Spain. In its last efforts to win support from the
democracies, the Spanish government had disbanded the brigade
and now, against their will, they were going home. I joined them,
and for the rest of the voyage, in the brotherhood of the bottle.

Before the great September hurricane of 1938 smashed New
England, it tossed our huge liner, sending most of the passengers
to their bunks. The Spanish veterans and I had the bar to ourselves. They talked. I listened. They told how they had left the
corpses of their friends on the banks of the Ebro and among the
olive groves of the war-torn republic. They talked bitterly of the
democracies that were letting another democracy die, and I was,
as usual, drinking brandy with them when the death of still another democracy was announced. The bartender told us the news
just flashed from Munich: for peace in our time, Czechoslovakia
had been sold to the Nazis. That night we mourned together.

When the ship docked in New York, we said goodbye, giving
each other the *embraso*. The example of these young men, more
than any words I had heard all summer, had changed me. The
last shreds of any remaining pacifism in me had dissolved. While
these fighters had gone hungry, thirsty, had faced guns and
death, I had scarcely risen to my feet from bed or café table.
Bloated with twenty extra pounds, experienced as a woman, I
loathed myself as I walked down the gangplank.

11 "Your own hands shaped me, modeled me; and would you now have second thoughts, and destroy me?"

Perhaps it was guilt over the summer that made me eager to work and work hard. I got a job in the research department of the National Youth Administration.

I did not slip into Washington unnoticed. Drew Pearson announced in a paragraph about the name and me, opening the way to all sorts of invitations to dinners, cocktail parties, and lectures given by brilliant, attractive New Deal activists. I was wined and dined by these exciting intellectuals whom I admired without reservation. I did not realize that one day even knowing them would prove a fateful liability. I filled my after-hours with volunteer committee work for the American poor, black and white, for the dying Spanish republic, and for the victims of Nazism and Fascism.

In Washington I felt closer to Aunt Susan than ever in my life. It wasn't simply the humanitarian causes, but because I was literally following in her footsteps, right on up to Capitol Hill. These Halls of Congress had been her stamping ground for nearly forty years.

Now in the twentieth century I would walk into the ornate, gilt lobby of the Senate where she had skirted the brass spittoons of the man's world. I'd send in my card with "our" name to flush out a senator from the floor. In Aunt Susan's day the senator knew exactly whom to expect when he read that name. But today, when I would send in my card, the senator would emerge

124

from the floor looking baffled. He would search the little clusters of earnest pleaders in the lobby, until I stepped up to him.

'Senator, I am Susan B. Anthony, the one who sent the card in to you." Often he would seem confused.

"But my dear young lady, you look too young to have been through all that—" His voice would trail off; clearly he was not sure just when and what "all that" was. Of course neither of us had been around when Aunt Susan strode through the Capitol, shuttling from Senate to House and back, sitting erect in the visitors' gallery, glaring down at her quarry. And luckily he had never had the experience of being cornered at his home, something Aunt Susan reserved for the more elusive lawmakers.

On the very first day I began lobbying for unpopular causes on Capitol Hill, Aunt Susan's unbroken record of rejections by the Senate helped me feel better about mine. That day I went to see a senator about urging France to open her borders to desperately needed arms for the Spanish Loyalists. The senator was charming; in fact he invited me to join him for cocktails; but he refused to help. Like Aunt Susan, I was never victorious.

As the autumn advanced I was whirled from Spanish Loyalist fund-raising parties at smart art galleries and Georgetown homes to mass meetings at the National Press Club auditorium. I would listen to speakers such as long-time prisoner, labor leader Tom Mooney. I'd attend the intellectual feasts provided by the Washington Cooperative Bookshop. At the bookshop, I could find the volumes I wanted on the anti-Fascist cause and there I could meet the leaders of the various movements who gathered for forums, lectures, and cultural events. Only four years before I had been asked to become a Republican. Now I had moved to the left of the official Democratic Party platform, especially on foreign policy. My heart was with the handful of House and Senate members, columnists like Pearson, and former Ambassador to Germany, William Dodd, who urged an immediate united front against the Nazis and Fascists. I was also fired by the even smaller handful who predicted that the recent establishment of the House Un-American Activities Committee spelled the beginning of a native American repression. I went everywhere, was in everything, even helping to organize the new Federal Workers' Union at the National Youth Administration.

As soon as I had returned from Europe, I had gone on the

wagon. I wanted to keep my head clearer for my job and crusades, and I needed to slim down from my summer bloat. I had
never been totally on the wagon before. Even with Richard, I
had merely cut down to social drinking. Now I was unprepared
for the uneasy feelings that stirred inside me when a Washington
matron said, and said seriously: "Why Susan, going on the wagon
at your age? You're like a hardened old drunk! Can't you simply
cut down?"

I knew that I couldn't just cut down. I had to take all or nothing where booze was concerned. I tried to ignore this clearest of
all symptoms of alcoholism, that I couldn't control my drinking.
I either drank up everything in sight, or I had to stay away from
it altogether.

As soon as I lost the weight I wanted, though, I returned to
drinking with my Washington dates. We danced, we ate, we
went to my favorite joints to listen to black combos of trumpet,
clarinet, and bass. But the main purpose of all these evenings was
simply to drink.

Neither did any of the men move me until I met Ralph Wheatley. True to her shipboard threat, Sarah Watson invited me to
the first meeting launching the Washington chapter of the Descendants of the American Revolution. She and the other
transplanted New Englanders, Pennsylvanians, and even a few
liberal southerners from the original thirteen colonies, met in a
comfortable Georgetown drawing room one Sunday afternoon
in October. We were trying to single out the most important
issue for the fledgling organization to focus on in the coming year.

There were more men than women at the meeting, yet only
one man stood out. This was Ralph. He sat back quietly during
most of the discussion. Then when our confusing chatter had
gotten nowhere, he sat up and spoke out. In his deep and
authoritative voice he simply took over. He urged us not to
diffuse our energies on a general defense of civil liberties. That
only duplicated the work of the American Civil Liberties Union,
he said. We should focus on the most flagrant violation of civil
liberties and human rights, the plight of the Negroes and poor
whites disfranchised by the poll tax in eight southern states.

I was fascinated watching him take command. This is the kind
of man I like, I thought. This is the kind of mind that I am
drawn to. While the others had been circling around the mul-

berry bush, he had used his mind to think, plan, and weigh alternatives. More than that, he easily brought that roomful of about twenty people around to his point of view. Those who disagreed with him he maneuvered onto the defensive; and then, politely of course, shattered their arguments.

I did not take my eyes off this amazing man, so impressed was I by his leadership. Besides, he was very attractive. His deep-set hazel eyes were shaded by thick, straight eyelashes; his gold-tinged eyebrows were lighter than his light brown crewcut. He was slightly built, but he emanated the controlled power of a resting lion. He was not only master of everyone at the meeting, but complete master of himself. Despite his crewcut and ruddy face I knew he must be much older than I. Surely such a catch must have long since been snapped up by some predatory Washington female.

During cocktails, Ralph himself answered my question. He made it plain almost at once that he not only was a divorced man, but by his manner, that he was available; one always knows. He drew out of me information about my job, my committee work, my hobbies, sports, in fact my life history. He promised we would get together soon.

On Aunt Susan's birthday, February 15, I saw him again. The Descendants, along with women's organizations and other groups, commemorated her anniversary at a luncheon. I sat at the head table and made a few remarks to the assembly. Ralph quickly took me over at the end of the luncheon and drove me to the U.S. Capitol. There he squired me down to the crypt and stood watching while, with senators and congressmen, I placed a wreath on Aunt Susan's statue. I was aware of his intense stare even as the flashbulb cameras of *The New York Times* and Washington papers caught me stooping with Senator Key Pittman to lay the wreath.

After the ceremony Ralph warmly congratulated me on my poise, "so unusual," he said, for a twenty-two-year-old. He seemed impressed by my national publicity and association with the friendly congressmen.

"I wonder if you realize your tremendous potential," he said as he bought me a drink afterward. "I think you are going to surpass your Aunt Susan in the fight for freedom." The way he said it thrilled me.

From that day on it seemed that wherever I went in Washington, Ralph Wheatley went too. We were together at the climax of the Descendants' first campaign. The Daughters of the American Revolution had refused the Negro singer Marian Anderson permission to perform in their Constitution Hall. We and other liberals had combined to win a permit for her to sing outdoors. We had chosen fittingly enough the steps of the Lincoln Memorial. On a spring day Ralph and I heard Marian Anderson's glorious voice ring out, enthralling the thousands of awe-struck listeners who stretched from the feet of the Great Emancipator to the tall, white obelisk of our first president. This day was especially important to Ralph in his mission to finish the task of freeing the Negroes that had only started, he said, with the Civil War. Ralph had not only drafted, but done all the necessary research for what would later become the Twenty-fourth Amendment to the Constitution, the law abolishing the poll tax as a prerequisite to voting.

"The south lost the Civil War, but won the peace," he said. "I want to see that the Negroes and poor whites get their true freedom!"

Soon I wanted to know everything about Ralph. Every detail of his life was, and would be, important to me. How easy it would have been for him to lead the life of his own Boston Brahmin class. He could have spent his time preserving his family fortune or enjoying some Beacon Hill club. Instead Ralph had made every minute of his well-ordered life count toward increasing his knowledge of the universe around him. Even as a child he had become a stamp-collector, then an astronomer, then his lifetime love, a birdwatcher. At Princeton he dug under the earth's surface to get to bedrock for his geology courses. He trained his mind in science, as well as in great English literature. After Princeton he went on to Harvard Graduate School to earn himself an M.A. in Economics.

At Harvard, Ralph joined with some classmates in the John Reed Club, founded to discuss the Marxist philosophy of the Harvard revolutionary who had witnessed and written the classic *Ten Days That Shook the World,* the account of the Bolshevik Revolution in 1917. A few years later when his marriage to a Boston debutante broke up, he solaced himself with his first trip to the Soviet Union. He wanted to see for himself the socialist state he had studied and discussed. Again when his textile mill, inherited from his father, folded in the 1929 crash, Ralph journeyed once more to the Soviet Union to learn how a government-controlled economy might prevent such disasters. He returned to Washington to give his talent with that of his classmates toward saving Depression-ridden America from revolution.

"Right from the start we were all working together for something greater than we were," he told me of those early New Deal days. "We didn't care how hard we worked—right around the clock. We believed we could save America by the NRA, the WPA, the NLRB, FSA, and all the other Roosevelt agencies."

Life in those pioneering days had not been all work, however. Ralph was the perpetual dinner guest, in demand not only because of his bachelor and social status, but because he could talk on any subject that would ever come up at a Washington dinner table.

In the exciting chaos of those times, Ralph had been a center of calm. He knew what he wanted and with undeviating realism he went after it. His goal was Capitol Hill. But he knew he lacked the extraverted personality to run for Congress, so he determined instead to become staff director of a major Senate or House committee. In those days the center of government power was still solidly on Capitol Hill, not down on Pennsylvania Avenue in the White House.

While watching for this coveted opening, he established a reputation for brilliance in a series of jobs in the downtown New Deal agencies for conservation, farmers, labor, and wages and hours. But his main energy was directed to his after-hours activities not only for the abolition of the poll tax, but for the eighteen-year-old vote and full civil rights for Negroes. His days were further packed with his voluntary work to save the environment. Decades before most Americans became aware of conservation, Ralph pioneered with Bob Marshall and others to fight for the preservation of soil, animals, forest, and wild-life areas. Almost single-handedly he halted the slaughter of migrating birds by hunters in Pennsylvania, dramatizing in photographs and print the charnelhouse of hawk and other bird corpses along the great eastern flyway.

"Don't you ever stop thinking and working?" I asked him on July 4th weekend.

"There's so much to be done. I find by planning I can use minutes that other people waste by daydreaming," he said. "I get my relaxation birdwatching or hiking—or having my back rubbed."

He was lying on his bed in a little summer hotel at Point Lookout, Maryland. He had asked me to come up and put sunburn lotion on his back, taking me away from my date for the weekend party. Val Wylie, my Englishman, had sailed over true to his promise to take me to Mexico. But Ralph soon convinced me that my place was in Washington manning the freedom fights we espoused together, not flitting off to Mexico with Val. My newspaper friend Webb Miller was also in the United States covering the visit of Their Britannic Majesties, George and Elizabeth. Ralph was pleased when Webb flew back on the first transAtlantic Clipper. He openly cheered when Britain's mobilization, following the Nazi-Soviet pact, sent Val back to England.

Ralph's treatment of my Washington drinking partners was even less subtle. Generally I had my first cocktail date at five, my second at seven, and my dinner date around nine. Usually the first and second dates would linger on so that by ten I was drinking with not one, but three men. Suddenly Ralph would appear in whatever bar, lounge, or restaurant we happened to be and simply and without apology waft me away from the startled men who had been providing—and paying for—the drinks.

With the coast cleared of my overseas friends, Ralph invited me to a Labor Day weekend party that he thought would make me happiest. Knowing my love of sun, swimming, and sea, he chose the narrow strip of dune-ridged sand, the Outer Banks of North Carolina. He permitted two other bachelors, who had invited themselves along, to buy me drinks at the old beach hotel and to dance and sing with me. But the late night he reserved for himself. He wanted, he said, to be alone with me on this most momentous weekend of our lives, for on Friday of that weekend, war had broken out in Europe.

Ralph blotted out the others, even as he blotted out the war and the seascape around us. He led me up and over the steep sand dunes, then down into their depths like the bottoms of bowls scooped out by wind. We stood like a primeval couple surrounded by walls of sand obliterating all but the bright stars directly overhead.

In that bleak Lear-like sandscape, he stretched my mind to
horizons as infinite as the sea beyond us. Ours, he said, was not
to be the ordinary marriage. Ours would be a partnership for
posterity, for emancipating the Negro, the unemployed, the foreign born, the voteless, the oppressed wherever they were. He
inspired me to reach for the stars of altruistic achievement instead of selfish, sensory goals.

In a state of high exaltation I said "yes" to his proposal. I felt
fulfilled because Ralph cared for my mind as well as my body.
He believed I could amount to something: all he required was
that I follow his leadership and become sober and responsible.

No sacrifice seemed too great to make for him. I went cold on
the wagon. I knew that cutting out the drinks he considered a
sheer waste of money would please him more than anything I
could do. Because I had missed Mexico with Val, he suggested
that we spend our honeymoon there—and take a month for it.

Then one day his voice came triumphantly over the phone:
"Sue, it's come at last! The job on Capitol Hill with a new
House committee on migrant workers. But I have to start almost
immediately—that means no Mexico. Could you bear giving it up
and going instead for just a week to the Gaspé?"

I thought only momentarily of sun-filled, tropical Mexico and
quickly agreed that the long-awaited plum was far more important.

We were married at Easton by the mayor in a simple ceremony. Joyously I received my husband's embrace, and held out
before me the plain gold band on my finger. As we left for our
honeymoon we stopped at the bank for some travelers' checks.
Standing at the counter where I had stood as a child depositing
my tiny savings, I proudly started to sign the checks with my
new name, "Susan Wheatley." But as I began to write, Ralph
gently put his hand on mine, and said something I would understand only years later.

"Darling," he said, "before you sign, think of this. Yours is such
a very great name—we need it in the cause. I am not asking you
to change it. I'd like you to keep it."

I did not question his decision. I even let him add the Roman
numeral "II" to distinguish me from Aunt Susan.

I did wonder, though, at his choice for our wedding night. It
was an isolated, broken-down, frame tourist cabin with a large,

sagging, iron-railed bed lighted by a naked overhead bulb. It seemed odd spending our first night of marriage in such a place, and without even a glass of champagne to celebrate. But, of course, I was on the wagon. Ralph probably didn't want to tempt me at a motel near a noisy bar.

At 7:00 A.M. I discovered the true reason for his choice. On the very first morning of our wedded state, I couldn't believe it when my bridegroom said cheerily, "Come on, get up, Sue! If we want to see the white-breasted nuthatch we have to get out now!" He threw the covers off me and I dressed in the early morning chill.

That night, and the next, we spent at bird sanctuaries. We took bird walks after dinner. We listened to records of bird calls played by one ornithological innkeeper. He and Ralph imitated the songs and did not appreciate it when I burst into laughter at the weird contortion of their faces. I, in turn, was not amused as we continued to rise at dawn each morning en route to Percé in the Gaspé Peninsula. Nor did I relish having to trade my white chiffon bridal nightie for a Mother Hubbard flannelette in the cold, late, spring of Quebec.

I did love the sight of the giant pierced arch of red rock from which Percé got its name. I begged Ralph to check in at an adorable hillside inn overlooking the Rock. We looked at its luxurious cabins complete with wood laid in the fireplaces, home-spun blankets, and satin eiderdowns.

"Why waste money? We'll be outdoors most of the time. Besides I've already booked us down below."

We went to a plain, wooden hotel on the flat, into a dark bedroom with another sagging bed. But Ralph was right. We did spend most of our time outdoors, though not swimming. The St. Lawrence was ice cold and the northern sun was scarcely warm enough for tanning. But it was just the right temperature for the colony of rare birds he had come to see.

The gannets bred on the rock cliffs just off Percé on Bonaventure Island. Ralph rejoiced as we strolled around, carrying his inevitable field glasses, his bird cards to check off, and his camera. I, who loved brisk walks, learned to slow down to the pace of the birdwatcher. I learned how to stalk, hands behind back, with no motion to frighten birds away. On my honeymoon I learned an entire semester's worth of ecology, biology, ornithology, botany, sociology, and economics of the Gaspé. Even at dinner Ralph always had something to read and discuss with me. I used my new knowledge to write and sell my first free-lance piece to *The New York Times*.

One afternoon when the rain barred our birdwatching, Ralph said it was a good day to plot out our first year. He decided that I should get my master's degree. Many times in our courtship he had laughingly said that the only thing virgin about me was my brain. I was glad to begin training it.

"An M.A. would be another string to your bow and add a thousand dollars to your earning capacity. Also it gives you status. It will help us in whatever we decide is to be your mission."

I looked over his bare shoulder on the bed to see what he was writing. In his careful, minute handwriting, he had jotted down figures. He was, he said, trying to fit the cost of my tuition into the budget. Henceforth it would be my job to budget. I wondered if I, who could not even add or subtract properly, would be up to the task. Then he continued the lessons he had begun the first day of our wedding trip. He quizzed me on the names of every town we had passed through from Pennsylvania right on up and out to this land's end at Percé. He insisted that I start memorizing, as he did, every river, state, town, bird, plant.

"You never know when these facts might be useful to you," he said. "You must train not only your memory but your observation. Start taking notes." He always held up to me the example of a friend who went all the way through the Soviet Union with him. "He never jotted down one note—yet he claimed to be a writer," Ralph would say in disgust.

When we arrived home at his large house in Washington after our brief but busy honeymoon, Ralph's Negro maid Elva reminded him to carry me over the threshold. I slipped from his arms when I heard girlish voices coming from what had been Ralph's, and now would be our, bedroom upstairs.

For the time we had been away, Ralph had rented the four upstairs bedrooms to a covey of young typists and secretaries from his Capitol Hill committee. They would double up in the other three bedrooms now that we were home and needed our room. Their rent gave added income, offsetting the new cost of a wife, particularly a nonworking wife going to school.

I forced a smile in time to greet the six girls, my own age and a little older, who chorused a giddy "Welcome home!"

Any dreams of marital solitude were shattered by these, the first paying guests of hundreds that would always clutter our home. We never spent one night alone under our own roof and we seldom dined without a "boarder" or other guests. This constant flow of people bewildered me at first, but of course it was all right since it was Ralph's custom. Yet, in the years to come, long after these many people had left our house, they were to return to play a strange and crucial part in the greatest crisis of my life.

On that first day, Ralph led me to the room off the kitchen, a bright, glassed-in sun parlor. There stood a large desk, a wooden posture chair, and a brown metal typing table.

"Your wedding presents," he said, hugging me. He was very proud. Then he took from his ever present briefcase a yellow legal-sized sheet with items written opposite the hours of the day.

"Here is your schedule for your new life. If you are going to stay at home you must follow a plan to keep you from woolgathering."

My very first act as a bride in my "own" home was to sit at my wedding-present desk and type out the daily program that he had ordered for me. Before he left for the Hill, he pasted it on the wall at the exact level where my eyes would see it every time they rose from my typewriter:

SCHEDULE FOR SUSAN B. ANTHONY II, 1940–41

7:30 A.M.	RISE.
8:15	Breakfast.
9–1 P.M.	WRITE. If nothing comes SIT at TYPEWRITER ANYWAY. KEEP THE SEAT OF YOUR PANTS ON THE SEAT OF THE CHAIR.
1	LUNCH.
1:30	WALK.
2	RETURN TO STUDY and edit morning's writing. Work on thesis, or study.
4	MODERN DANCE—twice weekly.
5	ICE SKATING—alternate days.
5:30	DINNER on nights of classes at American U.

6   DINNER other nights.
7   DINNER when guests.
6–10 P.M.   CLASSES four nights a week—American U. Other nights
               committee meetings, or dinner guests, or out to dinner.
11   RETIRE.

He did not write "11:30—Sex" on the schedule for fear Elva
would see it.

My devout adherence to the schedule was to contribute to
the annals of medical history. After six months of sitting at my
typewriter, seven days a week, I developed a pain in the left
cheekbone of my bottom. The doctor called in a colleague in
bewilderment. Together they slapped me, tapped, thumped, and
consulted. Suddenly the younger one burst out laughing.

"It's Weaver's Bottom!"

"But I am not a weaver!"

"Do you sit long hours on a hard chair, crossing your legs?"

I admitted that I did, never less than four hours, usually six
or eight on my hard, wooden posture chair.

"It's called Weaver's Bottom because weavers used to get it
at the loom. You have sort of housemaid's knee of the bottom.
Get yourself a rubber tube to sit on. Your bottom is too thin."

It never even occurred to me to cure my Weaver's Bottom by
cutting down on my long hours at the typewriter. Nor did Ralph
suggest this. He himself spent his time at home at his own desk
in the large master bedroom. He was compiling statistics about
the eight million people disfranchised by the poll tax. Proudly
I saw him show the same dedication to universal suffrage that
Aunt Susan had given woman suffrage.

Relegated by Ralph to my own study, only once did I break
our rule that we must maintain total silence during our sacred
hours of work. That day I ran upstairs with a wonderful idea.
He must write a book on the poll tax and the eighteen-year-old
vote, and all the voting restrictions that remained. He not only
liked the idea, he went ahead, found a publisher and wrote the
book on weekends and nights after he came home from the Hill.
He dedicated it to me.

My own mission appeared in a most unexpected, yet logical
way. Mary Margaret McBride, then dean of American women
radio commentators, called me up from New York and invited me

to appear on her nationwide broadcast to celebrate the twentieth
anniversary of the Susan B. Anthony amendment. When I asked
Ralph what on earth I would talk about, he replied: "Tell what
the vote has done for women and the country as a whole."

I really didn't know what woman suffrage had done. But I
went to work to find out. In a week I had gathered plenty of
facts for a fifteen-minute interview. As I entered the New York
broadcasting studio, a large lady in a navy blue tentlike jumper
greeted me maternally. She was Mary Margaret McBride. She
pointed to the sheaf of papers in my hand and asked what they
were. I told her they were my notes, that I feared my mind
would go blank.

"Nonsense," she said smiling. "You're a born performer. I can
tell by your voice, and of course you're a chip off the old block.
You don't need notes. Just listen to my questions and answer me."

She proved right. When the red signal flashed, she and I
seemed suddenly alone on an island of electronic excitement. I
forgot myself completely and loved every minute of talking into
the microphone. I learned many lessons that would help me
eventually with my own New York and Boston radio shows. But
of far greater significance, those minutes on the air led me to my
cause, a cause that had been waiting all the time for me to cham-
pion.

A flood of warm letters after the broadcast responded to my
statement that Aunt Susan had achieved only the first step in
emancipating women. The vote was just a beginning.

Ralph's crusade for Negro rights in 1940 was twenty-five years
ahead of the civil rights movement of the 1960s. In 1940, though
I didn't know it, in my efforts for women, I was laying some of
the foundation for the 1970's "new feminism."

With Johnny Danton, my retired gangster friend, in mind, I
helped organize committees, first in the United Federal Workers
Auxiliary, and then nationally, to win child-care centers for children of working mothers. I lobbied for the passage of the Lan-
ham Act which would give Federal funds for day-care centers.
Later I helped found the Congress of American Women for the
purpose of mobilizing women to win these and other services,
to finish up the work Aunt Susan had started.

Whatever had happened to the militant suffrage movement
after its success in 1920? My research disclosed that that night of

August 26, 1920, with bands playing and flags flying, the mammoth suffrage victory parade marched through Manhattan, with the tall ghost of Aunt Susan at its head, into American history. American women's altruism, their unity and prodigal self-giving for a cause greater than themselves disappeared like the parade, almost overnight. They did not go on, as Aunt Susan had prophesied, to use their newly won vote either to make the world their home, or to make the world a home of peace and prosperity for all mankind. Only a handful of remnant feminists urged women out to paid work and the professions. The vast majority of adult American women continued as unpaid domestic servants in the home.

Ralph lavishly praised me for the achievements I chalked up. In our first year of marriage I published my first feminist findings in national magazines and obtained my M.A. in political science, writing a thesis on "The Status of Women in the Executive Branch of the Federal Government."

One day Ralph took me on one of our hikes in a nearby wood. The bare, black slickness of the trees sprang out from the white glare of the snow. Ralph's voice was as bracing as the air of the clear, cold, Sunday afternoon.

"You have no idea, dearest, how proud I am of your progress. You are a wonderful student, young, supple, devoted."

I put my footprint in the snow, looked back, and saw it quickly melt. A shadow darkened that brilliant moment. Suddenly the transient, now vanished footprint, brought me to the great abyss of death. I had never thought of death, my own death, before. All my learning, what good was it? My thoughts, my ideas would vanish in death as surely as my footprints in the snow.

Timidly I shared the thought with Ralph.

"But, my dearest, our immortality, yours and mine, is assured. Not some individual immortality, that's a myth that the church teaches."

To Ralph, immortality was the good we leave after us, the good for mankind. Aunt Susan was immortal because of woman suffrage. He and I would live on after death in Negro suffrage, the eighteen-year-old vote, and in my own work for women. We might not live to see the freedoms we fought for, but posterity would benefit.

I listened to what Ralph was saying and I nodded in dutiful agreement. I loved Ralph for his wisdom in all things. But, as we walked away, I looked back to where we had been standing. Not a trace of our presence remained in the unsubstantial snow.

In those first two years of our marriage our social life was busy. But the people we saw and those we entertained were always tied in with our work. They were senators and congressmen, foreign officials, diplomats, war correspondents. The only exceptions were bird friends. Except for these, Ralph never invited people to the house unless they were "useful." Nor did we ever go to a party unless it could "help." Ralph memorized the names of hundreds of people at Washington cocktail parties, a feat he could accomplish because of the Roth Memory Course he had taken. This gave him the ability to retain instantly first and last names, occupations, connections, and whatever else he learned from them.

One day in March, during the second long winter of our marriage, a strange thing happened. I was walking down the stairway at home after lunch, returning to my study to be back at my typewriter at the scheduled 2:00 P.M. when all at once I stopped. I simply stood stock still where I was. I had no feeling at all. I was numb. I felt as though I were not on a staircase at all, but on an escalator. I could not walk with my own legs. I could only be borne along mechanically. I was like a wooden Pinocchio.

Within minutes I was back at my desk. The numb feeling had passed quickly. But I was bewildered by the experience nonetheless.

That night we had only one guest at dinner. Ralph had brought her home because he was curious as to why a woman of her background and speech had become a destitute migrant worker. He had met her at one of his hearings. Sitting at our table that night, Eleanor Rice looked anything but destitute. In her neat black dress, once good, she told us with quiet charm and cool honesty about her rehabilitation. She owed her sobriety entirely to a newly formed fellowship for alcoholics. She had lost everything, her husband, her children, her home, because of booze. Cast out, she had drifted around the country washing dishes, picking fruit, anything to get the money she had to have for the drinks she had to have. In an alcoholic stupor she had wandered into a meeting of recovered alcoholics in Washington.

"I have been sober one day at a time for three weeks, by the Grace of God and those wonderful people," she told us.

Impulsively I confided that, young as I was, my own wild drinking had put me on the wagon during the past two years.

"Sue is a brand-new girl since she stopped drinking," Ralph added, "mature, responsible."

Two weeks later I caught cold. And then it was that I realized that my rigid work schedule had, despite three good meals each day, carved twenty pounds off my already skinny body. Ralph ordered me to bed immediately. He himself always stayed in bed three weeks with his annual cold, propped up in bed with a blue sweater, while he reread *The Decline and Fall of the Roman Empire*. I had never been able to afford the luxury of bed for a cold; now, upon his order, I lay beneath a pile of blankets.

Elva appeared at the bedroom door and announced that a Mrs. Rice was downstairs and wished to see me.

Weaving on her pin legs, with bleary bloodshot eyes, clad in a ratty old fur coat, her hair stringy and matted, Eleanor Rice filled the room with the smell of vomit, urine, dirty flesh, and stale whiskey. She was clutching a half pint of cheap rye.

"You're drunk!" I exclaimed in disgust.

"I need help," she slurred.

"Why don't you get help from those people you told us about?"

"They say they can't do anything once I've taken the first drink, and I sure have done that! They say go and finish up the drunk, then they can help. But," she leaned over me, wobbling, her foul breath smothering me, "the joke's on them, and on me. I can't get off the stuff without some more whiskey to taper me off." She drank bottoms-up and finished the bottle. "I have no money, no place to stay to taper off. I need your help!"

"I can't help you, I never was a drunk like you," I said. "Just because my husband felt sorry for you and had you to dinner when you were sober doesn't give you the right to come to our home drunk. Use your will power! Just stop drinking! But not here. I'm ill and I need rest."

She shook her finger at me like a witch, blazing forth in rage, "You, you Susan B. Anthony the Second, with your rigid life, your nice little tin-god husband, your great plans for saving the world. You think you have it made being on the wagon now, but I have news for you. My alcoholic friends say, and I know it's true, your own will power never works. The wagon always breaks down." She sat heavily on the bed. "You'll fall off the wagon with a bang. You'll hit bottom, beg someone for help, and I hope you get turned down as you are turning me down now!"

"Elva!" I called. "Help me get Mrs. Rice out of here!"

But it was too late. Eleanor had slithered off the bed onto the floor and passed out, limp as a bundle of filthy clothes, snoring with a ghastly postnasal rattle. I phoned Ralph at his office on the Hill.

"Call the public hospital and have them send an ambulance for her immediately," he said tersely. "Get her out of the house now, before our guests arrive for dinner. Sorry, dear, you had to put up with her."

When the ambulance drivers tried to roll her onto the stretcher, she suddenly revived, thrashing her arms like a windmill, cursing them and me. They finally forced her into a straitjacket, and carried her out like a corpse.

By the time Ralph got home my conscience was troubling me. He shook his head. "Forget her. Helping her just keeps the system going. Our job is to change the whole sick society that breeds derelicts like her, not to perform individual acts of charity."

That night sitting at our food-filled table, sober, surrounded by Ralph and our guests, waited on by Elva, I could not forget Eleanor Rice. Once she had sat there as sober as I. Now she was writhing in alcoholic anguish in a welfare ward. Were we really right ignoring her suffering while claiming to help mankind? Eleanor, a human being, had begged me, another human being, to help her. Yet I had ignored her.

Ralph's deep voice interrupted me, urging me to return to my bed. I looked pale, he said. He escorted me tenderly up the stairs.

"I think that awful mess this afternoon has set you back. I'm packing you off to Florida for a couple of weeks to soak up some sun and really get rid of your flu."

After he returned to our guests, I had an urgent impulse to call the hospital and learn how Eleanor was. But I knew Ralph would not approve. Instead I called Western Union and wired my old friend Rippy in Fort Lauderdale, asking if I could visit her.

Her answer came quickly.

"Welcome if want quiet repeat quiet visit."

Proudly, I wired back, "Dry as bone two years."

On the day I was to take the train to Florida, Ralph said he had a surprise for me. Though it was Palm Sunday, it was snowing, unusual for Washington so late in the season. I couldn't imagine why he was driving me out into the country in such weather and with gasoline rationed, and he wouldn't tell me.

We turned off the highway onto an icy, rutted, rural road. Finally we drove through a grove of giant evergreens and up to a large white frame house. Then, without warning, he said, "This is ours, Sue. I have bought this lovely place for us."

I couldn't believe it. He had bought a house without even discussing it with me?

"The former owner is still here. Come in. She expects us."

Still in shock, I walked onto the verandah which listed sharply and like the rest of the house was badly in need of paint. A maid answered the door. Mrs. Crawford was upstairs ill in bed, but she would see us.

An old lady in an old-fashioned knitted bed-jacket sat up weakly to greet us as we walked into her bedroom. She held out her hand. It felt very frail as I took it.

"So this is Mrs. Wheatley?" she said, smiling, "My dear, I hope you grow to love White Pines as much as my late husband and I did. He planted every tree, every bush, every flower on the place. We built the house when we were married fifty years ago.

Diplomatically Ralph let Mrs. Crawford know that I had to catch a train to Florida. She hurried to a favor she wanted to ask, that she be permitted to stay longer than they had arranged at the time of the sale. "I must move not just me, but my entire life, you know."

But Ralph was firm. He explained his own problems with wartime carpenters and painters. She would have to leave as agreed.

She sank back as though fading into the huge four-poster bed. I wanted to assure her she could stay in her home as long as she wanted, but I was still too dazed to say much of anything. I let Ralph show me the six bedrooms, the sleeping porch and bath on the second floor, then take me down to the drawing room, dining room, and huge old-fashioned kitchen, with its maid's room adjoining. Every room of the old house needed redoing, especially the kitchen with its old coal range and the bathroom with its antique fixtures.

This remote country house was exactly the kind of housekeeping trap I had been crusading against for two years! Deep in the country, far from shops and services, I would be a virtual prisoner. We were dropping back from twentieth-century Washington to nineteenth-century Maryland country life, without the money or manpower to help us. My studies of the rural and urban housewife had taught me that the farm wife spent far more hours shopping for the simplest item, and waited longest for the simplest repair. How could Ralph, in the midst of wartime rationing and shortages, even dream of such a step?

But more serious, the question kept recurring, how could he have bought a house without even consulting me? It was the exact opposite of the feminist crusade he had praised so. He had ridden roughshod over me like a nineteenth-century patriarch, making all decisions for his voteless little wife. And then to order that sick old lady out of her lifetime home in two weeks!

All these thoughts filled me with forebodings as he put me on the train for Florida, coach, not sleeper. I sat in the crowded wartime train holding unopened the book he had given me for "holiday reading," Tolstoy's monumental *War and Peace.* Try as I would I could not blot out the incarceration that awaited me on my return home. I scarcely heard the rousing singing of the drinking soldiers around me. Though several of them invited me to join them, I didn't even see them as men. They were just neuters to me, as all men had been since I had married Ralph, just khaki uniforms with pink, tan, or white faces above them.

That week at Rippy's new, beautiful, waterfront cottage, I began to open up to another human being for the first time in two years. At first, she, like my other Fort Lauderdale friends, congratulated me on the new sober, lean, purposeful Susan. But then she began with her old sharpness to probe beneath the surface. She walked into my room one day and saw stuck in the mirror of the dressing table the schedule that I had written down. It numbered the hours I would spend on swimming, walking, reading, drawing, napping, sunning, eating, and calling on old friends.

"I thought you were supposed to be on holiday!" she rasped in her metallic voice.

At first I defended my overorganized life. She laughed at me. "What are you trying to prove?" she said. "Who are you trying to impress?"

That opened the bulkhead that had for so long shut off my feelings. Out poured my forebodings about the remote country house, the guilt I felt at ousting the old lady, the dread of years spent on renovations and repairs. Immediately I tried to close the bulkhead again. I felt disloyal to Ralph. It seemed like a betrayal of all his wonderful training, his patience, his kindness to me. But Rippy broke in.

"You used to have spunk and imagination. Humor. Yet here you are being ordered around by this guy like some nitwit child bride. Come off it, Susan. You've got lots on the ball. He sounds like a mechanical man to me. Don't you become mechanical too!"

I knew I had changed in my two years of marriage to Ralph. But I hadn't become mechanical. Or had I? I remembered that day coming down the stairs. I had been as feelingless then as an automaton.

"Why not try freeing yourself before you free all those other women you write about, kid?"

She left the room to get dinner for us and some old-time friends. I had known them in those far-off days when I was very young, five years before. Now I was a settled old matron of twenty-five.

12 "...for lo, the winter is past...
the time of the singing has come..."

The night before I was to leave Fort Lauderdale for Washington, I felt I could unbend a bit. A group of us, all light-hearted relics of my drinking past, went to The Deck for dinner. I sniffed the familiar aroma of beer, whiskey, and cigarettes as we stood at the bar. Hank, the bartender, smiled broadly.

"Susan B., I do believe!" He reached across to shake hands. "Wouldn't recognize you, looking so well. Whatever you're doing, do more of it. What'll you have? It's on me."

"Thanks, Hank. I'll have a coke, straight."

"Good girl," Hank said as he served it. "The hard stuff never agreed with you." He reminded me of how I used to hand him my purse as I walked in for a night of drinking; I'd known I would lose it otherwise.

I stretched my coke while my friends stretched cocktail time from one hour to two. Hungry, and bored with their drink-time chatter, I ordered a second coke. Then through the dense and smoke-clouded gloom, I saw the first man that I had looked at in two years. He was staring at me. He had blue eyes and he towered over everyone at the horseshoe bar.

I looked away, then looked back again, strangely unable to do anything else. And he, in answer, came over to me. My friends welcomed the handsome stranger in barroom camaraderie. He maneuvered in next to me.

"What will you have?"

144

"Another coke, I guess."

"Don't you drink?"

"Not any more."

"Which one is your husband?"

"He's not here."

"Who are you? Why are you here? Why don't you drink?" He wanted to know everything.

We all had dinner. He managed to sit next to me. We talked about Thomas Wolfe, Dostoevski, and D. H. Lawrence.

During coffee, he asked me, "Do you like the sea?"

"I love it."

"Let's go look at it."

He took my arm and led me out into the tropical night, past the sleeping yachts along New River, under moonlight dappling the sidewalk through the coconut trees. As we walked we could hear the moiré rustle of palm fronds, the creak of a mooring line, the rubbing of wood against rope. He took my hand. I did not pull away.

His name was Tom. He was twenty-five. He was a merchant seaman off a tanker on the South Atlantic run where his ship played hide-and-seek among the Nazi U-boats. His rolling sea gait should have told me he was a sailor.

But in addition Tom was a reader, a thirsty reader, and what's more a writer. Fragments were already down on paper: fragments of the life in the steel mills where he had worked; of his year-long transcontinental hitchhiking; of the year that he spent lying across his bed reading and reflecting, until the war sent him into the Merchant Marine; and now the wartime voyages and his shipmates, those still living and those he'd never see again. His talk was pure poetry, rhythmic and colorful.

It seemed natural to be walking hand-in-hand with this young man on the soft smooth sand with the Atlantic rolling in. It seemed natural to listen to him, to feel his arms about me, blocking out my northern self even as he blacked out the stars above his head. We said goodbye as the sky was lighting up.

As I glided through the sea next day in my final swim before taking the train north the following morning, Tom's loping prose, like his loping walk, formed a rhythm in my mind. My flesh felt tender in the salt water as though layers of numb dead skin had been torn off in the night. Nor was my flesh alone now sensitized.

Some part of me, submerged so long, leapt up iridescent like a dolphin on the line. And like that dolphin, I was boated by love. Lying on my stomach, letting the sun bake me on the hot sand, I saw a pair of black shoes, dark pants legs, then heard his voice, and felt a light kiss on my forehead.

"We're not sailing till later. How about lunch?"

I rose and threw myself into his arms. I danced in to change and out again to a table by the sea. So high was I on love for this man, it did not occur to me that the drink before me broke my two-year abstinence. Nor did I even pause to think what that one drink could mean.

Instead the drink became the thing, the first, the next, and on until it was another day. Awakening in our hotel room, Tom informed me that he had jumped ship. He would ride northward on the train with me and board his tanker in New York.

We sat up all day and all night in each other's arms in the crowded wartime coach. We didn't sleep, trying to hold back the minutes racing to the time of parting, he to his ship, I to friends I had promised to visit in Augusta. To blunt the knife of separation, at Tom's suggestion we drank martinis in the diner. With all the drinking in my life, I had never had a martini. I soon found, as many have before, that they are quickest.

My final glimpse of Tom was as he stood tall, unsmiling, on the train steps. At the same moment that he disappeared into his coach, a long, black box was loaded on the car next to his. The train pulled out bearing the coffin and Tom. I walked heavy-footed to a wooden post, leaned on it and cried.

After a few days in Augusta, I boarded the train that would carry me back to Ralph. I had come south by coach in obedience to his thrift. Now I bought myself a Pullman ticket. The soldiers on my journey south had been neuters, now my fellow passengers got the unspoken message that I was a woman. Coming south I had carried *War and Peace*. Going north I chuckled over *A Sub-Treasury of American Humor*, a collection of pieces from Tom's favorite magazine, *The New Yorker*.

I felt light as a bird as the train carried me north. I simply put out of my mind the imminent meeting with Ralph. Somehow I felt no remorse—not yet. I compartmentalized the time with Tom as an interlude, never to be repeated. It was a gift that I would savor and cherish, like the handful of golden sand

I carried in my suitcase to take out and sift on a cold January day. What I could be sure of, as the train rushed toward Washington, was that I was a very different woman from the rigid, mechanical being who had journeyed south.

As the train pulled into the gloomy shed of Union Station, I began to be alarmed. How could Ralph fail to notice how different I really was?

I shouldn't have worried. Ralph commented only on two changes in me as he led me out to the car. First, he wondered why I had wasted money on a sleeper. Second, he congratulated me on my deep tan. He was consumed with plans for White Pines, and the importance of his new job as staff director of the Senate War Industry committee. He handed over the wheel to me at his new office on the Hill, saying cheerily how glad he was to have me back, especially since we had dinner guests.

At cocktails before dinner, instead of my tomato juice, I took a healthy-sized martini. Ralph looked at the drink with some surprise, but didn't comment till bedtime. Then he said he was glad I could relax a little now with a drink or two. For me, drinks before dinner, and after, had made all the difference between a deadly serious dinner party and actually enjoying our guests.

After Florida, and while we were waiting the long months for White Pines to be ready, I determined to do what I had always wanted to do, write not just my feminist articles, but news stories for a Washington paper. Tom had stirred me into motion. I wrote a fictionalized story of our three days together. Then I wrote three feature articles on women in the war. As a result of these stories, I was hired as a city desk reporter for the *Washington Star*, the third woman in their history to become a straight news reporter.

Ralph was delighted at my new job, partly, of course, because it would bring home more money. Even more important, I would meet celebrities who would be useful to him. I loved life in the news room filled with editors and male reporters, learning under City Editor Bill Hill how to be a good working journalist.

I did not, could not forget Tom. I bought records of the songs we had heard together. I drew sketches of his intent face. I gulped down great drafts of his favorite author, Thomas Wolfe.

And then a letter came. Tom had written it in iambic pentameter. I carried it with me everywhere. He wanted to see me again.

Then he telephoned. He was coming to Washington on Sunday. I had to arrange to see him.

I had had no training in the double life. I could not think of where to meet, or what to do with a lover on a Sunday, but now I learned the advantages of a reporter's flexible schedule. It was easy to tell Ralph I had to go downtown on a story.

As I walked into the bar to meet him, Tom sat sipping a beer and reading *The New Yorker*. I wanted to throw my arms around him right then and there, but I waited until we got into the car. We drove out into the country. Like children in paradise we laughed and loved and drank, reveling unabashedly in our moments stolen from his wartime voyages and my other life.

When we could not find a hotel room in wartime Washington that night, I had to take him home. Even there we lacked a spare room because of our boarders. I had to put him up in the only part of the house that Ralph had not rented, the attic. Bare-raftered and unfurnished, it was used only as a maternity ward for my cat and kittens.

At breakfast next morning, Ralph looked the country squire with his ruddy, just-shaved cheeks, his immaculately combed hair and tweed suit. Filled with morning vigor and talk about his upcoming important day, he noticed nothing amiss in my hungover manner. I was terrified that he might sense something between Tom and me should they meet. I had hoped Ralph would be long gone to his office before Tom got up, but even as I rushed through my breakfast I heard Tom's footsteps. He peered into the bright dining room, fighting the light with his bloodshot eyes, his cheeks and chin gray with unshaved stubble. His jacket and pants looked as though he had slept in them, which he had.

Hastily I introduced my lover to my husband, explaining Tom away as my interview of the previous day. Ralph greeted him with, "Got to go. See you later, if you're still here."

Tom burst out, "Some fleas your cats have. I'm covered with bites!"

And then we began laughing like two naughty children as our elder smiled his apology for the fleas and left. I gathered my purse and clipboard and told Tom I'd be back at three, Elva would take care of him, he could go back to sleep on the couch, or on the bed of one of our boarders, all of whom were out working.

I thought I had felt no guilt about Tom, but I must have. For when I got to the *Star* city room, Bill Hill barked, "What on earth are you doing here on your day off?"

In my clandestine confusion I had totally forgotten the day of the week. Once more I realized my lack of experience. But I was learning fast. After that first brief encounter with Tom on my own territory, we decided we would from then on meet in New York when his ship docked. It was just too risky in Washington.

I told Ralph the incredible story that I must occasionally go to New York at the end of my twelve-hour Saturday trick at the *Star*, leaving at 6:00 P.M. to see my literary agent and meet potential publishers, all on Sunday. I will never know whether he believed me, particularly when on one of those furtive train journeys to New York, I saw arriving at Union Station the very agent I had told Ralph I was going to New York to see!

In New York near midnight, I would rush down to the Village Vanguard to meet Tom. When we closed up the bars we would go to one of those ghastly hotels that merchant seamen choose in midtown. We didn't care what the hotel looked like so long as we could lie in each other's arms until late next morning. Then, after our eye-openers at a nearby bar, we'd ride the ferry to Staten Island. I will love forever the smell of oil on a great port's waters. Tom and I stood on deck holding hands, inhaling the brackish harbor air. With the superhuman energy of those who love, I would board my return train at 2:00 A.M. to get to my 7:00 A.M. job at the *Star*.

Slowly guilt and remorse began to set in as the summer weekends with Tom went on. One Sunday morning the phone rang in our hotel room. Forgetting I was not supposed to be there, I answered it. "This is the house detective," a gruff voice said. "Why are you not registered?" Scared and frantic, I hung up and flew to Tom, who was in the shower. Tom roared with laughter.

"They're only worried about the extra money for an extra room guest. Forget it, Susan." I couldn't forget it.

We went walking on West Street, by the great ships, then across the Brooklyn Bridge to the harbor bars and to the Heights where our Thomas Wolfe had lived. But I had been badly frightened.

In September Tom went off to sea again. While he was away we moved to White Pines. The renovation was still in progress, which made life complicated, especially since Ralph already had the house filled with roomers and a steady stream of weekend guests.

My brother Dan, now an army officer at nearby Fort Washington, usually came with four or five fellow officers and their wives. I often invited Allied officers, Czech or Free French press attachés. And these on top of our never-absent paying guests. Adding to the confusion on weekends and nights were the painters and carpenters who could only fit in our work when free from their high-paying war jobs. One housepainter became a part of the family and was present every weekend for more than a year.

One Saturday in October Tom joined the crowd. Ralph accepted him as just one more visitor. I picked Tom up at the airport and he talked all the way out in the car about a gigantic battle at sea he had just survived. Next day he was still going on about the pounding his convoy had taken on the Murmansk run. Finally I sat him down with restorative whiskies and got him to dictate to me on the typewriter. Next day I took him and our story to my editor. Scanning it quickly, he informed me that we had the first eyewitness account of the biggest convoy battle of the war, a scoop! He sent me to clear it through censorship. It was wired everywhere in the world and Tom later expanded it into his first book, which he dedicated to me.

The *Star*, noting the bouquet of job offers from *Life* and other publications, immediately tripled my salary. I was an "expert" now on merchant marine survivor stories, and given many other choice assignments.

One Friday I went out in the rain with a bad cold to cover a story in a drafty armory building. The next night Tom was expecting me in New York again, but the cold grew so much worse that I almost didn't go. By now, though, Tom was a compulsion. Feeling weak and miserable, I took the train trip up and we went as usual to his seedy hotel room. As I began to undress,

I saw on the bureau a lipstick that was not mine. I was too hurt even to mention it to Tom. In all these months, I had never dreamed that deceivers might one day deceive each other. Above all, I felt a sense of my own cheap shoddiness. The next after noon I sat like a stone over our drinks at Jack Delaney's down on Sheridan Square. In the diner going back to Washington I drowned my misery in many brandies.

Next day the doctor said my flu was serious and sent me to bed. Lying there day after day looking out at the dying leaves, I knew that my own "little death" was mainly pride. Like so many other lovers, I had deceived myself that our affair was "different," a distinctive, exalted emotion. Now I knew that what had begun as the golden and the singing in Lauderdale, had degenerated only into weekends of moving from bar to bed and back. What had I done to my marriage with my cheating?

As I got back my strength I began to jot down the account of my split, the split between Susan B. Anthony II, hard-working, crusading feminist, versus the adulterous drinking female who grabbed for instant pleasure and excitement. Perhaps some women were so "emancipated" from Victorian shackles that they could flout the double standard and embark merrily on affairs, liberated from the inner toll of guilt. But as I reviewed the past six months, I knew that I was not one of them. My present illness, psychic as well as physical, was proof of that.

I sensed too that my slip from chastity, like an alcoholic's slip from sobriety, was premeditated. It was not some sudden impulse on the spur of the moment. My own subconscious had prepared me long before I fell into Tom's arms. Even though Ralph did not seem to suspect I had been wronging him, I resolved that I would make it up to him. I would become the perfect wife, the dedicated crusader.

I threw all the energy that had gone into the affair with Tom into a spate of magazine articles and talks. I led the Newspaper Guild negotiations for a new contract at the *Star*. It was almost like the pulling-myself-together I had done after returning from Europe. A New York publisher asked me to rewrite my book in six weeks for fall publication. I knew I could not do it if I were clouding my brain with booze and so I set that aside too. The publication of *Out of the Kitchen—Into the War* got nationwide attention because of my name and its militant message: housekeeping and care of children should be taken completely out of the home so that women would be freed to win the war. Wire services, newspapers, and radio shows carried stories and reviews throughout the country. At the age of twenty-seven, I seemed to be measuring up to Ralph's expectations for me. I was also fulfilling the phrenologist's prophecy: ". . . like her Great-aunt Susan she will want to do all the good she can for the largest number of people . . . . "

Part of my recognition was an invitation to do a prestigious study for Bryn Mawr College on a grant from the *Ladies Home Journal* and Curtis Publishing Company. They wanted objective research on what the postwar American woman would do, eat, demand, buy. But the job would mean living on or near the campus.

On a rare night that we dined alone Ralph said to me: "Now that the Senate committee is running smoothly, I feel it is the right time for me to go into the army. Would you ask your friend, the general, to see if I can get a commission—the highest rank possible—and posting to overseas duty? It will look well on my record after the war."

In early 1944, when he got his majority plus immediate overseas assignment, I accepted the Bryn Mawr job. I was not to see Ralph again for two years. As we said goodbye he issued his farewell orders—

"If you are going to sleep with anyone while I'm away, make sure it is someone who will help my military career."

13 *"...if I make my bed in hell, behold thou art there."*

MONDAY MORNING—DOWNTOWN

Slits of sunlight piercing the venetian blinds pried my eyelids open, stabbing me into awareness of another day. The duel of two French horns warring on opposing scales told me I was at least in my own apartment, adjacent to the Greenwich Village Music School on Barrow Street. I could hear and I could see but I could not remember. Who had brought me home, when, and from where? I did not, and would not ever know. So many different men had brought me home, friends of the night, men whom I didn't know and couldn't remember. One of them had tried to kill me. Jock. Even now, lying in bed, I put my hand to my throat where he had placed the knife.

In two short hours I had to be uptown, bright and glib before the microphone so I could tell the women of New York how to live right, on my radio program "This Woman's World," built in part on the research I had done for the Bryn Mawr study.

Moving my steel-encircled head just enough to grope for a cigarette on the bedside table, I saw the glass of pale, pale green martini, left there at the unknown hour when my light went off. Its stale perfumed stench formed a resolve in my numbed brain. I would not touch it. Cold on the wagon I would go. I had done it before. I could do it now. With trembling hands I lighted the cigarette. I'd throw the drink out. After all,

153

I had proved my will power for two long years. True, the wagon had broken down, but I could go on again. I would lay to rest once and for all that drunken curse.

"You'll hit bottom," Eleanor Rice had shrieked at me four years before. "You'll beg for help."

I shook my head, dismissing her ravings for the madness they were. I tried my voice.

"Good morning, this is Susan B. Anthony."

A hoarse whisper came out. I tried again.

"Good morning, this is Susan B. Anthony. Now is the time for all good men . . ." Still no voice for radio. It worried me. It worried me so much that I began to shake and sweat. How could I get to the studio and on the air today? Surely a small medicinal drink wouldn't count. I needed it to cure the shaking. Just one to get me out of bed. I reached over and gulped the leftover martini, jerking upright in the bed as the fiery gin hit my empty stomach. Again I tried to speak, but still a baritone croak was all that came out. I put one foot tentatively out of bed onto the black linoleum floor, and then the other to feel if my feet would carry me to the phone. Squinting, I found the number of the throat doctor on the Square, dialed, and begged his nurse to work me in on my way to the studio. I clutched the phone while waiting. "Yes. Come in at ten-forty-five," the nurse's voice said. Good, now, just one more drink to sharpen me for that chore. I got out the ice, poured a three-ounce shot from the gin bottle, waved a drop of vermouth in the tumbler, and carried it back to the desk. The gin took hold and at last I could begin to read and write. This is the last drink for the day. I will come home, eat a big meal, and go to bed.

Fortified, I showered, dressed, doused my red eyes with strong drops, finally located my dark glasses and purse, walked down two flights, hanging onto the banister, out into the light of day.

I hurried past the news vendor, standing, felt hat on as usual, behind the counter of papers. He was the first human encounter of my day, and seemed to set the tone of it with a sullen disapproving glare. I finally caught a cab at the corner of Seventh Avenue, where the morning traffic ground in from six converging streets.

The doctor chided me for burning the candle at both ends, as he put it euphemistically while spraying out my throat. This ritual behind, I rejoined my cab to be hurtled up Broadway to the studio. My legs buckled as I got out, but I made it to the safety of the lobby wall.

MONDAY NOON—MIDTOWN

Cautiously approaching the elevator, I drew a breath and straightened into a ramrod walk more suitable to the standing of Susan B. Anthony, commentator of a lively, controversial, daily radio show.

I pursed my lips tight to hide my breath from fellow passengers in the elevator, and proceeded to the next encounter. My young secretary, Doris—did she know I drank?—explained that my show's guest for the day had arrived already. I went into my office where the small, older woman was sitting.

I greeted the pioneer birth-control crusader: "Mrs. Sanger, I do apologize for keeping you waiting—an interview downtown, and the traffic you know."

"How nice to meet the great-niece of Susan B. Only my dear, I can't really see what you look like behind those huge dark glasses," Mrs. Sanger said.

I pulled them off, fearing that the tell-tale red still showed. Sending Doris for some branch water to keep my tortured whiskey-cigarette throat from breaking up the show with coughs, I led Mrs. Sanger into the ice-cold studio, mindful to keep my breath well above and away from the petite reformer. I nodded to the program manager as I passed him, but I avoided his eyes now that I had removed my masking glasses.

I also nodded to the engineer behind his soundproofed glass wall, wondering if he would suspect today that my husky, cough-prone voice was not really caused by the chronic bronchitis I claimed. The red light went on, forcing me to muffle a cough behind my arm, well away from the microphone.

I held on with both hands trying to steady the sheet on which I had managed to type the "News of Interest to Women." The engineer had warned me frequently about rattling papers.

"Good morning, this is Susan B. Anthony. Today for the first time on daytime radio, 'This Woman's World' launches a three-day series of discussions on birth control. Mrs. Margaret Sanger, pioneer leader of this fight, is right here in the studio with me.

She is an heroic woman. Mrs. Sanger has been twice arrested for woman's right to bear or not to bear children. She is, of course, a direct spiritual descendant of my Aunt Susan who was arrested for woman's right to the ballot."

As Mrs. Sanger spoke I felt a wave of guilt in the presence of such quiet heroism. Mrs. Sanger had been persecuted, harassed, arrested for daring to assert that women should have the right to determine the use of their bodies; that parents should be able to space and plan their families. Especially she grieved for the unwanted children who starved, walked the streets, wound up in jails and institutions.

The minute-hand on the studio clock swung around to 11:57. I prepared to sign off the air. Would I do what I should do? Would I invite this grand old fighter to lunch with me? Or would I drink my lunch alone as usual? The red light flicked off. I stood up, touching the table to balance my unsteady legs.

"I do wish I could take you to lunch. But I have a long-standing appointment uptown."

"My dear Susan, I am sorry that we can't talk more," the older woman said in a motherly tone. "I think you need to take better care of yourself. I noticed your hands shaking. Now maybe it's just radio nerves, but my dear, you have such a great tradition to live up to."

She reached up and tried to hug me. Her concern caused me a momentary pang, an urge to return the hug, an urge to break through the lie and say, "I am not well, I am killing myself, I am dying." But I didn't. I said instead, "Goodbye, and thanks." At Lindy's restaurant downstairs, I followed the senatorial maître d'hôtel to a table, peering to make sure I was not seen by anyone from the studio. For the waitress I pretended to study the menu, pausing as though in thought before I ordered my usual.

"A pastrami sandwich on rye. Guess I'll have a martini, no olive, lemon, or onion. Better make it a double."

The sandwich was for appearance only. When it came I pulled it apart to make it look partially eaten, unable to get down any of it save a piece of crust and a slice of kosher pickle. The double I downed, and even as I did, began lining up the reasons for another. I'll have just one more to get myself through the mail upstairs, but it will be the last today, the very last.

I kept my eyes on Doris as I dictated replies to fan mail and letters to forthcoming guests. Did Doris suspect that I had been downstairs for my daily doubles? Did Doris tell on me to the program manager, the producer? Was she too innocent to realize what caused the red eyes, the shaking hand, the thick voice? To cover my fears, I adopted an even more authoritative tone as I dictated notes for a program on the twenty-sixth anniversary of the woman suffrage amendment, August 26. I'd tell the story of Aunt Susan's arrest for voting in 1872, how women had picketed the White House for two years—the first pickets ever at the executive mansion . . .

Harder was the answer to the memo from my program manager. The salesmen were complaining again; it was too hard to find sponsors for "This Woman's World." The show was "too controversial" for a daytime woman's program. Soap manufacturers in particular objected to a program that wanted to take washing and housekeeping out of the home. Bless the diaper service that liked my show!

I gave up trying to answer the program manager. Leaving the studio, I dropped the cloak of my public role and descended into the suffocation of the uptown subway, to dwell for the next hour in a private past.

MONDAY AFTERNOON—UPTOWN

Dr. Gilian Lodge, psychoanalyst, opened the door of his suite and murmured, "Good afternoon, Susan." His vocal chords seemed husky from disuse, the obligatory silence imposed upon him by his orthodox Freudian training. He rarely spoke save to administer a carefully selected cathartic phrase to help the "free association" along.

Prison-pale from submersion five days a week in the underground of his patients' psyches, his feet as well as his throat seemed weakened from disuse. He always wore old, cracked bedroom slippers, and an ancient tweed jacket patched at the elbows, more suitable for a slim-salaried assistant professor than a Park Avenue analyst earning upward of two hundred dollars a day.

Not meeting his glance, I walked quickly to the couch, flung myself upon it, put an ashtray on my stomach, and lighted a cigarette. By a scraping of his throat he indicated that he had taken his chair behind my recumbent head. He was hidden from my view as completely as any priest is screened from a penitent in the confessional. As I recounted my traumas to the ceiling above my eyes, the only sound from him was the scratching of his pen upon a pad. Notes on my case, he said. But since, of course, I couldn't see them, I wondered if instead he might be using my hour to write a paper for a learned journal, or perhaps a Broadway play. I was often tempted to leap up, take him unawares, and grab the pad and read it. Instead I droned out my hates and fears of the hostile world encircling me in which there was not a living soul whom I could trust. . . . Dad, who loathed liquor, had long since cut me off as though I were already dead. I had slashed out at Mother, hurting her, ignoring her pleas to stop drinking. Whom could I trust? My husband? After Dr. Lodge had met Ralph he had surprised me by making the only judgmental statement of the whole analysis:

"Your husband is one of the most self-centered men I have ever met."

It was an extraordinary thing for him to say because it was so out of character. Ralph used me, he said, merely as a name, or as a hostess for those who could advance him. "Get rid of him, divorce him! You won't make any headway in your analysis until you do."

His advice had thrown me into a panic. I simply couldn't face the legal breakup of our marriage. Divorce had never entered my head despite the shattering events since Ralph's return from the war and his back-and-forth trips to South America for the government. I felt I deserved the infidelities I had discovered; I felt I deserved his cruelty, because of my own lapses. For there had been many others since Tom, and they were not the high-ranking generals Ralph had recommended. I could almost trace my descent to the bottom through the descending character of my lovers. I had plummeted to the depths with the one who had nearly murdered me. Jock was, I knew, exactly what I deserved.

Midway in the hour, I heard the familiar clatter of china and silver spoon. Dr. Lodge had put his pad aside to pour himself a cup of tea.

He was my third psychoanalyst in less than two years. I had rushed to find the first on the day of hungover remorse in Philadelphia, begging him to help me. "My hands are tied behind my back. Untie them for me please. Free me from whatever it is that is binding me."

He and the next and now this one discredited a discussion of the present. It was an escape, they pronounced. Only the remote childhood past was worthy of pursuit in a full-scale depth psychoanalysis.

Hesitantly, now, I said to the ceiling, "Perhaps it is my drinking that makes me so sick."

"It is just the reverse. Your sickness makes you drink. It is a symptom of your underlying problems. When we uncover the roots of those, your drinking will take care of itself."

Not satisfied, I cried, "But I may not survive to find the problems if I go on like this."

"Time's up. See you Wednesday." He ushered me to the door. He had given me what I immediately interpreted as a doctor's order. I ducked into the shop kept by the purveyor of my "medicine," the bar around the corner from Dr. Lodge's office. This drink was for the road, the journey back to the Village.

MONDAY EVENING—THE VILLAGE

At the top of the subway stairs I bought some kosher hotdogs, bread, and even milk in the Sheridan Square delicatessen. I had made a new resolution coming downtown, that from now on I would eat, not drink. I even crossed Seventh Avenue to the lending library to borrow a book as substitute for booze until my date came later. Though I searched the crammed shelves, I could not find a single book that appealed at all. Disgusted, I left and walked toward the store whose shelves were crammed with what I really craved.

Casually, as though to finish off a long shopping list, I said: "I'd better get a fifth of gin."

"The usual, Susan?" the too-familiar clerk said to his daily customer.

"Yes, they sure drink it up fast—my friends," I said. He handed me the fifth in its revealing slimline bag. I tried to stuff the bottle in with the groceries to hide its telltale shape, became nervous under his amused eyes, and to my horror nearly dropped it.

"Like a bigger bag?"

"Thank you, no," I walked out, I hoped with dignity, the bottle held tightly under my arm.

I hurried past the drugstore, the beery-smelling corner bar on Barrow Street, and home to begin the serious business of the day, mixing the martinis ten-to-one in a pint-sized jelly glass. My full attention was now on the drink while I held cocktail conversations on the telephone (on the phone you don't have to meet people's eyes) and waited for my date.

Dinner with Rick at the San Remo consisted of more martinis until at 10:30 I ordered my usual night-time meal, antipasto and Italian bread. Ignoring the plate loaded with provolone cheese, anchovies, and Italian sausage, I "dined" on one ripe olive. Anything more might dull the edge of the oblivion I had so assiduously moved toward since rising. Rick washed down his steak with whiskey as he kidded me about my "feminist" radio program.

We had met through the show after he had poked fun at "This Woman's World" in a paragraph of his daily news column. I had flushed the veteran forty-year-old columnist from behind his typewriter and challenged him to slug it out in person on the air.

When he appeared for the interview, his booze breath and glistening eyes revealed the training he had kept for the contest. Confident that I could gun him down on my home territory, I used very light ammunition for my opening broadcast question.

"Tell me, Mr. Anderson, are you married, or can you speak freely about women?"

He blinked and reared back from the microphone, both hands on the table, as though I had hit home. He seemed as tongue-tied as many writers whose wit deserts them when they leave their pen behind. In the split second of silence on the air, I was aiming my next shot, when enunciating clearly he said: "I am not married, but I cannot speak freely. After all I know which side my bed is buttered on."

Now it was I who was speechless. The engineer frantically gave the throat-slitting signal to cut. I tried to smooth over the risqué remark, the first ever to stain the pristine purity of my women's show, but his retort had scattered my wits like a covey of quail. Generous in his victory, he bought me a consolation drink after the show, followed by a drinking visit to the track and liquid dinner on the terrace of his apartment. Aside from his rather ponderous wit, and the roar of his laughter that somehow was like Tom's, his main appeal to me was that living in his own glass house of booze, he did not throw stones at mine.

We walked northward after dinner past the squares of yellow light in old loft buildings and cold-water flats where youngsters were singing, or painting, or pounding out first novels. In Washington Square young lovers embraced on benches in the leafy stillness of the summer night. We turned down Eighth Street with its moving stream of tourists and young natives in denim.

"Look at those kids!" Rick said in scorn. "Aren't there any bathtubs in the Village?"

But far from despising them, I envied them the high spirits of their fresh young lives. Perhaps I had made it too late to Greenwich Village. Perhaps, if it hadn't been for Aunt Susan's scholarship to Rochester, I would have reached here while I was still awake to the beauty in life.

Somehow, now the urge to paint or sing or write had been replaced by one urge only, the urge to drink. As we walked toward that drink, across Sixth Avenue and past the fortress of the Women's House of Detention, I felt that I was locked behind doors as securely as those women prisoners. Like them I was filling the summer night with raucous shouts. But my shouts were silent.

After weaving our way along Tenth Street to Julius' for the serious drinking of the night, we pushed our way into the bedlam of drink-loosed tongues, through the crowd two and three deep at the bar. Other people's bodies, not my own legs, now supported me as we held high the drinks in our hands. No room at the bar for one more elbow. And then the nightly blackout curtain dropped.

TUESDAY MORNING—DOWNTOWN

Slits of sunlight piercing the venetian blinds pried my eyelids open, stabbing me into awareness of another day. How I had gotten to bed I could not remember. And now in two short hours I must be uptown once more. I needed a drink badly. I put one foot out of bed, then the other, and then almost stumbled over the typewriter table. I must have written something at that unknown hour when I came in.

A pillar of sunlight spotlighted the yellow sheet in the typewriter. I stared at the words I had written in my blackout but my eyes wouldn't focus. I ripped the sheet out of the typewriter, and threw it on the desk in disgust. I took out the gin and poured some into a glass with a smidgin of vermouth.

TUESDAY AFTERNOON—MIDTOWN

Miss Anthony regrets that she cannot have lunch today. Already I was composing my excuses as I went off the air with my guest, a rabbi.

"I must go cross-town for a tiresome appointment," I said. "Thank you so much for coming. I was really impressed and I am sure our listeners were with your ideas on birth control."

I almost pushed the rabbi to the elevator in my haste to get to Lindy's. I made it, and started priming the pump. I felt in my purse for pen and paper. I would put on an act—appear to be working, making sense, jotting notes. I drew forth the yellow sheet I had found in the typewriter that morning. I must have picked it up from the clutter on my desk along with my news summary. "I'm not really this bad . . ." No time to read that drunken scribbling now. I turned the paper over and wrote on its back the names of those I'd invite for the suffrage anniversary show. I ordered just one more to carry me through the ordeal of dictation upstairs.

Fighting for oxygen in the humid office, I heard myself ask Doris to get me some people on the phone who, it seemed to me, would make a good program. They were recovered alcoholics.

Doris handed me the receiver. When a friendly woman's voice came on the line, I pulled myself together and in the brisk tones of Lady Bountiful touring the slums, I said: "This is Susan B. Anthony. I have a sudden opening on my show. I'd like to help you people. I could interview a couple of your men."

WEDNESDAY NOON—MIDTOWN

I clutched the doorway of my office for support. Two well-tailored men leaped to escort me to my chair. Behind my dark glasses, I studied them. Did these experts see through them to the red swollen eyes?

For the show I called the older man, Mr. Y. In his forties, he was a senior executive in an advertising agency, bald, ruddy from weekends of tennis. Mr. X was younger, with dark glowing eyes and smiling lips. He leaned toward me and his manner seemed to ask, "Are you all right?" For a moment I felt as though I could collapse into his arms.

The show began. Almost from the start, Mr. X and Mr. Y took over the mike in a rollicking, happy-hearted performance as good as any I'd ever had on the show. They joked in a sophisticated way about "how to be happy though sober." Yet they came over as good men; that was the only word I could find, good. Not goody-goody like the "Christers" and YWCA types I had scorned at college, but simply good. I listened intently, nearly forgetting myself as Mr. Y said, "The only thing you need is the will to live, the desire to stop drinking, that's all. You must take the first step—that's the only absolutely necessary one."

"What is that? Er—ah," I caught myself. "I know our listeners would like to hear."

"We admitted we were powerless over alcohol, that our lives had become unmanageable," he replied.

"You mean your own will power isn't enough?" I asked.

"That's right," said Mr. X. "Will power will get you nowhere. We have all tried it—going on the wagon, trying just beer, just wine, just weekend drinking, just two drinks each night. Our will power always breaks down, if we are alcoholics. We have to admit we are totally powerless."

"But if you're totally powerless, how can you stop drinking?"

"We rely on a power greater than ourselves. We also have the group—the fellowship of men and women—and our twelve steps."

"Much as I'd like to hear more about your program, our time is up."

I rushed over to the attractive Mr. X.

"Would you have lunch with me?"

While he ate his lunch, I drank mine. But even as I poured in the martinis, I began pouring out the sickness of my double life, the uptown commentator, the downtown drunk. I unburdened myself of the lies, the cheating, the lust.

Instead of shocking him, he said lightly: "My dear Susan, I have done so much worse. Remember, I am an alcoholic. We're all alike. Some are high-bottom drunks—never get into jail or nuthouses or skid row—but we're all the same under the skin."

His brown eyes commiserated with me. More, they seemed filled with real concern. I leaned across the table, knocking over my drink, trying to reach out to that love, pleading: "Do you think I am an alcoholic? Do you?"

"Can't tell you that—only you can answer that question for yourself."

He poured me into a cab.

WEDNESDAY NIGHT—WESTCHESTER

I dived into the quarry pool, thinking to show off my swimming prowess to my radio b.'ss's dinner guests. Out in the middle of the water, my arms became leaden. I of the eight-beat crawl was sinking while a few strangers idly wondered what Susan was doing, alone, out in the middle of the quarry. Some training from my childhood rolled me over on my back and kept me from swallowing too much water. Somehow I got to shore where I lay shaking and panting on the grass. In the bathhouse at last I took my half pint of gin from my beach bag and drank it straight. The rest of the evening was a blur. But I was certain as I rode back to town on the train that I had fatally exposed my drunkenness to the station owner and his wife. Had I sounded the death knell of my job?

THURSDAY NIGHT—DOWNTOWN

I went out to meet Jock. A year ago he had raised a breadknife to my throat, cutting off a button at my neck. My life was not worth a nickel, my then-psychiatrist had warned me, should I ever see him again. Now as though drawn to a barracuda on the reef, I had said "yes" to his call.

The last time as we drank together in my apartment, I was getting ice out of the refrigerator when I told him that he would never write his novel. He had gone wild. It had happened so fast, his reaching for the knife, his swirling around. I had not moved. I felt the knife; I stood motionless. I knew if I flickered an eyelash that I would be dead. I stared at him. The knife clattered to the floor.

Tonight we did the bars. At one of them, I left him. I had a vague memory of wandering alone through the early-morning Village streets.

FRIDAY AFTERNOON—DOWNTOWN

I had awakened in my apartment so sick that I barely made it through the broadcast. Nearly fainting afterward, I had fallen into a cab and fled home to bed.

Now I lay dying. It had all gone wrong, every single thing in my entire life. And now I was alone. I had hit bottom. Could I make one last effort to live? Was it worth trying to live, trying to call for help? Dying I was, quite literally. I had been drinking steadily since talking with Mr. X.

I knew the fate that waited me was death; if not death by drowning or Jock's knife, death by drinking.

"Help me, someone!" I moaned. I was sinking. The pit was deeper than the quarry pool. The face of Mr. X once more surfaced. Mr. X would help me. I groped for my purse and dialed the number. The girl who had arranged his appearance on my show was on vacation; the one who answered the phone didn't know Mr. X; but I could try another number. The second voice said she didn't know, but gave me a third number to try, just in case. And now I feared I had forfeited my hope for help years ago when I had turned down Eleanor. She had put her curse upon me, damning me to share her own fate.

If I don't reach him now, I know I'm meant to die and die alone. But then the voice of Mr. X came on the wire.

"Tim here—"

"Tim!" I grasped the phone with both hands, "Tim! I'm dying! Come right over! I'm dying!" Even as I cried I could see him arriving with medicinal whiskey; could feel his protecting, comforting arms around me. A man, a sober man, someone to watch over me!

"Put off dying till tomorrow. Men handle men. Women handle

women on this program," he said cheerily. "Tomorrow I'll introduce you to some gals who really can help you. They'll take over."

My dream of romantic rescue was shattered. I hated him for not running to me, for not breaking his foolish rules.

"Susan! Still there? Did you hear me? You need a lady sponsor, not me. She'll tell you why. Be a good girl and get a pencil and write down this address for lunch tomorrow."

Who wanted to meet some woman? Reluctantly I found a piece of paper in my purse and scrawled on it the address.

"See you tomorrow—don't stand us up," he said. "Try and get some rest tonight. It may be asking too much, Susan, but remember, I've been—we've all been—exactly where you are now. We know how you feel and we can help if you want to stop drinking."

His words "stop drinking" spelled out a void intolerable to me now. He, who wouldn't come to my rescue, how dare he suggest that I could face the rest of this day without another drink? Rebelliously, I grabbed the martini from the bedside table. Beneath it was a sheet of yellow typing paper. *The words stood out on it as if they were illuminated medieval script. There was no way not to read them:*

"I am not really this bad—underneath this drunken, disgusting self, there is another self—someone who is not as bad as I am now."

This is what I had written two nights before, written in total blackout, written to myself.

Reading it, I cried.

14 *"...as you did it to one of the least of these..."*

I woke up sick and shaking the next morning, but I did not reach for my usual wake-up martini. I tried coffee instead. After all, Tim had told me that his sponsor had bought him a drink. I would try to hold out for my own first drink until we met uptown at that address he had given me.

I was still shaking when I got there at noon. Tim introduced me to Rosalind Petry. I barely paid any attention to her. Now the two of them would take me out to a restaurant where they would buy me that drink. Instead Tim waved a hasty goodbye and left—left me flat, alone with this woman. She was warm and friendly enough, but I wanted to bolt from her as we walked out onto the street. My hopes for a medicinal pick-me-up were blasted when she led me into a cafeteria. I knew what that meant, no bar, no drink!

I could not get down the lunch before me. But I did somehow force myself to listen as Rosalind, smiling good-humoredly, told me her own drinking story. She continued it for the next three hours, giving completely of herself, openly, honestly, never putting me on the spot. Shifty-eyed, wishing at every moment to get a drink somehow, I was nevertheless held by her words. Their shock value alone was enough to hold me. This sparkling, clear-eyed patrician who moved and talked with such assured dignity once had hidden gin in peroxide bottles in the family medicine closet. This immaculate Rosalind had slopped around

167

Third Avenue bars in a dirty old raincoat, drinking boilermakers with derelicts. Her story made mine seem as innocent as an Elsie Dinsmore book. Rosalind suggested that I try staying away from a drink, not tomorrow, but just for today, just this twenty-four hours. She told me to buy the book describing the alcoholic fellowship on my way home. She urged me to meet with her and other recovered alcoholics that very night.

I did buy the book and carried it along Eighth Street, turning the telltale jacket inside out so that no one would see what I was reading. I carried it up to my apartment, sweating, dying for a drink after our three-hour talk. I grabbed my bottle of gin as I walked into the kitchen, still holding the book in the other hand. As I was about to pour a huge hooker, something took me by the back of the neck. It led me to the bathroom where I poured that perfectly good bottle of gin down the toilet! Then I sat down and read about myself in every page of the book, leaving it only to meet her and the others that night. Though I was much too hungover to understand what they said, I grasped what they were. They were love-in-action. They seemed to say by every word and expression: "We love you no matter who you are, what you have done." They loved me unconditionally, as Aunt Nell had loved Uncle Sydney. I soaked up their love like the starved and dying woman I was.

Three days later Rosalind called and said she wanted me to go with her to help an alcoholic sober up. I protested. How could I? I was barely able to walk sober myself. I couldn't be of help to anyone else. She was firm. She said this was part of my recovery, going out to help another, and that now was the time to start. She took me to Number One Fifth Avenue, into a darkened suite reeking with stale alcohol and half-burned cigarettes. Mrs. B lay between linen sheets. Around her were icebags, bottles, barbituates, untouched breakfast, lunch and dinner trays, ashtrays and two (not one) burning cigarettes. She moaned and opened her red eyes. 'Thank God you're here," she gasped, grabbing me like a sick child.

I recoiled and tried to withdraw my hand from her clammy, sweaty one. I was revolted by the stench of her and of the room. I wanted to bolt from contamination. Then suddenly I really looked at her. And looking, I saw myself in her, and I also saw her in me. I could help her! I, who had been at the same bottom just three days before, could actually help another human being!

Rosalind sat back and let me carry the message. I patted the hand of Mrs. B: "It's pretty rough, isn't it?" I said to this former self with whom I could now identify. "I know how you feel. I've been there. In fact, I was there just three days ago. But today I'm not drinking—I feel fine and you can too."

Cautiously she opened one eye, then the other, and I began to tell her my own story. Rosalind called room service to send up coffee, no brandy on the side, please. We got Mrs. B into the shower, dressed, and took her to meet others that night in a Village hall south of Washington Square. Mrs. B remains sober to this day.

Mrs. B was the first of hundreds of person-to-person encounters that I was to have and continue to have to this moment. She was the first of those I have come to call my children of the spirit.

My own brand-new sobriety was put to the test a few days later when I was fired from my radio job! The station informed me that my show was being taken off the air; it was, they said, "too controversial to be commercially feasible." I thought it ironic that politics, not alcoholism, had killed my show. Despite my drinking I had never missed nor flubbed a program. After the initial shock I remembered what Rosalind had drilled into me. "Share all your troubles with us. Don't try to handle any crisis by yourself. Use nickel therapy: call me up. If you can't reach me, call another recovered alcoholic. But don't fight it out alone."

I did what she said. I called Rosalind and rushed up to her apartment. Over cups of coffee I told her of my very serious situation, with a financial problem now added to the one of sobriety. Take one step at a time, she advised. The only thing that really mattered was my sobriety, one day at a time, and if necessary, one minute at a time.

"Remember your first and only problem is staying away from the first drink. And that means trying to get some balance, some peace of mind. Don't let anything get you too low or too high. Just because we're sober doesn't mean everything in our outer world will go smoothly. It is how we handle the outer problems. There is no problem that a drink won't make worse."

I did as she said. I doubled the number of meetings with her and other recovered alcoholics. I kept a full stomach so I would not mistake hunger for a drink craving. I carried chocolate bars with me at all times on Rosalind's theory that no one ever took a drink after lots of chocolate. I talked with her and others on the phone at any hour I felt jittery. The result was that I got through this first major crisis without taking a drink.

Shortly afterward I came down with flu. I was still in bed, quite weak, wondering what I should do next, when Ralph came into New York between overseas assignments. I hadn't seen him in four months. I knew that there was nothing left in our marriage. He was leaving the next day for still another of his trips to South America. As he stood at the foot of my bed, I asked him for the first time in our marriage to lend me money. I asked for the loan only to tide me over until I could get well, and back on the air again.

He stood over me, looking down at me coldly, cleared his throat and said: "If you say you are returning to be my hostess in Washington, I'll lend you something. Otherwise, to me you're just another liberal."

At last it became clear to me that he had no concern at all for me as his wife, or even for me as a person. I got out of my sick-bed the very next day and went downtown to begin the divorce proceedings I had never before even contemplated.

Facing the end of my six-year marriage, the end of my radio career, I tasted real insecurity. But just as I was dipping into a panic, another radio station put me back on the air with much fanfare, claiming in a *Variety* advertisement that the Susan B. Anthony show was "not too controversial for us!" Rejoicing at the chance to broadcast again, I was happy to be sober, clear-voiced and clear-eyed as I interviewed my five-day-a-week stream of "controversial" guests in what was hailed as a very lively show. Six weeks later I was sitting at the typewriter at home when there was a knock at the door. A registered special delivery letter was handed to me by a postman. The letter was brief. It was from the station. It ordered my show off the air by the end of the week.

No explanation was given. Twice in three months my liveli-hood had been abruptly shut off. What was behind it? To whom could I appeal? What could I do?

Only gradually I realized that while I had groped in the haze of alcoholism, the world had moved from the alliances of World War II into the new battle lines of the cold war. No longer were the Fascists and Nazis the enemy; in 1946 the new enemy was the Soviet Union.

President Roosevelt had been in his grave less than two weeks, in April 1945, when the preliminary shots of this new war were fired at the San Francisco meeting of the United Nations Organization. With one voice the American press seemed to turn overnight against Russia. Now in December 1946 the attack on liberals and leftists was gaining momentum through official and unofficial agencies. I myself had interviewed some of the victims of these attacks on my radio programs. Now I was one of the growing number of liberal commentators being "purged" from the air, and blacklisted for future programs in New York.

It took me two years to get back on the air. And then it was not in New York and certainly not on controversial issues. I returned to radio in Boston, pioneering with a program on alcoholism, and later one on psychogenic illness. The shows reflected a general retreat forced by the purge of political commentary shows. But in my case they also reflected a transformation in my personal focus. By 1950 I had learned from my recovered alcoholic friends that my job was to change myself first, before trying to change the world. Further, I could change myself best by helping others on a person-to-person basis. "Each one reach one," was the way to get sober, and to stay sober.

But as I clung to my little weekly radio program on psychosomatic causation of illness, called "The Turning Point," I could not help wondering where I stood in the threatening McCarthy atmosphere of 1950. I put down on paper an analysis of my own situation.

1. I am not and never have been a member of the Communist Party.
2. During the war I gave my name to and worked hard on all sorts of committees and organizations whose area of concern I agreed with.
3. Even though I still feel these concerns, I have changed my fundamental point of view from mass crusades to person-to-person work.
4. Many of my former crusades are now listed as "subversive" organizations by the U.S. Attorney General. They were highly regarded at the time I worked with them.
5. In the present public and private attacks on all liberals, and in the "guilt-by-association" doctrine, I might be classed as "suspect."

The attitude of government and press seemed to be that if the Congress of American Women, which I had helped found in 1945, was listed by the Attorney General as "subversive," then anyone on its letterhead, or in association with it, was also subversive. Or if a friend or relative was accused of being a Communist, then his friends and family were also Communists. I thought of the earnest, profoundly patriotic people with whom I had worked for women's equality, for civil rights, for childcare centers—people any country was richer for possessing. Many had not only been purged from the news media, as I had been, but subpoenaed by the House Un-American Activities Committee, and now by this new and unabashedly publicity-seeking committee of Senator Joseph McCarthy's. New blacklists barred many from jobs in publishing, lecturing, the theater. Eventually these blacklists were to crystallize in the "Red Channels" newsletter, just one of many new and frightening methods of thought control.

And yet sick as all this made me, I had no impulse to get back into the fight. I became aware of how far my views had shifted, on New Year's Eve 1948, in an old Victorian mansion on Cape Cod. Sitting next to me at a splendid dinner party was a noted Marxist theoretician, an important member of the American Communist Party. At one point I mentioned to him that I was shocked at the slaughter of the Chinese people then taking place in the Mao-led revolution. He turned his face full toward me, with its late-night-meeting pallor.

"What does it matter if millions of Chinese are wiped out, if it forwards the cause of the revolution? It is a small price to pay."

I stared at him, unbelieving. He was speaking from another world, a world in which people were ciphers, to be wiped out, without feeling or compassion. It was exactly the opposite of my motivation in working for liberal causes during the war.

Since getting sober, my concern for people had become even more specific. I remembered the day I had been sitting on the steps of the New York Public Library watching the anonymous, blurring faces hurry past me on Fifth Avenue. All at once a remarkable change took place. As I watched, my focus shifted, and suddenly I was looking at people as individuals. I saw noses and ears and eyes and hats and colors and shapes—and each individual had his unique glory.

I knew then how different I had become. Now the individual came first, not the vast impersonal society, state, or class. And the individuals I had hurt were my business now. In the general clean-up of my household of character defects, I must make amends to each person I had hurt, starting with my own family, especially with my father. Like the prodigal son who had wallowed with the swine in the far country, I determined to "arise and go to my father," and ask his forgiveness for the seven years of our estrangement. He had every reason to turn me down as I had turned him down during the agonizing years when he and Mother had been reaching the dead-end of divorce. Now I knew I must board a train and go to Raubsville and apologize to him.

The locomotive worked its way through the familiar rolling green hills of Pennsylvania. As the train drew in at the Lehigh Valley station I scanned the platform looking for Dad. And there in the distance I saw the familiar old Plymouth coming down the road. Within minutes my father was embracing me, saying, "Welcome home, Sue."

I blurted out that I was sorry for everything I had done, and that he had every right to reject me. But instead Dad took my bag and put it in the car. He drove me home to Raubsville where a feast awaited me. We celebrated and made merry in our reconciliation, while he played the old songs on his banjo, singing in his never-to-be-forgotten voice. I was no longer lost, but found, no longer dead to him, but alive again. In the next years we often feasted at Raubsville and rejoiced in each other's company in New York on gala weekends.

Seven years later I was thousands of miles away on a Jamaica hillside when news reached me of his sudden death at Raubsville. He had evidently been cleaning the autumn leaves out of the chimney flue in his bedroom. He had had a heart condition for some years, but had kept it a secret from us. Neighbors found him on the floor.

Moved by the same amends-making effort that had led me to Raubsville, soon after the reconciliation with Dad, I boarded a train for Boston. I carried a particularly heavy burden of guilt toward Aunt Nell. I had ignored and neglected her during all the years that she needed me. She had reaped no reward for her unconditional love of Sydney, nursing him during his drunkenness, putting up with his temper. Instead, on one of his drunks he had gone to a private nursing home to dry out. When he emerged he told Nell that he had decided to divorce her and marry his nurse. Aunt Nell suffered her first angina attack at the shock. She asked for nothing from his huge income and estate. She accepted a pittance only when her lawyer insisted that she at least have that. In ten years I had deigned to give her but two hours of my time, when she was in New York once, at lunch in the Algonquin. I drank that lunch just as Sydney used to do.

Now I sought Aunt Nell's forgiveness for my years of neglect. Like Dad, she welcomed me with open arms and rejoiced at the miracle that had turned me completely around to sobriety. The only shadow for me on the weekend was that she asked me to accompany her to a Palm Sunday service at her Anglican church. But in my new tolerance I could even bring myself to attend my first church service since childhood. I was amazed that this frail old lady could survive without another angina attack the constant kneeling, rising, standing, kneeling. And all this on a foolishly fasting stomach!

"Part of my prayer has been answered, now that you are sober," she said as we parted. "But, Sue, I shall keep on praying until it is completely answered."

I did not learn what complete answer she meant until I spent a month with her at Rockport, Massachusetts, close to her lovely old home at Bass Rocks. Now at a simple summer boardinghouse we had our meals together, but each of us followed her own schedule otherwise. Her mornings were spent in prayer. I spent mine soaking up the sun and swimming in the numbing New England Atlantic. For practice in keeping my mind off me, I memorized the entire Sermon on the Mount—three whole chapters—from Aunt Nell's Bible.

As I accompanied Aunt Nell back to her Boston apartment, she put her hand on my shoulder, saying, "Darling Sue, this has been the happiest month of my life since Sydney and I were young together. You have no idea what your sobriety means to me. I will keep on praying that you will meet the One Person who loves you most."

I cried as the train carried me back to New York.

In the violent transition from the old to the new I committed all kinds of mistakes. So single-tracked was I on the rule that I must put sobriety first (a rule that would cause me great suffering a few years later in Jamaica) that I injured most the person closest to me of all. Mother had rejoiced in my new way of life. She had rushed to New York and hovered over me anxiously lest I be tempted to take a drink. Her visit had been followed not only by letters of good advice, but soon by another visit. She managed to quicken every anxiety in my mind, all the old insecurities and self-concern.

At last I said to her, "If you really want to help me stay sober, stay away from me. You stir up everything that's immature in me, and please don't write either. Your letters upset me."

As she left, I hardened myself to her tears with the rationalization that I had to do this to protect my sobriety.

Most people grapple with their identity search in their teens and twenties. I postponed mine with alcohol. Now, in my thirties and sober, I started in.

"Who are you?" I asked myself.

"Susan B. Anthony," I answered.

And that answer led me directly to the original owner of the name. I wanted to study this strange, powerful force in my life. I carried my typewriter up to the typing room of the New York Public Library, and while living on unemployment insurance settled down for six months of intensive research on Aunt Susan. I read and typed notes on everything available: nineteenth-century newspapers, Congressional documents, letters and books. I made a six-week literary field trip to her birthplace at Adams, Massachusetts, and to Battenville, New York, where she had lived as a girl; to Canajoharie, New York, where she taught and led her brief life as a belle. Rochester, her home after 1845, I knew already. I went to Seneca Falls, the birthplace of the American Woman's Rights Movement; and to the Rare Book and Manuscript Room of the Library of Congress where I pored over the scrapbooks she had kept for sixty years.

The experience, as truth inevitably is, was freeing.

I was beginning to find that "I am I," that I belonged to myself and to no one else, not even to the ghost in my life. And as so often happens, it was a seemingly small incident that led to a crucial breakthrough.

In November 1950 I was spotted in a New York hotel lobby by
a former coworker from my mass-crusading days. She rushed
up to me and gushed, "Why, Susan B. Anthony, how marvelous
to see you! I'm running for Congress, you know. How about
coming up and giving some talks for my campaign?"

"Honestly," I replied, "I wouldn't know what to say. I don't
even know what the issues are, I'm so out of touch with politics."

"Why Susan, it doesn't matter a bit what you say. It's your
name that counts. That's what I need for my campaign!"

For a moment I stared at the woman, dumbfounded. Perhaps
I should have been angry. But I felt like throwing my arms
around her, for this was the most liberating thing that had ever
been said to me. She did not need me, not my hands, my brain,
my voice. She needed my name!

"Thank you," I said. I took her hand and squeezed it warmly.
I left the somewhat startled woman and walked without further
word into the free night air.

That very evening I made a decision. I had put it off long
enough. I would go some place where I would no longer be
Susan B. Anthony II. I would go where I could be myself for
the first time in my life.

I flew to Key West, Florida, the southernmost point of land
in the United States, and got a reporter's job on the Key West
Citizen, using another name. I abandoned not only the name but
my whole northern past as a youthful crusader. I was kept so
busy reporting city, county, and state news that I didn't even
have time to read the AP teletype in the newsroom. For me,
to know had been to act. Now I simply shut out knowledge of
international and national events. I knew I would wind up as
insular as the island itself, but I was glad. Not only had events
on a huge scale ceased to absorb me, but I wanted to avoid the
kind of involvement and controversy that might lead to a drink.

It was an idyllic period. I rented an apartment, a darling place
over a garage, and settled down to work. I liked the role of the
reporter who by 1:00 P.M. knew just what was happening at all
levels of the island, two miles wide and five miles long. I loved
the profusion of bougainvillea and hibiscus that spilled over the
stately Bahama houses in the white light of the tropical city. I
loved the sprawling banyans and flaming poincianas. I loved
swimming daily after work in the flat, calm, blue-green sea.

Within ten months I proved that I could not only find a job unaided by Susan B. Anthony's name, but make a social life for myself too. And my byline, pseudonym though it was, was known up in that remote north country far from Key West. The Associated Press kept me busy writing copy on everything from my three days spent with Ernest Hemingway as he revisited his old Key West home and bars, to plane crashes and criminal cases. I worked for nearly ten hours a day during President Truman's semiannual visits; the rest of the year there were always murders, rapes, and celebrities. With authority and confidence I walked my beat from the newsroom to courthouse, police station, and sheriff's office.

I resolved to stay away from local political issues such as gambling as well as big national issues racking the land in 1951. The cold war was now flaming into the hot war in Korea. But one day quite innocently I wrote a story that was to bring current policies into my own life. I wrote up what I thought was a strictly factual account of police brutality on a tiny B-girl, arrested for indecent attire by a burly cop. As a reporter I had no alternative than to write the story after stepping across the pool of blood that resulted from the policeman's beating. I didn't know that in writing up this seemingly nonpolitical incident, I was stirring up forces that would nearly destroy me.

Instead, I turned to another writing project, rising at 5:00 A.M. each day before my reporter's duties began. It was an adieu to a ghost. A long one. Before I had finished I had rapped out a not-very-kind 100,000-word book. I called it *Farewell to Thee, O Susan B.*

I thought this book signaled my freedom from my aunt. But one day a friend, an invalid writer, challenged me about what I had done. "If you're really through with that ghost, why do you write a whole book about her? You are making Aunt Susan the scapegoat of all the past mistakes and heartbreaks and failures in your life."

Of course my friend was right. By accusing Aunt Susan of being the cause of my troubles, I had created an atmosphere of resentment and self-pity about my life. And ghosts thrive in such a climate. No, I would somehow have to find still another way.

One day, a week after the anniversary of five years of sobriety, I had a strange impulse. I went for my coffee break with some of

the reporters to the USO-YMCA building. When they returned
to work, I did not. Instead, I found myself walking up to the
secretary. Assuming my reporter's tone, I asked briskly, "Do you
happen to have a Bible anywhere here, please? I need one for a
story."

"Why of course," she said, handing me a big black book. "Keep
it as long as you want."

I was out on the street before I realized what a sight I must
make. I would not be seen dead carrying this big black Bible
down Duval Street. I tried to hide it with a piece of copy paper
from my clipboard. The paper was too small. I tried to hide it
under my clipboard, but still the telltale words *Holy Bible* stuck
out. Finally I went into a Cuban grocery store and begged a
paper bag. When I returned to the newsroom to write my stories
I put the bag on the floor as though it contained mangoes.

That night at home I began searching the Bible, not for a story,
not for memory training as I had done that summer with Aunt
Nell. I thought this book might contain the key to my battle for
my own identity. Where was I going? Was there some sense to
life? What or who could give me the answer?

But though I suspected the key was there, I failed to find it
in the Bible, even when Aunt Nell had sent me, at my request,
a beautiful leather-bound King James translation. It seemed so
remote from actual life. I simply could not force myself to take
the time to read it.

On a humid October night I was in my little garage apartment
putting on my lipstick before going out to cover a meeting of the
County Commissioners. I gathered my clipboard, my pen and
purse. Then I heard footsteps mounting the outside staircase.
There came a tattoo of sharp knocks on the thin, glass top of my
door.

15 *". . . rather fear him who can destroy both soul and body in hell."*

A male voice said, "Major Murray, Naval Base Security Officer."

I opened the door and saw a wooden-faced marine officer standing there. He was practically clicking his heels together in military precision. Major Murray, whom I had often seen on the base, while covering navy ceremonies, cocktail parties and promotions, said, louder than he had to, "Would you please come with me to the naval station. I have a jeep outside."

Surprised, I said I couldn't. I had to cover a night County Commission meeting in a few minutes—maybe he could drop me off there? I'd be over at the base as usual tomorrow.

He stood straighter in the doorway and said even more stiffly, "I've spoken with your editor. He's made other arrangements to cover the meeting. You are to come with me."

It then began to dawn on me that something must be wrong. It was not only unprecedented for the navy to send a jeep for me; it was unheard of for Norman, my editor, to let me miss a County Commission meeting.

"Major," I said, "what's the matter?"

"That's not for me to say. Bring your navy pass with you."

I followed him down the outside stairs and climbed into the open jeep. As we drove up Whitehead Street, I had the strange feeling that this stern officer was my captor. It was as though I were riding for the last time past Norman's old Key West house, past the lighthouse, the Ernest Hemingway mansion.

We turned in at the navy gate where the sentry saluted the Major and proceeded to a building marked "Marine Security Guard." Major Murray did not open the door for me. I followed him into his office where a navy commander was waiting for us. The major and the commander stood at attention as though some kind of ceremony was about to follow.

Then the Major said formally: "Please hand over your navy press pass."

I gave it to him, feeling as though I were being stripped of epaulets and sword.

"What's this all about?" I asked.

"You are hereby ordered off this base. You will never be given another pass," Major Murray said.

"But this is ridiculous! I have been on and off the base every day for nearly a year! What's up?"

"You're a poor security risk," Major Murray said while the navy commander stood stiffly beside him. "That is all. I'll drive you back to your apartment."

I asked to see the captain commanding the base but was refused. The major drove me home. I walked through the bougainvillea garden that led to my little garage apartment and once inside I locked the door quickly. Instinctively I did the first thing that any recovered alcoholic does in crisis. I made myself some coffee. And then I paced.

Early next morning I rode my bicycle down to the *Citizen* office to see Norman before the other reporters came in. I told him what had happened.

"Yes," he said, "they called me last night and told me they were going to lift your pass. I told them you were the best reporter I ever had and no matter what the navy did, I was keeping you."

Norman asked me if I would like him to drive me over to the captain to try to find out what this security-risk business was all about. First, Norman had to get permission for me to be admitted to the base. And then on the way over, Norman said to me, "Susan, before we see the captain, I must know the answer to this question. Are you now or have you ever been a member of the Communist Party?"

"No, Norman, never."

And then I went on to tell him about the long list of committees I had worked with from 1938 to 1948.

"Have you had anything to do with them lately?"

"Not for the last three years," I said. We were ushered into the C.O.'s office. The captain was deferential to Norman as editor of the sole newspaper on the Keys. "Sorry, Norman," he said, "I'd like to do you a favor but Susan is finished as far as this naval base is concerned."

Norman explained that I wanted to find out who were my accusers; what specific accusations had been made; how to clear myself.

"It is not for me to disclose the source of charges against her."

"But there can't be any charges!" I burst out. "What evidence is there for calling me a poor security risk?"

"I'm not required to give you an explanation. I am commanding officer here and I am ordering you off this base."

All that week I felt shaken by the experience. I began to wonder about people I knew: who would wish to hurt me? It was like the feeling one gets from an anonymous hate letter—helplessness against an invisible enemy, suspicion, fear . . .

When President Truman's Air Force One arrived at the Naval Air Station, Norman had to send out the society reporter while I sat chafing at the typewriter. An hour after the President had landed, the captain called Norman and told him, in some confusion, that I was to proceed immediately to the navy base to pick up my White House press pass.

The same Major Murray handed it to me.

"The President's press secretary, Joe Short, says he knows all about your activities going back fourteen years. The Secret Service had cleared you to cover the President at his press conferences. You will be allowed onto the base during the presidential visit. But the navy's ban goes back into effect as soon as the President leaves." He was very cold.

"Don't you think it's ironic, Major, that Secret Service says I'm safe enough to cover your Commander-in-Chief, yet you don't think I'm safe enough to cover your routine handouts?"

"All I know is that the President asked for you when you weren't there to cover his arrival," the Major said, and then dismissed me.

In spite of the President's kindness, I still had the feeling of being an outcast. It wasn't helped by being granted the coveted White House press pass again when Mr. Truman came down in

March. The President did what he could to throw a few little
scoops my way, and even one good one.

I was standing at his last press conference at the naval base
before his flight back to Washington. I asked him, "Mr. President, will you be returning to Key West as an official visitor?"

Beaming, he laughed and said, "No, Susan, I won't."

Every reporter in the room rushed to the telephone to call in
the news that President Truman would not be running in the
1952 election.

Eventually I confided my problem to the late Merriman Smith,
dean of White House correspondents. Merriman or "Smitty" as
we called him, knew a lot about me. In fact, he had done some
real checking. He startled me when he said over a drink at the
Casa Marina that the stripping of my navy press was a local matter. He said it was undoubtedly a retaliation for my inadvertent
expose of the alleged Bolita collector, the policeman who had
beaten the bar girl. Smitty said that the county boss probably
warned the navy that he would publicize my past history as
being a threat to navy security unless the captain barred me
from the base. The county boss made it his business to learn of
everyone's Achilles' heel. Mine was, Smitty said, my "pinko past."

I stared at him in disbelief. But it did explain several odd
incidents.

I remembered the night shortly after the police-beating story.
A local policeman had burst into my garage apartment at midnight, barging in on a flimsy pretext of trying to find the *Citizen*
photographer. As he flashed his light around I remembered
thinking that he was hoping to find the photographer in my bed.
Immediately after this, one of the town's leading lawyers took
me for a ride up the Keys, saying I would "leave Key West on
a shutter," if I didn't stop writing stories about gambling. I
thought, of course, he was kidding.

I told Smitty about these experiences. It only made him all the
more urgent in his advice.

"Get out of town, Sue, before you really get hurt. This navy-
pass-stripping is just a sample of what they can do to you."

I might have taken his advice if I hadn't had a strong reason
for staying. The reason was—as so often in my life—a man, Lieutenant (Senior Grade) Robert Milford, U.S. Navy. We had fallen
in love. I knew when we did that I was violating a cardinal rule

of my own recovery from alcoholism. For he too was an alcoholic. Rosalind had warned me that the quickest way for a woman alcoholic to slip was to fall in love with a male alcoholic.

But I blotted out her words with the conviction that our love was different, that my six years of sobriety would actually be help to Bob. And they were helpful. This handsome man, immaculate in his navy uniform, admitted to me on our very first date that he had gone on the wagon only recently, that he was glad to date a girl who didn't drink. After that I became a guide to his sobriety and he, in turn, became my guide to the marvels of the underwater world. I fell in love with him and his silent sea at the same time. He taught me to glide with him in mask and snorkel and flippers twelve miles out on the reef. Together we dived and swam in this element so utterly new to me. This was a world of splendor, of dazzling light filtered through turquoise, of silky water, of silent motion, of gleaming tarpon and parrotfish, of lacy staghorn coral, of waving purple sea fans. Ten, twenty feet down I looked through my mask and saw, not beauty alone, but the golden light of illumination. Never again would I be satisfied to remain a swimmer on the surface. I would now always be aware of the supernal life beneath me.

Bob owned a 40-foot cabin cruiser called the *Molly Lou*. Every evening when I didn't have night assignments, we boarded the *Molly Lou*, and sailed her out into the Gulf of Mexico so that Bob could fish for tarpon while I sauteed crawfish in the galley for a drink-free dinner.

Our chief love was diving in the gin-clear water off Key West. Bob taught me how to handle a school of deadly barracuda inches away. He taught me to stay motionless, keeping my masked face towards them. They, being cowards, he said, would not strike if they could see all of me: that I was bigger than they.

One Sunday I tested his instructions. I was alone far out on the reef while Bob was off trying to spear a huge jewfish. All at once, immediately in front of me, was a barracuda. Remembering Bob's teaching I did no splashing. I stared at the predator. He looked at me, his powerful, submarine-shaped body momentarily still. I wanted to swim away from the threat of those daggerlike teeth, that snarling mouth. But I forced myself to keep my face squarely toward his. To my utter relief he turned tail and swam away.

These days when I was examining my life for its strengths and weaknesses, the experiences I had in the water took on a meaning for me quite beyond the actual adventure.

Staring down the barracuda was not the memorable lesson; it was his return from another direction moments later, when I didn't expect him. My character defects were like that. Once I thought that I'd erased them, they would came back on a higher level in a subtler form, to be dealt with all over again.

This world of the underwater, what did it say to me? Sealed from the problems of land, there was peace. Down under, I felt a oneness with the rhythm of the deep, with the waving sea fans. In this luminous seascape, I knew the first total silence of my life.

Yet, the time always came when I had to surface. Even then, amphibianlike, I carried some of the silence to the shore. I carried it inside me. And I carried the lessons I had learned, the knowledge that no matter how rough the waves on top, in the depths it was still and calm. In these Key West days I began a primitive kind of meditation, diving to my own center when the surface of my life roiled up.

On the return voyage of a long diving weekend at Dry Tortugas, Bob proposed marriage to me. Bright visions of our life together skipped before my eyes like the flying fish on our bow. But a cloud on the horizon had to be dispelled. For Bob, a career officer, the navy was everything. It would not be fair to marry him without his knowing my entire past. So I told him the whole story. I finished by saying, "I cared about the causes I supported during the war. And I cared about the people I worked with too. A few of them were undoubtedly Communists. But that's all past now, and it has been past for years." Still, I urged him to think seriously before marrying a woman whom the captain had called a "poor security risk." I also urged him to tell everything to his own commanding officer, so that if anything ever did come up about my past, his C.O. would be informed.

"Look Sue, my C.O. thinks you're wonderful. He knows the job you've done with me, that you've helped keep me sober for five months. The C.O. knows you saved my navy career."

Bob urged me to go back and apply for a new navy pass. It would be convenient to have one so I could come and pick him up at the base. Less than a year after my pass had been lifted, I was granted a brand-new one overnight. No explanation was offered, which made me think that Merriman Smith had been right about local political pressure. Or perhaps it was because there was a new C.O. at the base, an admiral. At any rate, it seemed that my troubles were over.

Bob and I went ahead with our plans for a wedding in January. We spent our nights and weekends getting the *Molly Lou* shipshape for our cruising honeymoon to Tarpon River. I moved out of my little garage apartment into a larger one on the second floor of an ancient, beautiful, white Key West house overlooking the sea. We wanted the apartment ready for us when we returned from the cruise.

Two days before the wedding, on the evening of January 14, 1953, I was getting dinner ready for Bob. I had just filed my last story at the *Citizen* and was looking forward to the moment when I would hear Bob's footsteps bounding up the outside stairs. He was late. I wandered around admiring our wedding presents: a shiny new clock barometer for the yacht, the new underwater camera, a huge volume on tropical fish. Then I walked to the closet and took out my wedding dress, not white, but a lovely periwinkle blue with hat to match. I moved the coffee table, straightened some lamps.

I began to worry. Bob was always navy-prompt. I was pouring myself a coffee when I heard him, but he was not taking the steps two at a time as usual. He walked in, his face ashen under its tan. His dark eyes were sunken, the pupils large.

"The admiral says we cannot be married!" he said hoarsely.

"What do you mean?"

"He says that I cannot marry a red like you, that you are a threat not only to my naval career but to the navy itself."

I stood rooted to the floor. "Bob, he's known for months that we were getting married. Why did he wait until two days before?"

"He claims he didn't know that we were serious until the news of the wedding appeared in the Miami *Herald*."

Bob sank down on the sofa. "Honey, I don't give a damn about him. I love you and if the navy doesn't like it, there are other ways to make a living."

"Perhaps so, but we can't let your career be wrecked because some unknown person is trying to destroy us. Let's get to the root of it."

Bob waved away the cup of coffee I had poured for him. "I know what I'm going to do, Sue. I'm flying tomorrow to Norfolk to see the head of the Naval District. I'm not letting some local admiral stop us. I'll fight this right on up to the Secretary of the Navy, even to the President, if I have to. I'm not going to give up our life together."

But in Washington this was inauguration week. I had no friends at court at all any more. President Truman was leaving the White House to make way for President Eisenhower. Joe Short who knew everything about me had died. There was absolutely no one in Washington to whom we could turn for help.

Bob kissed me and held me away to look at me. "I love you, and I'm going to marry you."

Bob flew out early the next morning. The hours dragged by until 10:30 that night when the phone finally rang.

"Honey!" Bob sounded urgent, "it's been hell. You have no idea. Norfolk, no dice, nothing to be gained here at all. I'm flying on to Washington first thing tomorrow. That's our only hope now, Washington."

"Bob," I shouted, "I could fly up to be with you!"

"Absolutely not. This is strictly navy business. Stay where you are. I'll be flying back tomorrow, I hope with good news. I'll call you and tell you which navy plane I catch a ride on. Pray if you can. We need prayers even though we've never prayed, Sue."

"Yes," I said. "Goodnight, Bob. I love you."

Next morning I went to Norman at the *Citizen* and told him that even though my honeymoon leave had begun, I wanted to work: I couldn't bear sitting around waiting for Bob's call. Even so the evening seemed to drag once I got back to our big new apartment. The phone rang. I snatched it up.

"This is a friend of Lieutenant Milford's. He's already airborne, flying to Key West. His plane will arrive at twenty-four hundred."

"How is he?"

The voice was guarded, "A bit tired."

I made myself a thermos of coffee and drove out to Boca Chica airfield at eleven, checked with controls, and waited.

Finally, the plane came in for a landing. I rushed out to greet Bob. He walked off the plane, spotlighted by the tower lights. His face looked dead white against his navy blues. One look at his eyes and I knew we had lost.

He kissed me, took my arm. "It's no good, Sue."

He got behind the wheel. "They said if I go ahead and marry you, I'll regret the day I ever joined the navy. They hinted at a court martial."

The white highway before us looked blurred and wavy. Bob grabbed my shoulder: "Drop your head and breathe, Sue." Then he went on. "They said that an officer in my classified position, marrying a woman with your record—they said they'd transfer me to some remote outpost where I would break down and go back on the bottle."

I straightened up in the seat. I suddenly realized, by his tone, by his expression, that Bob was more desperate than I. I wanted a drink more at this moment than I had wanted one in years. I knew this was the most dangerous moment we had yet faced.

"We have to get some sleep," I said. Alcoholics are not supposed to take sleeping pills, but this was an emergency. We drove to the local doctor's house. He was not in. We finally found him, out on call at the Casa Marina. He gave us six sleeping pills, all that I would accept.

Bob and I slowly mounted the stairs to the apartment. This was to have been our wedding night. Instead of newlyweds, we were like two departed spirits. I took one of the pills and sank into fitful unconsciousness, awaking at six with parched mouth and burning eyes, to see Bob dressed in his navy uniform drinking a cup of coffee.

"I'm going to see the admiral. I'm going to wring a special permission from him to marry."

"Anything, anything," I said.

"I'll call Norman and tell him you won't be coming in. You look awful, honey. Try and get some more rest. I'll be back in a couple of hours."

The bright sunny morning stretched out as I wandered around the apartment. I drank some coffee, smoked dozens of cigarettes. In my hoarse voice I mumbled words of an old song that ironically kept running through my head: "It's a Great Big Wonderful World."

At 11:00 A.M. Bob walked swiftly through the door, his face grim.

"The Admiral has ordered me to Japan. He's lifted me right out of Key West and transferred me to a base out there where no women are allowed. Do you hear me, Sue?"

I couldn't answer, I couldn't cry, I just sank down on the sofa.

"They can't order you out of Key West," Bob went on, "because you're a civilian. This is what they meant in Washington—they're banishing me instead."

I still could say nothing.

"They're saying all sorts of rotten things about you, not only about your politics. They asked me how do I know you're not a Communist? You've never made an official statement, they say."

He sat down beside me on the sofa. "There's just one thing, honey, that you can do, one thing that might save us. It might *even* stop my orders to Japan."

Hope rose fast, "What?"

"There was an FBI agent there with the admiral this morning. And he said, that to prove good faith, you should make a full statement to the FBI. He said he couldn't promise this would influence the navy, but it was a necessary first step. Go to the FBI." He put his arm around me. "Honey, it's our last chance."

"I simply couldn't do it," I groaned. "I couldn't live with myself, Bob, if I went to the FBI to repudiate all the work I did—"

"Who said anything about repudiation?" he asked.

"The very fact that you go to the FBI suggests that you did something wrong. I did nothing wrong. I worked hard on all those committees to help people, other human beings."

"It's our future versus your stubbornness. Honey, if you don't do this, you will always be suspect. Don't do it for me, but for us. Do it, Sue. Go up to Miami tomorrow and see the FBI."

For the next hour Bob argued, never letting up. Finally, he went out to get us some hamburgers. I flung myself down on the bed. Oh for a God, I cried out. Oh for something, some faith that would carry me through this nightmare. Oh for some way to know what is truly right.

Bob came back, balancing hamburgers and milkshakes. "You've decided to go to the FBI! I know you have!"

And then at last I burst into tears.

"Honey, I have to go to the base," Bob said. "I'll be back at four o'clock." Bob had pulled himself together, the navy officer in command. He left me with a kiss.

But at four he did not return. At six I went to the phone and called the base. A yeoman said he had left hours before after a surprise farewell party given him by his fellow officers.

Hours later I heard the screeching of brakes below. The door slammed open. Bloodshot eyes, tousled dark hair, Bob was drunk. Inside the door he stumbled and fell to floor. Out cold, he was too heavy for me to move him. I covered him with a blanket and put a pillow under his head.

In an hour or so, he pulled himself up and stumbled out in his rumpled clothes, down to his car. Too late I heard him gun it in the stillness of the night. I walked five blocks to wake Bernard, a recovered alcoholic friend. We drove about Key West looking for Bob and his car. We found him slumped over the wheel out by County Beach. I drove Bob's car home while Bernard took him along in his own. Bernard put Bob under the shower, slapped him conscious. Bob had to take the *Molly Lou* to Miami that rainy morning to sell her. And I had to drive to Miami to keep my promise about the FBI.

I couldn't blame Bob for drinking. After all, he'd had less than a year's sobriety. I, who had been seven years dry, knew all too well how precarious my own sobriety was at this moment. How I would have loved a martini to ease the anguish ahead.

I wept most of the way up the Overseas Highway, crossing its forty-two bridges, seeing through the windshield wipers the familiar channel where we had spent sunny days diving off the *Molly Lou*.

I drove in the rain-flooded streets to the FBI headquarters in Miami on Biscayne Boulevard. "Don't go!" everything within me said. I saw a neon-lighted bar. Did Miami bars serve liquor in the morning? I drove on. As I entered the office of the district director of the FBI the feeling of doom deepened.

I waited in a cell-like room for Eugene O'Brien, FBI security specialist. A pale man in a dark suit, O'Brien came in and lit a pipe as he sat down. I blurted out the story of the navy's ban on my marriage to Bob, and Bob's insistence that I make an official statement.

In his quiet voice, O'Brien asked me rather pointedly why Lieutenant Milford was not with me now. I told him that Bob would join us as soon as he docked the boat.

O'Brien apologized. They were short of help. He asked me if I would write my own statement. When the big typewriter was wheeled in, I began to feel faint. O'Brien sent for a cup of water. Then he handed me a sheet to sign declaring that I was making the statement voluntarily. He asked me whether I would be willing to testify in public court or hearing. I wrote a large "NO."

My life drained out of me into that typewriter. As the recounting of events went on, the physical energy drained out of me too. When I stopped, O'Brien simply sent out for coffee. Then I picked up the story of the navy's action, starting with the night the Major knocked on my door.

After a long while, the phone rang. O'Brien handed the phone to me. It was Bob asking me to drive over to the dock to pick him up. My spirits lifted. Bob was here. But the moment I saw him, I nearly wept. His dark eyes were red, vague, shifty. He had been drinking. He had not been able to pull himself out of his binge.

Back at FBI headquarters, Bob sat down and labored over my typed statement as O'Brien and I sat silent in the little room. Halfway through, Bob stopped. He frowned. O'Brien spoke quickly.

"Lieutenant Milford, you probably want to delete Miss Anthony's mention of your name and the marriage story, since this brings you into her statement. The statement will, as you know, be circulated in the navy. If you are implicated it will go on your official record."

I held my breath waiting for Bob's reply.

Bob looked out the window, he did not look at me; he dropped his eyes, then he looked at O'Brien, though talking to me.

"I know I told you, Sue, to put all this in about the navy and me. I was good and mad at the time. But I think Mr. O'Brien here has a point. Putting me in the statement needlessly brings me and my career into the picture. The main story is yours, not mine. I think Mr. O'Brien is right; it serves no purpose to tell my story here . . ." His voice trailed off into nothingness.

O'Brien looked at me with no expression. He had known this would happen, even before it happened.

O'Brien shook my hand. "You have done the right thing," he said. I think he really meant it. His voice went on but I was barely hearing. "No matter what happens in your life, or to your marriage, you have done the right thing."

With leaden legs I walked with Bob out onto bright, white Biscayne Boulevard. The rain had stopped. Bob was holding my hand, saying, "We'll find a way, Sue."

A few days later back in Key West, I drove Bob to the bus which would take him on the first leg of his trip to Japan, up the Keys to the airport in Miami. I waved goodbye as the bus pulled out.

Then I drove along Duval Street, past the old stone Anglican church, controlling a sudden impulse to go in and throw myself on my knees and ask mercy from a God in whom I didn't believe.

The lonely days began. For over a year Bob had been my daily companion. Now he was gone. I had promised him that I would date no one, knowing well that navy men, often long away, need this reassurance more than other men. I was busy. I had my newspaper work. I went out to alcoholics whenever they were in need. I scheduled regular visits to others, visits to an old man in a wheelchair; a young navy wife tied down with a new baby; a fat divorcee who lived in an expensive, hideous house, whose problem was boredom. I filled my off-time with trying to help these people, hoping that human contact would be enough. It wasn't. I wanted to reach for something beyond human relationships, but I didn't know how or what.

One empty night I took a crucial step. I was reading a book that had drawn my eyes at a bookshop the day we were at the FBI, a paperback anthology of the American psychologist-philosopher William James. In it I came across the example of a mountain climber who could neither reach the top of a mountain nor descend to the bottom. He was standing still, confronted by a yawning crevasse that looked too wide for him to jump.

Commenting about this, James said, "Often enough our faith beforehand in an uncertified result is the only thing that can make the result come true. . . ."

The mountain climber, James was saying, had two choices.

If he made the jump without faith that he could do it, he would fall; but if he believed he could do it, the adrenalin in his body would respond and carry through to his muscles and to his coordination, and he would leap safely to the other side.

"Believe, and again you shall be right, and you shall save yourself."

Was I like the mountain climber before the crevasse? I could refuse to believe that I could make the leap of faith. Or I could believe, and save myself. I could even pray as if I did believe. The theory interested me. But somehow I could not bring myself to pray. Then one day the thought came to me, "Why not *write* to God?"

Writing had always been my private voice, the way I expressed my innermost thoughts, whether in diaries or letters to friends or even on yellow scraps of paper when I was drunk. Now one evening I decided to write God, even though I did not believe God was a person. I believed only that there was some impersonal higher Power, a life force. Despite my disbelief I wrote to God *as though* He (or it) did exist. I wrote on the clipboard that had borne all my other writings for seven years. To my great surprise, It or He answered, not with a crashing experience, but with a tender, almost humorous experience in caring.

The first prayer I wrote was to save the life of a little one-eyed, tiger cat.

A raccoon had almost ripped the eye out of the cat's head. Badly infected, it had wandered into the yard of a friend of mine, Mary Hudgins, where I was spending the day. Mary may have sensed my need to get away from thoughts of Bob and naval orders. She asked me if I would take the animal to a veterinarian in Key West where it could be put to sleep. She placed the tiger in my car and said goodbye. As I drove home, he mewed pathetically, as though knowing the fate that awaited him. I realized I simply could not have him killed. Instead I would beg the vet to save his life.

But I had a problem. My slim newspaper paycheck had long since vanished on groceries and rent. How could I get a vet to look after Tiger if I had no money? So it was, driving homeward on the Overseas Highway, that I resolved I would write God. I would pray specifically for Tiger's cure and for the money

to pay the doctor. I carried him up to my apartment. Then I
sat down and wrote on my clipboard:

Dear God,
Please save this cat's life. Please let me have the faith to take him
to the vet's even though I don't have the money to pay the vet. I
accept that you can make all things happen if I have faith. Help
me in my lack of faith.

Then, wrapping the tiger cat in a towel with his poor eye
hanging on his cheek, I took him to the veterinarian. The vet,
who was no sentimentalist, was almost brusque as he allowed
that he'd see what he could do. On the way out the door, I
asked, as if an afterthought, "Oh, by the way, Doctor, what will
your fee be?"
The vet looked at me carefully.
"You say it's not your own cat? It's a stray?"
"Yes."
"Five dollars," he said and closed the door with a smart click.
I was amused at this nonsentimentalist. The fee was lower
than it would have been for a bona-fide pet.
Still, I had to find even that five dollars.
Next day I paid my weekly call on an old Key Wester, an
invalid who was house-bound. Andrew Brown and I always
chatted about Key West news and politics. Then it was our ritual
to have a dish of ice cream. On this day Brownie astonished me
by referring to his own personal life for the first time in our two-
year acquaintance. Andrew Brown's wife, much younger than he,
breezed by on her way out of the house to go shopping. The old
Key Wester's eyes followed her as she left, and for a brief second
those eyes seemed sad. Then, suddenly, his wife returned. She
had forgotten her shopping list.
It was then that the old man leaned over to me and said in a
jocular, between-you-and-me way, "I'd give five dollars to anyone who could get my wife to kiss me as she runs out. She never
does."
I blinked hard. It seemed like some sort of quiet, cosmic joke.
I wondered if God really had a sense of humor!
"I'll take you up on that," I said. At that moment his wife

swept by again. "Please," I called to her, "come win five dollars for me. I need it."

Mrs. Brown came back and I told her of her husband's offer. She gave a hearty laugh, leaned over and kissed Brownie resoundingly. He was delighted. Laughing even more, she pointed her finger at him.

"Now, Brownie, you be sure to give Susan that five dollars! Don't you dare weasel out of it, you old skinflint," and she sailed out of the high-ceilinged, old drawing room.

Brownie took the five dollars out of his pocket and handed it to me, still beaming. Full of strange, sudden confidence that my prayer for Tiger, too, was going to be answered, I rushed to the vet's to learn the fate of the cat. I waited nervously while other patients, dogs, cats, and even a monkey, were treated. Finally the vet came out, holding the cat. One eye was shut tight, the other greenly gazed at me.

"Well?" I said.

The vet fairly shoved Tiger at me. "I took his eye out to save his life," he said. "He'll be fine."

"Thank you! Thank you!" I paid him. Then hugging Tiger I shouted, "It works!" to the astonished veterinarian and carried my new pet to his new home.

"It works!" I said to myself over and over as I mounted the outdoor wooden stairs to my apartment, place the cat on the couch, and gave him milk and meat.

I loved the cat not only for himself and for his companionship, but because he was the ever present affirmation of my first answered prayer. Then one day I came home from the *Citizen*. My eyes were drawn to something just off the curb. I walked over and saw lying, utterly still, my beloved Tiger. A trickle of blood had dried on his fur. I picked him up, his one good eye sightless in death, his body stiff. I ran up the outside stairs to my apartment, now hatefully lonely, crying at the loss of my cat, symbolizing as it did for me the loss of so much else in my life.

Still sobbing I took my clipboard and wrote a second prayer:

Dear God, if there is a God, send me a friend, a real friend, a long-time, old friend to whom I can open my heart.

There wasn't much time. I had to rush to the airport to cover the arrival of the navy's "Mother of the Year." With my prayer still on my clipboard I walked forward to the plane to interview her. Descending the ramp was not only the navy's "Mother of the Year," but also my own spiritual mother, Rosalind Petry, my oldest recovered-alcoholic friend.

I could not believe in such a sudden answer to prayer, but there she was, my loved and long-time friend. As soon as I finished my coverage of the navy mother, I drove Rosalind to her motel, telling her excitedly that she was indeed the answer to my despairing prayer of only an hour before. Then began a fortnight of the sharing I had hungered for. I poured out all the things that had been happening to me, including the two prayers that I had written that had been answered.

"The time has come when you must really start practicing prayer all the time. You must pray," Rosalind insisted, "instead of simply talking about your problems. Pray with me now."

Right then and there in the restaurant, with her eyes open, she softly spoke a spontaneous prayer. I was much too self-conscious to pray out loud. But for the next ten days we had dinner together every night and she told me what prayer had done for her.

"Sobriety gave me back my life. Prayer to God taught me what to do with it."

I felt lonely when I saw her off at the plane. She was flying to visit a planter friend in Jamaica.

Then, in June I received a letter from Bob. The letter said quite simply:

Dear Susan,
I have met a lovely girl, a schoolteacher. She is unlike you, very simple. She is warm and very loving. Much as I hate to give up our plans for the life we wanted in the Keys, I must stay in Japan because she wants to continue her teaching here. We are to be married next Tuesday. I am sorry it had to end this way, but it is for the best. I hope you will some day find happiness.

Bob

P.S. Please send me the underwater pictures I took. I'd like to add them to my Japanese collection.

16 "... or what shall a man give in exchange for his soul?"

Rosalind Petry rescued me again.

When the meaning of Bob's letter sank in, I went right to Norman and asked if I could get away to recover. He took one look at my face. "Take a week," he said.

I flew to New York, to Rosalind and her familiar East Side apartment. I wanted to be close to her while I struggled to stay away from drinking. And this time I wanted to learn from her about prayer.

During the week I was with her, we talked for hours at a time. She gave me books to read. She took me to her church and introduced me to her minister. Later I had a conference with him in which he refused to let me feel sorry for myself about the things that had been happening to me.

When I left New York, I flew back to Key West loaded down with books on prayer and Scripture. I had absorbed the advice given me. I did not return to play the role of the jilted female. I was a forward-looking, prayer-supported woman. Now I couldn't find time enough for all the studying I wanted to do. I also set aside half an hour each morning for prayer—writing my prayers on my clipboard—a habit I continue to this day.

Rosalind had another therapy in mind for me, a new man. And she had a man in mind: Jack Lewis, whom she had visited recently in Jamaica. Again and again she urged me to fly over to see him—and I was tempted. Besides, I had always wanted to see Jamaica, the island on which my mother's family had lived for more than a century. At last, one day I flew to Montego Bay.

Jack and Jamaica hit me with the same impact. I was stunned first by the beauty of the island and then by the beauty of the tall, tanned man who came to greet me. He was wearing stiff-starched Indian army shorts, bright madras shirt. He was well-built and graceful, with a handsome head and marvelous legs. I had met enough men in my life to know when one appealed to me. He drove me up the steep, white, marl road, past green sugar-cane fields and bamboo trees. We arrived at his mother's mountaintop plantation, Antrim, in the sudden tropical dusk.

A year later I returned to Jamaica as his bride. On credit and crop potential, we bought Rose Hill, an ancient, neglected plantation three miles down the hill from his mother's. Jack made light of my observation that Rose Hill lacked a road, a kitchen, electricity, telephone, running water, and furniture.

"The crop's the thing," he said, his eyes glowing with pride at owning the three-hundred-acre farm. The crop was pimento and allspice. There were also cattle. "And besides, Sue, the roof is in good condition."

We moved in during the chaos of crop time, on Friday, the 13th of August. We were accompanied by masons, carpenters, cattlemen, and then pickers for the allspice crop, small berries with the flavor of cinnamon, nutmeg, and clove. Sometimes while scratching tick bites or yearning for a glass of iced coffee—there was no ice because there was no icebox—I would wonder what I had ever found romantic about the tropics. But if life at Rose Hill was strenuous, it was also wonderfully rewarding.

There were adventures too. The threat of Hurricane Hazel sent us to batten down and board up, rushing our limes to the still before they rotted. We made predawn journeys by Land Rover to recruit allspice pickers, driving five hours one way to back-a-bush villages never before visited by a white "Missus."

On the morning of the fifth-month anniversary of our marriage I set out on one of the duties of a planter's wife. The child of one of our pickers had to be taken to the hospital twenty miles away—and rain had made the roads almost impassable. Skidding and slipping in the jeep down the steep muddy trail I inched down the mountain through flood waters to the hospital in St. Ann's Bay. With the mute black mother, I waited in the fetid front room while the doctor examined the child. When he finally called us, he said wearily: "Mrs. Lewis, you will have to leave the child here. He is dying—something is blocking his nutrition. We'll do what we can, but I don't offer any hope."

The grieving mother and I drove back in a race against time before the torrential rain washed the road to her home completely away. Finally, with the rain still pouring down, I slipped and slid on our own steep cowpath to Rose Hill. Weak from lack of food, I put on coffee water, munched left-over fried ackee and roasted breadfruit, and ate avocado pear I picked off the tree by the house. Grieving for the dying child and the poor, bony mother with her huge terrified eyes, I let my eyes roam over the rainy hillside.

My eyes stopped. At our gate three hundred yards beneath me was something I was not sure I was seeing.

There was a man laboriously climbing the hill, up our steep, rain-washed drive. A raincoat protected his head and shoulders, but not his face. And his face was white. It was unheard-of in Jamaica for a white man to walk. White people drove or rode horseback.

I peered through the slackening rain as the man approached our house. At last puffing and panting he stood at the foot of our stone steps. I stepped out on the verandah.

Catching his breath, he wheezed, "Mrs. Susan B. Anthony Lewis?"

Why *Susan B. Anthony* Lewis? Why not Susan Lewis?

"Yes," I said. "Do come in out of the rain. You're an American!"

He walked onto the verandah and took out of his jacket a black wallet with a card showing through a gleaming transparent front. I peered at it in the fast falling dusk. It had an eagle on it.

"U.S. Department of Justice, Assistant Attorney General John Mahoney."

I stared in bewilderment at the bland, baby-blue eyes, the fresh pink face.

"May I fix you a drink?" was all I could find to say. At that moment Jack ran up the steps. He looked questioningly at the man.

"I'm John Mahoney, U.S. Assistant Attorney General," he held out his hand to Jack, who took it.

"Well, whoever you are, you're to be congratulated getting

up here on a day like this. Sorry you had to walk up the hill. We haven't had a chance to make a road yet, been too busy with the crop."

Mahoney relaxed into a wicker chair. "The driver said he couldn't make it up here in his cab. We want to talk to your wife about some people she knew once. We have no right to talk to you, Mr. Lewis, since you're a British subject."

"You have every right to talk to me if you want to," Jack said, sitting perched on the verandah railing. "My mother is an American. My great-grandfather on her side was one of the first graduates of West Point. Won't you have a drink?"

The assistant attorney general turned to me and asked in a low voice, "Do you want to talk in front of your husband?"

"Of course," I replied, "Jack knows everything about me." It seemed to me that my voice was unnaturally thin and high.

"Well," said Mahoney, settling back in the rocker, "waiting down at the foot of the hill in the cab is the American security agent for the Caribbean. I can't stay now because we're in this cab with some tourists who got off the plane at Montego Bay. We'll be back tomorrow, if we may.

"But why?" I asked. "Why will you back? What's the purpose of this?"

The blue eyes veiled as though a film had dropped over them. "I'd rather not say tonight, Mrs. Lewis. We just wanted to make very sure that you really were here. We'd like to come back and talk tomorrow morning."

"Come to lunch," Jack said in his host-planter's manner. "We'll be glad to have you and your friend both. And now we'll drive you down in the Land Rover, it's the only thing that can make the hill."

As we walked down the stone steps toward the Land Rover, it came to me that his visit might have something to do with my citizenship, since I was married to a British subject. "Is it my citizenship?" I asked him. "Is there some trouble with that?"

"You're still American!" Mahoney answered quickly. "You remain American unless you formally renounce your citizenship, or vote in a Jamaican election or bear arms for them." I wondered at the time how he knew so certainly.

We rode down past the white-trunked pimento trees, twisted by the trade winds in a westward dance. At the big black limousine Jack said cheerfully, "Honk your horn tomorrow and I'll come down for you."

"Oh, Jack," I cried as we drove back to the house "what irony that our first guests for a meal at Rose Hill would be the last people on earth I want to see."

"Sue, you're building this all up."

"But I'm not important enough to warrant top officials coming all the way over to the island. This has something to do with going to the FBI."

"Darling, you know I don't care about politics, left or right. The only thing that matters is you and me and Rose Hill."

But these keepers of my dossier had invaded Rose Hill. Next morning the sound of their horn hundreds of feet below shook me like a gunshot. Jack got out the Land Rover and brought back Mahoney and a sallow man with glasses, Norton Wilson, the American security officer for the Caribbean. He had flown over from Havana to meet Mahoney.

"I am here to represent the American government on British soil at this interview," said Wilson.

They sat down on the verandah and Mahoney turned to me. "Mrs. Lewis, you remember, of course, that you gave a voluntary statement to the FBI in 1953. A statement of your political activities in the past."

A deep flush warmed my face.

"Something has come up about a few people, people you must have known in those days in Washington. They were active when you were there."

"Active in what?"

"Some of them are under investigation," Mahoney went on, ignoring my question. He then mentioned names of people I had not even heard of in ten years, much less seen. They were people I had worked with in causes I cared deeply about; what they were "under investigation" for he was not free to disclose.

"I am going to ask you an important question, Mrs. Lewis." Mahoney paused and looked at Jack and me intently. "Will you, Mrs. Lewis, come back to Washington with us this afternoon to testify about these people?"

The sun went under clouds, the sea turned gray.

Names, names, names to go into a secret file somewhere—to be used in some secret way. I thought of how "they" had lifted my navy pass. I thought of the accusers one was never to see face-to-face. All at once I had the craving, empty feeling of wanting a drink.

I shuddered, answering in a low voice, "I have already told the FBI everything, although I believe now that that was a mistake. I could not possibly go to Washington." I walked to the railing. "I don't believe I could survive such a journey."

Jack was standing on his feet now too. No longer the graceful squire, he stood his full six feet with RAF stiffness.

"I must tell you that my wife has an extremely serious problem with alcohol. Such emotional stress would indeed endanger her very life. She could never stand it."

"It is your duty to give evidence when called upon," Mahoney said to me. "And we call upon you now."

The cook chose that moment to announce that lunch was ready. We broke off our tense exchange while we lunched. Mahoney asked polite questions about Jamaica farm life. "I could never stand this isolation," he said looking at me. "I don't see how you can either, Mrs. Lewis. You were always in the center of things in America."

"I find it—or at least I did find it a wonderful change until last evening, at five-thirty to be exact," I said.

After lunch Mahoney returned to the matter in hand. "I don't want you to give a final answer now, Mrs. Lewis. I want you and your husband to discuss this matter."

"Mr. Mahoney," I replied steadily, "I have spent eight years recovering from alcoholism. I don't intend to throw it away."

Jack returned after driving the men to their car. He put his arms around me.

"Mahoney says that if you don't come voluntarily, they will serve you with a subpoena."

The word stabbed like a knife. Even on our island we had read of the reputations blackened, the lives ruined simply by the threatened use of this weapon. For the next three weeks I lived in an agony of fear and apprehension.

The day came for Jack to make the six-hour drive to the south of the island to bring back the huge allspice fanner for our now-harvested crop. I had felt nausea and pounding in my ears since Mahoney's arrival and Jack wanted me to go with him so that I could stop off at Mandeville and see his doctor, Melville Clark.

I was just closing our suitcase for the journey when Jack entered the room with an envelope bearing the words "Department of Justice, Official Business, Return Receipt Requested." The letter was from Mahoney. It stated that a subpoena would be served upon me through the American consul "in the immediate future" unless I cabled now that I would come to Washington. I sank down on the bed. Jack brought me a coffee and said it was more imperative than ever that I get to Dr. Clark in Mandeville. "We must get moving," he said, knowing that this was the best thing for alcoholics in crisis.

Hours later we were sitting in Dr. Clark's office. He seemed worried, repeating over and over that I must get some rest. At last I broke down and told him why I was not able to sleep. "Go to America?" he said, surprised. "You're in no condition to go anywhere, my dear. You are in a very precarious state of health. You have practically no blood pressure. I am going to write a statement which you can send on to Washington. You certainly are unfit to go anywhere. I also think you should get legal advice immediately."

We did get legal advice, from the best attorney in Jamaica, Carlton Parker. He agreed that we ought to send Dr. Clark's certificate to Washington. We did, and waited impatiently several days until at last a brief cable came from Mahoney asking us to call him immediately in Washington. Carlton Parker, our lawyer, told Jack to cable Mahoney instructing him to communicate with Carlton in the future.

A week of ominous silence followed. I tried to concentrate on my writing. I couldn't. Between stomach upsets, waves of weakness, and tears, I was degenerating fast into a helpless, passive state.

After a particularly bad night I begged Jack to take me out of the isolation of Rose Hill. Jack, seeing my state of nerves, drove me to Mandeville for a visit with his father. There I began to feel almost like a normal woman. I went to the beauty parlor and had my hair done. We even had a night out, Jack and I, at Mandeville's little theater. It was between acts that Dr. Clark came over and said quietly that he'd like to see me in his office early the next morning.

He came out to us the moment we entered his office. "A man named Schmidt from the American Department of Justice flew into Montego Bay last night. He called me during the play to say the Department will not honor my medical certificate. He tried to talk me out of the certificate on the phone. He is looking for you now to serve you with the subpoena. I'd better warn you that Schmidt is an unpleasant character. He said he would not leave the island until he has served you. I think you had better call Carlton right away, and also you'd better get a medical certificate too before you are served."

If the man was looking for me in Mandeville, the best place for me was back at Rose Hill. But as we reached the sanctuary of our farm, Matty, our headman, rushed up to us: "Two men them just now here in green pick-up car. Them ask for Miss Sue. Cook took them to the verandah and gave them a limeade—them Americans, but them not tourists them. Them say they be down the hill at Eaton Hall Hotel waiting 'pon you."

"I don't want them to see you, Sue," Jack said as we got back in the car, "not until we have reached Carlton and have Dr. Mayhew's new certificate."

The back road was washed away. So we had to take a chance on a dash for it over the main highway. But they were waiting for us. A green station wagon moved from its hiding place under some palm trees as we reached the highway. They started after us. Jack, his eyes gleaming with the chase, put his foot flat out on the accelerator until the Rover reached ninety on the narrow tarmac road. We lost them and made it to St. Ann's Bay where we parked in a side street and went to find Dr. Mayhew. He examined me and with no hesitation at all wrote out a certificate stating "Mrs. Lewis is unfit to stand any physical or mental strain. This, in my opinion, would include giving evidence in court."

We now rushed with the new certificate to find Carlton at a garden party. We barged right in with our travel-soiled clothes and told him of the arrival of the two agents. I must not—definitely not—be served a subpoena, he said, until he was present, next morning in his office. He warned Jack that they must be kept from dropping a subpoena at my feet.

We were new in the role of fugitives, pursued by the law. It was silly of us to go back to Rose Hill, but we did.

As soon as we mounted our newly cut dirt driveway, Jack spotted the freshly made tire marks, yet he kept on going. Standing in front of the steps were two men, one tall and one shorter, both in tie and jacket. The tall man was holding a folded white paper. Jack drove around to the door leading to the basement. I leaped out of the car and ran across three feet of lawn into the house just as the tall man reached me. But Jack was out of the car gripping the man's arm.

"We've got to speak to Mrs. Lewis!" the man said.

I ran upstairs to our bedroom and locked the door. I heard angry voices below, then the screech of car tires and the roar of an engine going down the hill.

The next morning early we drove the ten miles to St. Ann's Bay. When the two men arrived, we all five crowded into Carlton's small, inner office. Schmidt identified himself. Black, who was an American consul, remained silent. Schmidt, in his nasal accent, began hammering at us about why I should return to Washington immediately. Carlton stated mildly that I was medically unfit to go anywhere. He also said that if they would like to confer about my medical condition with Dr. Mayhew, he was home nearby at that very minute.

Schmidt ignored Carlton and turned to me.

"We'll get you to Washington yet, Susan B. Anthony Lewis."

It was as though he had rung a bell, sounded a familiar alarm. At that moment I saw everything clearly. Sitting there in Carlton's office I understood at last what was happening. *"Susan B. Anthony* Lewis." *I* wasn't the one they wanted on the stand in Washington. *I* could tell them nothing they didn't know already. It was—how long would the tragi-comedy continue to be played? —it was my name again. They wanted the news value of having Susan B. Anthony on the witness stand. As a newspaper person myself I appreciated the strategy, but they must be scraping the barrel for names and publicity.

Schmidt's insistent voice interrupted me.

"If Mrs. Lewis will not come voluntarily, not only will we subpoena her, but we will invoke the extradition agreement with Britain."

Jack reached his arm out protectively. "We'll also see to it that Mr. Lewis, who has been so uncooperative, is never allowed in America again. We will lift his re-entry permit."

Jack stood up, flashing with anger. The heated discussion moved further away from me as I looked in a daze out the window at the slow-moving Jamaicans with market baskets piled on their heads.

When they had gone Jack led me out to the car. "They're angry, Sue. They don't like being thwarted. I think they mean to break us up, to deport you out of Jamaica—to bar me from America. First Mahoney and Wilson, now Schmidt and Black—next the weight of Empire. But they will not do it." He took a revolver out of his shirt. "I've had this with me all morning. They may mean business, but I mean business too. They will not take you away!"

Jack was cracking. The weeks of strain had been too much. I had been leaning on him so hard, so fearful that my own state would lead to a drink, I had not seen how desperate he too was getting. I talked fast.

"We'll get help from America. Legal help. And we'll pray, Jack! We'll pray that this nightmare will pass." I began praying out loud, mixing Psalms and Daniel in the lion's den; and every prayer in distress that tumbled out my lips.

We made it to Kingston despite Jack's reckless driving. After hours of frustrated shouting on the always poor line from Jamaica to America, we reached Rosalind. She gave us a lawyer friend's number to call. We didn't reach him till late next day. The voice of Sam Phillips wavered thinly over the undersea cable from New York. Jack bellowed out the story of the threat to deport me, then handed me the phone.

"Susan," I heard Sam say faintly, "have you become a British subject yet? I should think you would want to have the same citizenship as your husband. I should think that would be the very first thing you would do."

"Become a British subject?" Give up my roots in America? Give up the family tradition, how could I?

Jack drove me for a milkshake, one of the first thoughts when an alcoholic's in trouble. "It's the way, the only one I can think of Sue."

"I can't do it. I simply can't do it," I cried. Why was I once more being told I must do something that was abhorrent to me.

The next three days were a total blur. I was limp, fainting, crying, sitting passively in the car while Jack raced us back and forth across the island with papers applying for British citizenship; to Carlton's North Coast office, back to Kingston three hours away.

There in the garden of a hotel, a justice of the peace told me to raise my right hand and say aloud the crucial words:

"I Susan Brownell Anthony Lewis, swear by Almighty God that I will be faithful to bear true allegiance to Her Majesty Queen Elizabeth II, her heirs and successors according to law."

I was still weeping as we took the papers to the colonial secretary; he said they would go to King's House for the governor's signature by next courier.

The next morning was the day I was to receive the subpoena. It was "Christmas weather" bright and sunny. Jack drove me to Carlton's office and we walked into the waiting room. There stood three men, not two. The two American agents, plus a khaki-uniformed British police officer. In a voice hoarse and unsteady, Black, the American consul, began to read from the subpoena ordering me to appear in Washington five days from then. I didn't hear much of it.

All I remember is someone holding smelling salts to my nose hours later as I lay on a sofa in Carlton's waiting room. He was wording the brief on why I couldn't comply. He roused me from time to time to ask me questions of fact. At four o'clock he took my arm gently and said, "Sue, do you realize that you are a British subject? You cannot be deported from Jamaica now or ever."

I blinked up at him, trying to focus his face through the haze around me. "The governor's secretary called," Carlton continued: "She said that H.E. signed your application as soon as it went to King's House. It took effect one minute after midnight this morning. You were a British-protected subject at the time you were served with the subpoena. They cannot deport their own subject. Extradition does not apply. But you must face the fact that you can never go home again—you can't go back to the United States even to visit your family, unless you comply with the subpoena and testify. You would be arrested for contempt the moment you put foot in America."

Our first Christmas at Rose Hill was a shambles. Despite the traditional gift-giving to our staff, the mounds of food and flowing rum, a pall hung over the day. Jack and I were like two soldiers with battle fatigue. I had taken it out in an exhausted depression. He had taken it out in rudeness to the people around us and violent outbursts of temper. Jack, who had stood by me so magnificently for these two long months, now—once the need for protectiveness was over—turned bitter and hostile. He had been so valiant in war; his partisanship could not survive the peace.

Nor could our marriage, although we did not yet know it. The strain we had been through dealt a deep wound to the new marriage. Soon I could not sit at home and write. His moods were so violent that they permeated my work room from the moment he put his foot on the step. I knew that to save my own sobriety, I had to get out of Rose Hill and work, work with people, turn outward. I took a job at the craft I knew best, reporting. In February 1955 I became the North Coast correspondent for the Jamaica *Daily Gleaner,* and later for the Associated Press.

My assignments were celebrities and disasters. I interviewed everyone from Marilyn Monroe to Groucho Marx, Princess Margaret to John F. Kennedy. I wrote of my love for the island and its gentle black farmers, cattlemen, and musicians. My love for Jamaica helped me blot out the feeling of separation from my own country which underlay every hour of the day.

And then even my reporting seemed to boomerang against me. The news became a horrible series of disasters. First, a railroad wreck killing two hundred and injuring seven hundred; then death by fire of a score of our Runaway Bay friends when a tanker truck exploded. The shock of arriving minutes after these and other tragedies weakened my resistance until I took to bed with pneumonia.

I lay convalescing in the old kitchen building, now converted into a bedroom-study, staring at the bright allspice wood fire that warmed the room against the February norther. Where was the peace I had sought in the years since sobering up?

Back in college I had almost failed biology because I didn't know one truth. I spent a year in the laboratory nearly smothered by formaldehyde, confused by ugly little creatures, protozoa, frogs, crawfish, all disparate trifles in a maze of microscopes, slides, and tweezers. I didn't know that these creatures had any relationship to one another. Monday, I peered at an amoeba;

Wednesday, at a protozoa; Friday, at a frog. I never glimpsed biology as the fabulous progression of living matter it is, moving from the simplest of cells to the complex organism we call man. Now it came to me as I lay looking up at the cathedral-like ceiling of the cottage blackened by the cookfires of two hundred years, that there just might be a similar progression in the growth of the soul. Perhaps the events, the mistakes, the disasters of my life were not unrelated episodes, but part of a pattern the end of which had not yet appeared.

Languidly I picked up a book I had bought two years earlier but had left unread. It was by Evelyn Underhill and it was called *Mysticism*. I started to read. I have never really stopped reading it since. For in the second half of the book there was spread before me the carefully documented evolution of the life of the spirit. She called it the mystic way.

Evelyn Underhill said that the evolution begins with a spiritual awakening to a Higher Power called God. This first stage I knew. The evolution moves on to what she called the purgative stage, a stripping and cleansing of the self. This too I had experienced, especially in these last Jamaica years. Beyond that, she wrote, comes the illuminative state. By reading deeper I began to see that I had at least tasted illuminations. Sitting there in bed I remembered what I called "Glimpses of God." I took out my clipboard and began jotting them down, reaching back into that long-buried memory of a childhood Christmas Eve when I saw a divinely beautiful face at the window at Raubsville. Excitedly I added others: the melting snow erasing my footsteps; the crystal-line moments of silence and calm underwater; the message on the yellow sheet of paper written when I was no longer in control. All these might be what Evelyn meant. But I knew from what I read that I certainly had not arrived at the exalted state she described as illuminative. That state contains more than mere glimpses of God. That state is permeated by the presence of God twenty-four hours a day. Few, she said, venture further than this state chiefly because few are willing to endure the next stage, the dark night of the soul, the final death of all self-will. But only the death of self-will in total surrender would bring one to union with God, the final goal.

I began to pray that God would lead me, would fuse the sporadic glimpses of Him into the illuminative state, and then take me by whatever means, by whatever surrender, was necessary into that ultimate relationship.

He answered in the last way my will would have chosen. He answered by using Jack as the instrument. Our marriage, which had been disintegrating since its early wound during the subpoena crisis, reached its end when he ordered me out of Rose Hill. I stayed with friends. It was a time of ordeal, for this was not only the total break-up of my marriage but of a whole way of living. Yet I stayed away from a drink, I stayed sane because somehow I sensed that how I reacted now would make or break me for the rest of my life. In some way I knew this experience was related to Evelyn Underhill's evolution of the spirit.

In the air-conditioned booth of a music shop in Kingston where I had gone to buy a record for the lady in whose home I was staying, I realized I must go even further. I must surrender, here and now, my own will to God. Suddenly I saw that the roadblock delaying my spiritual journey all these years had been *me*, my will, my refrain, "I want what I want when I want it." I knew that I must let go of everything. I had been struggling too hard and too long, I must totally let go of the marriage, of everything on the beloved island, and even the island itself. I would devote the coming months wholly to God to learn His will for me. I would stop the futile fighting for my marriage and my life here. I would go to America, accepting the invitation to speak in California on alcoholism that had been offered. That was a lead to follow. Perhaps out of it would come direction for a new life, directed not by me, but by God.

A few weeks later I risked going up to Rose Hill to say good-bye to my animals. My little foal came up to be nuzzled and followed me into the kitchen as I walked through it for the last time. Her dam, Cayo Hueso, neighed in the paddock, lonely in the rainy day. I walked upstairs to the drawing room and dining room. I shook hands with the headman and cattlemen. I got into the car and drove down Rose Hill common, down the steep red dirt and marl road, past the green allspice trees glistening in the rain. My foal followed the car down the hill. I tore my eyes from the green, green hillside, and drove slowly through Rose Hill gate, out into a world created not by will, but by God's will.

17 *"I have been crucified with Christ; it is no longer I who live, but Christ who lives in me . . ."*

I traveled light. I started my spiritual sabbatical stripped of marriage, property, even citizenship in the land of my birth.

In mid-June I entered the United States at Miami, on a British passport. As a visitor on a tourist visa expiring in three months, I knew I could not work for pay during my stay—and the money I had scraped together for the trip was limited. Yet instead of being apprehensive I was filled with a strange expectation. The speech in California was the only specific objective of the trip. But there were dozens of places I wanted to go, hundreds of people I wanted to see. By now, the chain of alcoholics who had received and were now giving help, stretched across the country. In towns everywhere there were meetings and prayer groups I wanted to visit. Exactly where I was to go, whom I was to see, where I was to stay, I did not know. I knew only that I wanted to be told as I went along.

As I flew from Miami it occurred to me that just as the jet's captain was piloting the plane to Los Angeles, so there was an invisible leader piloting me to a destination. For weeks my mind had been stirring with new thoughts and phrases, some of which were meaningful, some I did not understand at all. Now a line from Shakespeare kept running through my head, "Journeys end in lovers meeting." In some way it seemed to apply to me—yet what lover could I be heading toward!

In Long Beach, California, I delivered the scheduled talk on

alcoholism. And then I started moving about, accepting invitations for a night in Alahambra, a weekend in Monterey. I never
moved aimlessly, always with a set purpose for a set day, but
never much beyond that day. Without meaning to do it, I followed the route of Father Junipero Serra, the eighteenth-century
Franciscan who founded the missions along the California coast. I
followed the skein from San Diego to San Luis Rey, Capistrano,
Carmel, on north to San Francisco, sensing each time I entered
the cool dark sanctuary how saturated it was with prayer.

Still with the sense of being led by something bigger than I
knew, I continued my strange journey unconcerned about my
dwindling funds. San Francisco, Denver, Las Vegas, the Grand
Canyon . . .

The Grand Canyon was my first "nonspiritual" visit. No
prayer group, no recovered alcoholics had invited me; I went
strictly as a tourist. But there, at last, it seemed as though the
real purpose of my journey would be realized.

There in the time before dawn, I walked along the rim of the
greatest crevasse in the world. I watched the other tourists, their
faces like flowers, as they gazed at the vast splendor before us.
These were human beings as human beings should be, I thought,
rapt as I was in praising the mystery of creation, and the creation of mystery. I walked on to a remote ledge jutting out over
the drop to the canyon bottom and there in the cold air waited
for the light to break through. And as I watched I realized that
just as the peaks were waiting for the sun to give them form
and shape, I, too, was waiting for a breakthrough. The faces I
had just passed flashed before me again. Why couldn't they and
I maintain this contemplative wonder, this love affair with life,
not just on holiday before some great spectacle, but every day
of the year? Why couldn't we all make a breakthrough from
what we were to what we were meant to be; a breakthrough
that would unify our souls and make us whole—all of us—the
panic-ridden, drug-addicted, booze-addicted, television-addicted,
bored, lonely, cancer-fearing mortals of our time?

But how? What was the way? What—or who—could transcend
our split and divided souls? I only knew what had happened to
me, that I had been saved from death when I had admitted my
powerlessness and called upon a Higher Power for Its help. And
since the day of the very first answered prayer for the one-eyed

cat, I had tried to lead a life based on daily communion with this Power. There had been further answers too, for others and for myself. But standing before that great divide, I knew that I had somehow missed the heart of it. . . .

But now it was early September, My three-month visa would expire soon. I did not want to go back to Jamaica and risk losing the peace of mind I had been approaching. I did not want to leave America. The elusive spiritual goal I had come to attain had not been reached. Yet I felt I was close to it, very close.

I flew to Washington for advice on my citizenship status. With one day to go before my visa expired, an extension of another three months was granted.

Two days later in New York, my mentor Rosalind sent me to a friend of hers, the writer Adela Rogers St. John, for advice on how to communicate my thoughts on Breakthrough. Sitting with her in her hotel suite, I told her my hope that I could set up a pilot project for men and women with problems. They would practice the stages that had given me sobriety and a glimpse of the spiritual dimension to life. I wanted to test my hypothesis that Breakthrough, as I called these steps, worked for all people in need, not just for alcoholics like myself.

Adela became excited by the idea. But she said the east was not the place to launch the project.

"Go west, Susan," she urged. She had friends in San Diego who would help—San Diego would be the perfect place to begin—her friends might even help finance the project.

Go west—I had just been west. What madness to retrace my journey, I thought as I meditated in Central Park after our talk. But then, nothing, not a thing, really kept me east. . . .

On the eve of my departure, there was a plane crash in Boston, a bad one. In an instant the horror of the three air disasters I had covered as a newspaperwoman came rushing back. I watched the television reports and several times started to telephone to cancel.

Instead I went out to Idlewild the next day. It was like a morgue, as an airport is when one of its own has gone down. Again doubt gnawed at me. What was I doing going to California anyhow? I had no real prospects, only a letter to Adela's friend.

In fact, at forty-four all I really had was my sobriety, two small suitcases of clothing, my typewriter, and my ever present, green net bookbag. Once on board the plane, I took out two new books a contemplative friend had given me.

I started to read *Self-Abandonment to Divine Providence* by an eighteenth-century monk, Father J. P. de Caussade. His message couldn't have been more tailor-made.

Surrender this moment, Live in the sacrament of the present moment. It is not necessary or possible for everyone, he said, to make a total surrender of his entire life. *Simply surrender this present moment.* I had never been able to make a total, unconditional surrender to the Power I knew existed. That Power had been too vague in my mind. One minute I would surrender. Five minutes later I would start running the show again. For fourteen years I had wanted to surrender, but when I prayed for it, as earnestly as I could, I would fail. To surrender one has to trust. What I was asking myself to trust was too vast, too vague, too incomprehensible.

Now on the plane I started to practice moment-by-moment surrender. Everytime I started to tense as the aircraft bounced or changed its engine sound, everytime I started to worry about the void to which I was flying, I practiced surrender of the moment to God. That moment I could handle and, after all, that moment was all I had.

Later, when I finally opened my other book, *The Way of a Pilgrim,* I was disappointed. In this famous book by an anonymous nineteenth-century Russian holy man, I ran quickly into a stumbling block. His spiritual secret had been to pray ceaselessly, over and over, twenty-four hours a day:

"Lord Jesus Christ, have mercy on me."

That statement alone was enough to make me put the book aside. Since 1946 I had come a long way on my own pilgrimage, but that certainly did not include calling Jesus Christ, God. I did believe that he was the greatest man who ever lived. But my God had never worn flesh and blood, It was an infinite life force, a life force that worked in all men, not just in Jesus. I put the anonymous monk down and went back to Father de Caussade.

From Los Angeles, to stretch my few remaining dollars, I took the bus to San Diego. Financially I was at this moment in worse condition than I had been at any time in my life, even when I hit bottom in alcoholism. Miserable and broke as I had been then, I would never have stooped to stay where I checked in now. I awoke next morning in the one place I had always sworn dawn would never find me, the Young Women's Christian Association.

I looked around at the little room. It was as bare as a nun's cell and the dim light of the twenty-five-watt bulb did not brighten things. There was a single bed with a brown metal frame, one brown chair, a small chest of brown metal drawers, and a curtainless window through which I could see a dark rain falling. The institutional tan walls bore one picture, that of Jesus Christ.

Is this journey's end for me, a dollar-a-night room at the Y? Journeys end in lovers meeting? This is no lovers' meeting place, this chaste, all-woman atmosphere of the YWCA. From my room on the fourth floor, I looked down at the rain-swept streets. I felt the chill of the rain, the chill of the antiseptic room. Why had I come so far to be so alone? I had blood relatives in the east who could have provided at least a kinship warmth. That was what I needed more than the exalted spiritual fellowship I had sought all summer.

One second I was standing at the window watching the rain. In another second I was crying. I was standing at the window, sobbing, overwhelmed by sorrow. I was thinking of my mother, of the time during those tenuous first days of sobriety when I had hurt her, cut her bluntly off from me on the grounds that her constant concern might send me back to the bottle. For that long-buried cruelty of mine, I suddenly felt contrition. Not remorse, not the remorse of my drinking days when I would be sorry but know all the while that I would drink again. I felt true contrition, a deep decisive sorrow for having wronged her.

I crossed the room for the typewriter. I took off its cover and put the machine on the bed. I sat down and wrote a letter to my mother, begging for her forgiveness. I typed out the envelope, placed the letter in it.

And as I sealed it, the forgiveness came. I knew I was forgiven. I knew that I was forgiven by my mother. Then as I sat there, I was forgiven by another Person, the Person of Jesus Christ. In that split and blinding second I knew that Jesus was

*not just a man, He was God. I stood up, trembling and confused.
I went to the window. I turned. And He was there:*

"I am God. Before Abraham was, I am."

*He held out His arms, "Come unto me, and I will give you
rest."*

I answered as I surrendered to Him, "Yes, Lord, yes."

*The greatest of all experiences had happened to me. And it
had happened so simply.*

And now as I looked around the little room it no longer
seemed drab, nor did my few possessions seem meager. I drew
out of the green bookbag the Bible Aunt Nell had given me so
long ago. I hugged it to me, for this book contained His word,
His life. The typewriter on which I had written the crucial
letter leading to His forgiveness seemed to shine, drawing me
to it as the only way I knew of expressing the exaltation I felt.
I sat down and wrote and wrote, words of praise, of joy, repeating, "Jesus is God! Jesus is God!"

This then was the lovers meeting at journeys end. He then was
the invisible leader who had been calling me all this time. Human
lovers I had had. I knew the excitement, the rush of joy when
meeting them. Human lovers I had embraced and with them
breathlessly traced each minute that had led to our encounter.
Together we had checked the places and times we might have
met before we did.

Now the words poured out as I traced in my life this greatest
of all relationships. For this Lover had been in every milestone
of the journey. He did not go in and out of my life as did
human lovers. He was there all the time. He had been there in
that first vision of Him at Raubsville when I nearly recognized
Him. He had been there when as a half-blind girl I began my
first concern for the little ones through the inspiration of Johnny
Danton. He had been there when I made my bed in hell at the
bottom of my alcoholism. Then He had called me through that
yellow scrap of paper.

And now in having Him I had everything and needed nothing.
In belonging to Him, I belonged to His world. His viewpoint
brought order out of the seeming chaos of my life. For now I
knew that His viewpoint, the viewpoint of God, was that everything in our lives is a spiraling journey away from Him and

toward Him. Had I opened the door to His knocks, this meeting could have happened sooner, but the good news was that it had happened now, today, October 7, 1960.

I put on my raincoat, picked up the letter to Mother and left the little room. In quiet joy I walked out into the rain, out onto the sidewalk of a new world. I mailed the letter, then realizing I had had no breakfast, I stopped in at a drugstore. Crackers and coffee were all I felt I could afford. I sat at the counter enjoying the proximity of people. I enjoyed my chat with the friendly clerk as I took out my purse and paid the twenty-cent check. Money seemed suddenly a tremendous irrelevancy. As insecure as my outer world was, my inner world was inexplicably, unaccountably, unalterably safe. For the first time in my life I felt absolutely secure.

Out in the wet streets again, I wandered down to the Coronado Island Ferry. Impulsively, I went aboard.

Standing on deck near me were a young couple, his arm holding her close as they leaned on the rail. They seemed as oblivious of the rain as I. Nor did they shrink at the blast of the foghorn as the ferry pulled away from the dock. They were detached from everyone, everything, but each other. Nothing else existed. I wanted to say to them, "Enjoy your love, seal it in your heart and mind." They knew that human passion was beautiful. But did they also know that it was fragile, that it could be transient, subject to the ills of the flesh, tensions, separations, death itself?

I was happy for them, I was sad for them. I was sorry they didn't know *my* happiness. At last this day I had a Love who was stronger than the worst the world and my own folly could do. My Lord loved me unconditionally, regardless of what I was, what I did. And this love, unlike the human kind, cast out fear.

The ferry docked. I wished the young lovers well and we filed onto the misty island. I strolled along the ocean shore, circling the big white mass of the old hotel shining through the dim day, past sailors and official navy cars, a station wagon with a young mother, her hair in curlers, the children clambering on the seats.

On the green lawn of the Coronado Hotel, I saw a woman munching a candy bar, stuffing the paper wrapper in the pocket of her transparent raincoat. She was very fat. My heart ached for her. She made me think of my battle with fat as a child and the blow when Joel had called me "Fatty." I wanted to tell this woman how much God—how much Jesus—loved her.

Of course, I thought, as I walked on, she could diet, she could discipline herself, she could take herself in hand without this glorious knowledge—as I had starved myself for ten long years. We all have the ascetic drive within us; William James called it the "moral equivalent of war." He said that men have marched willingly to die in battle, undergoing incredible pain and suffering for some cause larger than themselves. I had proved that even I, even for the "high cause" of popularity, had will power to spare. Why hadn't it been enough to save me? Why had it not been enough to carry me through? Because, when put to crucial test, no human power was enough.

"Not by might, nor by power, but by my Spirit, says the Lord of Hosts."

Human power fails because there is only one Power transcendent enough to reconcile all the parts of man, his body, his mind, his spirit. In my own life I had permitted one drive to cancel out another. I had shaped my body with diet and exercise only to tear it down with alcohol. I had developed my mind with study and regimentation only to let the clamoring of my body in illicit sex and duplicity cloud it. As for spirit, I was offered the Holy Spirit, as all of us are, but again and again I rejected Him in favor of ghosts of my own making.

Aunt Susan was such a ghost. I had allowed myself to manufacture her out of my own needs and inadequacies. I tried to live up to her and tried to live her down. And when I could not measure up successfully, I let her take the blame. What the real woman may have been, I hope someday to know. But when Jesus comes, ghosts dissolve. He casts them out as He fills us with the Holy Ghost.

I was stopped suddenly in my walk by a Naval Station sign: NO ADMISSION. Without warning a surge of fear and hate swept over me. I was standing again outside the Key West installation—so like this one—my clearance revoked, my motives, my good name, my very loyalty in question. As I turned and fled from the hateful sign, self-pity and resentment began to poison the exalted day. The faces of the men who had hurt me passed before my eyes: the marine major, the navy admiral, the FBI agents, the assistant attorney general . . .

I stopped again. What was I thinking of? My conversion to Jesus Christ was only a few hours old. How could I claim to love Jesus, if I hated my brothers? For the terrible truth was that my brothers included these men, every single one of them. Jesus specifically commanded: "Love your enemies and pray for those who persecute you . . . ."

But, I argued, how could I possibly love those who had persecuted me for nine years? The answer came instantly. "You do not have to love what they do, or even to *like* them, you must only love them for themselves, forgiving them their trespasses against you, as I have forgiven you your trespasses against Me— your cruelty to your mother, your tearing down of your body, your adultery, your denial of Me since I first appeared to you when you were a child of eight."

And then there came to mind the most selfish sin of all, my running scared to the FBI, to save, as I thought, my marriage to Bob, at the cost of my integrity. If I wanted Jesus to forgive me that trespass, I must pay the price of forgiving these others. They shared with me the universality of our human condition, the solidarity of sin. I must be able to feel a kinship of mortality with each of these men, seeing that he, like me, knows the shadow of his certain death hovering over him. Indeed, to be free in Christ I must do more than forgive, I must pray for God's highest blessings on these people, looking upon them as the instruments God permitted to strip me down.

Into mind floated a strange little verse:

> The more the world takes from me
> The more will I produce for Thee.

Producing for Him meant not merely working for my private salvation or sanctity, it meant creating, bearing children of the spirit. It meant giving myself unconditionally, indiscriminately wherever there was a need I could meet. I could only keep what I had been given by giving it away.

The crucial day was ending as I returned to the dock. The sudden southern night descended on our ferry boat. It plied through the fast-falling dusk even as I knew I would have to ply my way through that other, universal dusk of an unknown future. But as the lights of the city drew us onward, so the light of Christ would illumine the remainder of my voyage, no matter what the darkness. And I might reach the mainland shore, the home port all Christians are meant to reach. Today's meeting with my Lord was not my journey's end. It marked only the entry, through the narrow channel of Grace, to the high sea whose far shore is union with the Beloved, so that ". . . It is no longer I who live, but Christ who lives in me."

I disembarked and went through the lights of the city streets to the Y, and took the elevator up to the fourth floor. Unlocking my door I felt a flicker of the old creature return. It said I must be practical; what would I do now, stripped of money, of nationality, of status?

But even as I entered the little upper room, He was with me. And so I simply asked Him: "Lord, what will You have me do?"

After

Catherine Marshall Writes...

This story has a happy ending. When I first met Susan B. Anthony, Ph.D., she was in imminent danger of being deported from the United States, thus becoming a woman without a country.

When I uncovered the fact that her citizenship plight in 1968–69 stemmed all the way back to the McCarthy era, I was appalled. Of course I had watched the McCarthy hearings at close range, since I was at that time living in Washington. But this was twenty years later. Could the roots of McCarthyism actually have survived so long to shoot up the poisonous plant of political persecution for someone like my friend Susan? At first it was difficult for me to believe such a thing possible in the United States of America. But finally I had to believe it because there the facts were before me: officials from the Immigration Department might knock on her door at any moment to escort her to a plane for deportation.

At that point I, who am no female militant, almost became one. I vowed personally to take Susan B. Anthony's fight for United States citizenship all the way to the President of the United States if necessary—or the Supreme Court or whatever.

That did not prove necessary, for first a group of Susan's Christian friends—Protestant and Catholic—decided to roll out the big guns of prayer. At our instigation, Susan sent out a letter

220

to several hundred of her friends asking for an Interfaith Prayer Vigil. The object? That she not be deported and that she be allowed American citizenship. Those receiving letters included editors, publishers, writers, professors, college presidents, archbishops, superiors of seminaries—just plain friends. In the end, there were about five thousand, all of whom knew Susan or had had some connection with her through the years. The letter had gone out April 14–16, 1969. The Prayer Vigil lasted for eight weeks.

On June 26, 1969, at 12:01 P.M. Susan got the news via a phone call from her lawyer in West Palm Beach, Florida: the Immigration Board in Washington had reached a final verdict— Susan B. Anthony had never lost her United States citizenship. She was a citizen. She is a citizen. She could not and cannot be deported.

Irony of ironies. One department of government working against another department of government with the citizen caught in the middle. I wanted to shriek to my friend, "You mean nine years of litigation, of traumatic legal efforts, of expensive lawyers, a special bill before Congress, all that struggle, all those affidavits—all that was not even necessary!"

Susan's viewpoint was different: "Let's just say that prayer accomplished in eight weeks what nine years of hard human effort from everyone whose help I had been able to enlist had not been able to do."

I was at Evergreen Farm in Virginia when I got the glad tidings. I was so elated to have the long battle over that I cannot recall all that I said. But Susan remembers and likes to quote me: "This is the time when you run out of words praising God."